THE SS DIRLEWANGER BRIGADE

The History of the Black Hunters

Christian Ingrao

Translated from the French by Phoebe Green

SKYHORSE PUBLISHING

Skyhorse Publishing books may be purchased in bulk at special discounts for sales promotion, corporate gifts, fund-raising, or educational purposes. Special editions can also be created to specifications. For details, contact the Special Sales Department, Skyhorse Publishing, 307 West 36th Street, 11th Floor, New York, NY 10018 or info@skyhorsepublishing.com.

Skyhorse® and Skyhorse Publishing® are registered trademarks of Skyhorse Publishing, Inc.®, a Delaware corporation.

www.skyhorsepublishing.com

10 9 8 7 6 5 4 3 2 1

Library of Congress Cataloging-in-Publication Data is available on file.
ISBN: 978-1-62087-895-8

Printed in the UK

To Roland Beller
To Xavier Escure
To Marie-Louise Prévot
To She Who Is Absent

"Chanter quelqu'un qui s'en va . . ."

Contents

Introduction

The Dirlewanger "Moment"

Military unit history, long considered a positivist anach-
ronism, has recently been relegitimized. In 1994,
Leonard V. Smith's study of the 5th French infantry
division on the Western front from 1914 to 1918 illuminated the
transactional relationships between commanders and troops,
finding that these relationships underlay both the acceptance
of combat by troops and a less brutal exercise of authority than
known before, influenced by the repercussions of the repression of the "great mutinies" of 1917. In his more famous mono-
graph on Poland's Reserve Police Battalion 101 and its participation in the Final Solution, Christopher Browning drew on the
social psychology work of Stanley Milgram and on the studies
of the Frankfurt School to emphasize the role of submission to
authority and of group dynamics in the acceptance of genocidal violence.[1,1] Unit history is, paradoxically, both one of the
oldest types of military history and one of the most promising,
if historians are willing to examine it with fresh eyes.

The present work proposes to do so by studying the
Sondereinheit Dirlewanger, a special unit of the Waffen-SS
formed in 1940 by Oskar Dirlewanger, a misfit SS officer poorly
regarded by his superiors. The idea was to recover from concentration camps certain types of prisoners whose abilities the SS

---

1   Notes will be found at the end of the book.

1

wished to exploit in very specific combat situations. Formed in late 1940, the unit operated through February 1942 in the eastern part of the General Government, guarding labor camps and combating the earliest partisan movements. In late February 1942, its troop numbers reinforced to bring it to battalion size, the unit left for Belarus, where it remained until the collapse of the Army Group Center in the summer of 1944. After passing through Poland, the Dirlewanger unit, which had in the meantime become the Dirlewanger Special Brigade, was enlarged and renamed the 36th Waffen Grenadier Division of the SS. After operating in Hungary and Slovakia, the division was annihilated by the Soviets in Saxony during the last months of conflict, while its eponymous leader plunged into hiding in his native Swabia.[2]

The *Sondereinheit* has been the subject of several studies. French MacLean, a soldier and historian, has explored the archives,[3] but his book, summarized by the narrative above, ignores essential elements: it says nothing of daily life; nothing of the relationships between men and officers; nothing of the fluctuation of morale. Nothing, finally and above all, of the lived experience of war: the individual and collective experience of violence. And yet for a decade historians have been exploring what war meant to those who lived it, at the front or behind the lines.[4] This concept, indeed, already suggests an angle of attack. The number of works addressing the issues of violence, death, mourning, but also of the social dynamics peculiar to wartime, has considerably increased over the past ten years.[5] Studies attempting to go beyond the usual chronological boundaries, boundaries sometimes more impenetrable than those between academic disciplines, have also known a growing success.[6]

The first mode of construction shaping the present work was the choice made in the 1980s to turn towards a history taking into account the forms of experience of war, the social framing of the transmission of that experience, and the diffusion of its interpretation. In short, the emergence of an analysis in terms of "the culture of war":[7] a concept that includes at once war itself, how it is experienced, and the discourse that arises from it. To address this culture of war, it was necessary to enlarge considerably the range of sources drawn upon. If military archives are far from neglected, battlefield archeology, everyday objects and images, but also the personal and familial discourse made accessible by war diaries and written or artistic production now enrich the palette available to us.[8] This type of history foregrounds bodies and psyches, reveals deterioration, affect, fear, hate, anxiety, trauma; but also habituation, banality, boredom, and release. The study of mutilation and its social treatment, psychic trauma and its clinical treatment, gave rise to the most recent major advances in the historiography of the two world wars.[9]

The second mode of construction involved the use of tools developed by French social anthropology in the 1980s; the detailed description and analysis of the gestural language of violence, which constitutes the irreducible heart of the phenomenon of war. To study these elements is to reach the profoundest depths of war. However, most illogically, the analysis of the material conditions and social practices of the exercise of violence in war remained unexplored territory until the 1990s. Only with the works of John Keegan, Victor Davs Hanson, and Stéphane Audoin-Rouzeau[10] was this new subject recognized in the discipline of contemporary history. The idea still evokes a certain resistance among historiographers of the Second World War, most often because it occupies an unexamined blind spot.[11] In other historiographic fields—pioneers in the matter—this type of study is now firmly established.[12] Students of contemporary history have thus only recently discovered that war is intimately related to the hunt and that in the construction of the image of the enemy phenomena of animalization come into play.[13]

The culture of war, the cynegetic and the pastoral imagination, the social construction of a gestural language of violence: these are the axes orienting our inquiry into Nazi policies of anti-partisan activity. The *Sondereinheit* Dirlewanger constitutes, in this view, a momentum that one might compare to those particle collisions induced by physicists within immense acceleration rings to reveal the subatomic structures of matter. The *Sondereinheit* was founded and led by Oskar Dirlewanger starting in the summer of 1940, at the express demand of Heinrich Himmler. It was originally intended only for action in the event of armed partisan resistance behind the German front lines. For specialized missions, specialized recruitment: the *Sondereinheit* remained for a long time exclusively made up of prisoners, then concentration camp inmates, convicted of cynegetic—hunt-related—crimes. All were hunters; all were poachers. The unit is thus an ideal observatory for those aspects of anti-partisan activity on the Eastern front that emerged from the image of the hunt and the animalization of the enemy. This impression is further strengthened by the theaters in which the unit operated. On the outskirts of Poland and the Ukraine, in areas mixing open ground and forest, the men of the unit were responsible, between late 1940 and early 1942, for guarding the camps in which Jews were held, condemned to wear the yellow star and compelled to the hardest tasks of road and bridge-building.[14] Penned, marked, and set to labor, the Jewish prisoners had been degraded by the Nazis to the level of beasts of burden. In Belarus, its second theater of operations, the unit was responsible for part of the clearing and combat action against the partisan units based, starting in early 1942, in the great northern forests covering the majority of the region.[15]

The Dirlewanger troops were, in short, confronted with situations evoking two fundamentally different modes of symbolization and interpretation of the image of the enemy and of martial activity. Poachers acting as hunters in Belarus and as

4

shepherds in Galicia, the Dirlewanger troops represent an ideal observation point for comparing the behavior and the practice of violence, to test the coherence of an interpretative model that may only be tested more widely if it proves their behavior was different in the two situations described and provides a satisfactory account thereof.

Anthropologists, however, have not limited themselves to the social image of the hunt. Bertrand Hell, in particular, has shown in his great book that the hunters crystallized, around their activity and their group identity, the essence of the social discourse defining the Wild, "representing" it and assigning it a place in Western societies,[16] while at the same time restricting it to specified physical and social spaces. The image of the hunter, like that of his different quarries, corresponds, according to Bertrand Hell, to a European imagination of Black Blood, which defines the "exact distance" from the Wild to these societies and, by a discourse interpreting hunters' behavior, inserts them in social organization and integrates therein the savagery and violence of that image. The decision to create the unit, taken at the highest level of the Nazi hierarchy, forms part of this imagination, as does the representation of anti-partisan action. It thus constitutes another ideal observation point of the anthropological interpretive framework formulated by Bertrand Hell, applied now to a Nazi society whose susceptibility to ideological discourse related to blood is well-known.[17]

Documentation on the *Sondereinheit* Dirlewanger is abundant but inconsistent and dispersed among a dozen archives. German archives in Berlin and Freiburg[18] constitute the basis of our documentation, to which we add elements recovered in the 1990s from Lublin, Warsaw, Minsk, Moscow, and Mogilev, consulted on microfilm in the Holocaust Memorial Museum in Washington,[19] except for those from Warsaw, consulted on site.[20] There are intervention orders, operation reports, collections of radio messages sent and received by the unit, and documents relative to its staffing, its internal life, and its day-to-day management. This documentation, however, covers only the two years spent in Belarus. Only the most fragmentary of documentation exists for the unit's first period of existence, spent in the Lublin district. Nothing is known of what the unit did there—nothing or nearly nothing of its activities guarding concentration labor camps. This absence made research particularly difficult, leaving its issue undecided until the very last. To bridge this gap in documentation, it seemed necessary to call upon a second type of source, produced by the justice organizations that reviewed National Socialist crimes post-war in the USSR, Poland, and Germany. It is remarkable in any event that this documentation was produced only after 1945: Starting in 1941, the special unit was the target of SS justice, its members suspected of numerous crimes and—particularly revealing—of cruelty, notably in their treatment of Jewish labor camp inmates.[21]

The consultation of these sources poses numerous methodological problems. The characteristics of the unit themselves augment this initial difficulty. This documentation was collected on the occasion of investigations of the crimes committed by the unit during large-scale search and sweep operations. Now, the men of the unit were habitual criminals, familiar with interrogation. Thus, contrary to the men of the *Einsatzgruppen* or police battalions, for example, the men of the unit were determined to reveal nothing of their participation in these crimes.[22] Out of some four hundred testimonies found in the *Zentralstelle der Landesjustizverwaltungen* (ZStL) of Ludwigsburg and in the Länder archives, only a handful include a confession. Almost none describe the crimes in detail. For what is intended to be a close study of the gestural language of violence, the problem is considerable.

In order to compensate for this missing element, we have consulted two additional types of source, they too of judicial origin: the reports of Russian and Polish commissions on Nazi crimes, which often include autopsy reports and reports on the exhumation of mass graves, and the testimony of survivors or witnesses. The first type of document allows us to address the materiality of the injuries to the bodies of the victims inflicted by their killers. Nevertheless, the injuries are extremely difficult to identify, and the reports are not exact enough for our purposes. The testimonies are, of course, dependent on the existence of survivors. For the sweep operations in Belarus they are relatively numerous and available either in Russian, in the Belarusian archives, or—as we consulted them—in German translation in the Federal court proceedings. For the unit's first period of activity, the victims are Polish Jews from the Lublin district. This region was the target of an early and almost total genocidal program, Operation Reinhard,[23] and there were hardly any survivors of the two camps guarded by the men of the *Sondereinheit*. Testimony on this first period is thus almost nonexistent. Two sources remain for us: the first is the inquiry led by the SS justice division on the extortion and multiple crimes committed by members of the unit in the Lublin district; the second consists of two inquiries, one by the *Zentralstelle* of Ludwigsburg,[24] the other by the Hanover prosecutor's office,[25] which include all the documents and testimonies available on that period of the unit's existence.

Documentation is equally sparse on the repression of the Slovakian uprising of autumn 1944 and on the last operations of what had become the Dirlewanger Division, in the area around the city of Cottbus. Military sources are few and judicial sources are almost nonexistent, due to the near-impossibility of incriminating the men of the unit in the criminal acts committed during this period of the war. Nevertheless, there are reports, memoirs, and diaries written by a very specific category of recruits to the Dirlewanger Division. Beginning in late 1944, the lack of combat personnel was such that Himmler,

Gottlob Berger, and Dirlewanger decided to add political prisoners, primarily communists, to the Division.[26] This was the decision that led, in the phrase of the historian Hans Peter Klausch, to "antifascists in SS uniform." This historian, alone in focusing specifically on this unit, details the history and the fate of these "politicals" in a book that is not exempt from a militant empathy for these men. He adheres to the antifascist ideal that constitutes the basis of the culture of the East German Left, merged with the SED (*Sozialistische Einheitspartei Deutschlands* or Socialist Unity Party) starting in 1947, but also to that pacifist ideal represented since the 1980s in German historiography by the *Friedensforschung*.[27] Everything becomes a prelude, for him, to the description of those last months, at once martyrology and heroic epic, which he describes for more than six chapters. Let us not be misunderstood: we criticize neither his position nor the perspective he has chosen. His work is sufficiently exhaustive to be a trusted resource for the last year of the unit's existence, the testimonies he collected in particular. Nevertheless, the thematic focus chosen by Hans Peter Klausch is not the unit itself, and we must admit that his interpretation does not bear on its practices of violence, nor on its experience of war.

For several years, the historiography of the First World War has been the stage of a bitter polemic. On one hand we have the historians of consent to war—through the interiorization of a culture giving meaning to the conflict—the principal but not the unique basis of the great endurance shown by European societies in the trial by ordeal of the war.[28] On the other hand, a group of historians see in this exceptional duration the result of a constraint obliging millions of men to fight in a conflict exterior to themselves.[29] Consent or constraint: the terms of the choice—one cannot speak of discussion, the tone of the attacks is such as to prevent dialogue—are set. These terms may easily be transposed to our study. All the members of the unit were, before their incorporation, concentration camp or prison inmates with little room for maneuver. The presence of political prisoners, ideological enemies of the regime and of the uniform they wore, and "comrades" in the struggle of the men they were supposed to fight, only reinforces the interest of the question, making the hypothesis of constraint seem obvious.[30] Were they "constrained" to war? Were they, above all, "constrained" to the atrocities they committed?

Killers who might in this case be victims, marginal men in a war—the war of the partisans—which itself is marginal, hunters or shepherds of men in black uniform:[31] whatever answers this work may suggest, it must be recognized that the poachers and political prisoners of the Dirlewanger Unit take us into disturbing territory. Let us try, nevertheless, to find our way therein.

Chapter 1

The History of a Brigade

From Berlin to Lublin

Oskar Dirlewanger was sent to Oranienburg in late May 1940 to take charge of the military training of eighty prisoners condemned for cynegetic crimes. Transferred from all over Germany, the prisoners had been assembled in an isolated barracks and had been put at the disposal of one of the regiments of the *Verfügungstruppe*, the future Waffen-SS.[1] If we consider the average age of the recruits—around thirty—the two months of training they were given must have been limited to the rudiments of military discipline and a summary physical training: something close to the Prussian Drill, but hardly going further, considering how soon they were sent into "action."

This training was selective enough that in the end only fifty-five of the eighty poachers were accepted in the commando. The others were returned progressively to their detention centers, without penalty: it was purely a question of physical unacceptability. The order requesting their reintegration in prison specified that no disciplinary measures were involved.[2]

In early September 1940,[3] the fifty-odd men and their leader were sent to the Lublin district and put under the command of the local SSPF (*SS und Politzeiführer*), Odilo Globocnik. There they were joined by some twenty new recruits and four Waffen-

SS NCOs, chosen both for their experience and, as was to become a recurring practice, for their disciplinary records, requiring that they be "put to the test." The troop thus formed would stay nearly eighteen months in Southeastern Poland and Galicia, divided among the Soviet-German demarcation line, the city of Lublin, and the Stary Dzików area.[4]

The Lublin district had an unusual status. As a frontier proconsulate directly facing the zone of Soviet influence, in the eyes of the Nazis it had not only an essential defensive function, but also a key role in the politics of reorganization of ethnic relations as decreed by Hitler after the invasion. The leaders of the RSHA (Reich Security Head Office) had decided to make Lublin a reservation for all the Jews of Germany and occupied Europe.[5] A final destination for deportees, the district was also the stage for very ambitious objectives on the part of Odilo Globocnik, in terms of both economic mobilization and the policy of Germanization. The question of territorial control was of crucial importance in this view.[6]

The men of the *Sondereinheit* weren't immediately concerned by the politics of Germanization. The question of territorial security, however, was central to their missions. These missions do not seem to have been clearly defined. The first missions under combat conditions, in particular, remain largely unknown. We do know that beginning in autumn 1940—and perhaps in December—the unit protected Polish rangers operating in the forests in the eastern part of the region, especially along the frontier. Gottlob Berger, the head of the SSFHA (*SS-Führungshauptamt*), Dirlewanger's close friend and faithful supporter throughout the war, testified before the American tribunal at Nuremberg and described the supposed activity of the unit in the beginning of the campaign, mentioning combat missions against snipers, former civil prisoners who escaped from Warsaw during the invasion.[7] Hans Peter KIausch challenges Berger's testimony on this point and believes rather that

11

it was a struggle against the first Polish underground resistance, formed by soldiers overtaken by the German advance and the Russian invasion, hidden in the woods along the banks of the Bug, in his version, to escape capture. This embryonic resistance movement, according to Berger, caused numerous losses to the occupation forces, and the Dirlewanger unit was called in to put an end to these incidents. Nothing in the sources contradicts this—ideologically marked—thesis of Berger's. However, nothing contradicts Hans Peter Klausch's theory either, and the latter has the advantage of making sense of the unit's activity, which thus has perfectly plausible adversaries. Nevertheless, action against real or supposed snipers was not the unit's main mission. Post-war testimony doesn't mention anti-partisan activity. Another very credible indicator of the total absence of danger is the fact that the unit suffered no losses.

The men almost never mention tracking partisans in the forests of the demarcation zone; all, however, say that the unit spent the majority of its time on the most ordinary surveillance work. Policing the civilian population and fighting the black market[8] seem to have been the group's main activities.[9] Unit reports speak regularly of the spoils seized by the men supporting the local police force (money, consumer goods, valuables).

Two facts must be noted. On the one hand, the detailed statements of goods seized often conceal numerous subterfuges for the personal profit of the men of the troop. On the other, these reports assumed a function of ideological confirmation: the value and abundance of the spoils confirmed, for the men of the Dirlewanger unit as for the occupying SS forces, Jews' supposed capacity for deceit and justified the measures that were starving the ghettos at that time.[10] One example shows the organization of both the men's behavior and the narrative they constructed around these activities. Among the dozen reports remaining from this period, one

12

tells of the search made on October 10, 1941, of a building in the Lublin ghetto, at that moment certainly one of the occupied territories with the highest mortality rate.[11] Famine reigns and epidemics are legion there. And yet the report describes the search of the building in these terms:

> The establishment is large, well lit, and relatively clean. A five-man orchestra plays every day. In the establishment itself were found the products listed (120 pounds of fresh meat, geese, chickens, ducks, butter, eggs, coffee beans, tea, cocoa, sugar, wheat flour, white bread, cigarettes, German red wine, French champagne, etc.). On a shelf under the zinc counter we found kilos of untouched sliced bread and scraps. On the counter itself we found three dozen custard and whipped cream tarts, as well as three dozen herring sandwiches. According to the ledger found in the desk, the takings for this establishment conceded to ghetto authorities as of October 9 were 4,100 zlotys, as explained by the fact that besides tap and bottled beer, we found twenty-five bottles of liquor and schnapps visibly emptied that day. In the course of this operation, neither the cellar nor the larder was searched.
>
> The fact that we found, in large quantity, in a Jewish establishment where jazz is played, goods that are not found in the Reich (coffee, tea, cocoa, white bread) or only in very limited quantity (meat, poultry, sausages, fish, cigarettes, etc.) made a great impression on the president of the popular tribunal and the director of the League of state employees. The order to restore to the Jews the goods thus seized is all the more inexplicable.[12]

The report continued by drawing conclusions confirming the image of the deceitful and manipulative Jew, always managing, according to Dirlewanger, to profit from economic conditions, even the most difficult. The report, however, was more than a simple empirical confirmation of anti-Semitic beliefs; it was also an institutional weapon directed against the SD.

According to Dirlewanger, the head of the Lublin KdS was protecting the establishment's owner and was using his position to establish a lucrative business. The objective, thus, was double: on the one hand, Jews were represented as manipulators, having succeeded even in getting seized goods restored to them; on the other, the SD's reputation was tarnished in the eyes of Globocnik.

The commando was also responsible for guarding the construction works that Globocnik set up along the Soviet–German demarcation line. Globocnik had found the way to build an economic empire based on the exploitation of concentration camp labor and convinced Himmler of the necessity of building an immense fortification, the "Eastern wall," composed of anti-tank trenches and structures built by Jewish prisoners. The men of the Dirlewanger commando were thus part of the teams guarding the prisoners, running no risks whatsoever. One detail speaks of the relaxation of the men of the unit and suggests at the same time another perspective for analyzing their behavior: the omnipresence of the hunt, to which Dirlewanger as well as his men gave themselves over in the forests where, until January 1942, one would have been hard-pressed to find a single partisan.

The reports of confiscations performed in the ghetto nonetheless suggest that this posting was marked—a euphemism to which we will return—by problems with the police caused by multiple infractions, misdemeanors of all sorts, accusations of extortion, and fraud.[13] The unit's reputation was damaged enough for it to be sent away from the region, despite the stubborn resistance of Dirlewanger and the intervention of Gottlob Berger, who opposed the SS judicial procedures directed at the unit. Berger, nonetheless, could not prevent an intervention by the HSSPF for the general government, Krüger, who issued an ultimatum demanding that the special unit leave. In late January 1942, marching orders were received;[14] three weeks later, Globocnik praised the unit in the most hypocritical terms, saluting its action in "delicate circumstances."[15] Dirlewanger took his time assembling troops and materiel, not to mention irregularly acquired goods. After a final exchange of letters in which Berger, exasperated, invited Dirlewanger not to refuse to obey an order from the *Reichsführer*, the unit arrived in Belarus where, placed under the command of Himmler's operational general staff and temporarily attached to the SS cavalry brigades,[16] it would finally be used as it was meant to be: in "anti-partisan combat."[17]

Belarus, February 1942–July 1944

Belarus, a land of forests and marshes with patches of subsistence agriculture, did not hold a central place in German plans. During the invasion, fighting was nonetheless fierce and the cities that fell into the hands of the occupiers were in an advanced state of destruction.[18] By the summer of 1941, Red Army troops overtaken by the German advance had taken refuge in the Belarusian forest and had adopted a survival strategy of obtaining what was necessary for their subsistence, without planning any definite resistance to the German occupation. Starting in early 1942, however, the Soviets began a patient labor of coordination, organization, and command unification of those troops, which at that time, according to the figures of the Moscow command center for partisan combat, numbered some 23,000 members.[19] Reacting to the noticeable increase of partisan unit activity, the combined forces of the military command for the territories behind the Eastern front, the police, and the SS modified their initial strategy of "passive resistance to partisans" (which had consisted until then of patrolling the roads and relentlessly hunting down wandering individuals and groups) and began to organize large-scale sweep operations.[20]

The pilot operation, Operation Bamberg, began in Polesia and, going north, finished near Babruysk.[21] The following week, the *Sondereinheit* was engaged. There was practically no transition period between the two theaters of operations for the men of the commando. During the thirty months they spent in Belarus, there were at least fifty-five large-scale sweep operations.[22] The unit participated in twenty-seven, either as a unit or integrated into different anti-partisan combat groups such as the "*Kampfgruppe* von Gottberg," named after the Belarusian SSPF. To these twenty-seven major operations we must add the "small operations" performed by the unit around its quarters, situated first near Mogilev then, starting in January 1943, on the same road, but a few dozen kilometers north of Minsk, in the village of Lagoisk. In total, and even if the unit journal has been lost,[23] it is reasonable to think that the group participated in more than fifty sweep operations.

In its first week-long sortie, the unit took by assault a partisan camp entrenched near Ossipowitsch, then near Klitschev and Tscherwakov. Other reconnaissance actions followed, from March 16 to 22 in particular, south of Mogilev and on the road from Mogilev to Babruysk.[24] The results of these first engagements were convincing enough in the eyes of the hierarchy for them to support the efforts of Dirlewanger, beginning late March, to reinforce the unit's troop strength, still limited to some hundred men. On March 23, the general staff of the HSSPF for central Russia wrote to the general staff of Himmler's command, to which the commando was attached,[25] a letter in which he mentioned that "the SS *Sonderkommando* Dirlewanger had proved itself with flying colors" and had shown itself "better suited than any other troop for anti-partisan combat on difficult terrain." He requested on these grounds that the troop strength of the commando be raised to 250 men, and that they be assigned "MG-34s [heavy machine guns], six light grenade-launchers, two heavy grenade-launchers, two infantry howitzers (identical to those used by mountain troops, to be carried on harnesses)," as well as transmission equipment and additional vehicles.[26] This unanswered letter from von dem Bach-Zelewsky's services constituted the starting point for Dirlewanger's stubborn efforts, which he pursued at the same time as an intense sweep activity.

The reports show the incessant work of reconnaissance and combat against partisan units, which began in early spring 1942 to sabotage German communication lines on a regular basis. Thus, during its first month of operation the unit's activity consisted of attempts to hunt these groups down and to secure the road and the railroad from Babruysk to Mogilev. After which, the unit dedicated itself, beginning in May, to ensuring through road work its own communications with Mogilev, the location both of the hospital where any wounded were to be treated and the command unit to which they were attached.[27] During the third week of May, the commando experienced its first losses: four men were attacked on the Mogilev road as they started on leave. Of the four men, three were killed. The reports of the circumstances of their death illuminate combat conditions: one was mutilated after his death, the second was burned in the car accident, and the third was apparently the victim of exploding bullets, illegal munitions also used by the unit itself.[28] After the burial, the men of the unit avenged the three deaths by burning a partisan camp and an apparently deserted village.[29] A few days later the commando was operating near Orscha, then was again sent into the Mogilev-Babruysk-Beresino triangle, where it performed a joint operation with *Einsatzkommando* Eight along the rail line between Minsk and Mogilev, apparently in reprisal for the death of seventeen German police officers killed by partisans.[30]

The next few days, after an interview between Dirlewanger and von dem Bach-Zelewsky,[31] just back from a long sick leave, were spent sweeping the forests west of Mogilev. The operations of May and June marked his return to action, in the context of the large-scale operations it was now his responsibility to coordinate, in his role as HSSPF with authority over Waffen-SS troops, *Sicherheitspolizei* units, and uniformed police, but also, to a certain point, over Wehrmacht units having received "instructions" concerning the handling of operations. This coordination on the ground must have been confirmed no later than summer at the Berlin level by the recognition of the *Reichsführer*'s abilities in anti-partisan combat and, as of autumn, by the nomination of von dem Bach-Zelewsky to the position of "plenipotentiary for anti-partisan combat."[32]

July passed in operations along the railroad line. Dirlewanger was wounded July 9 by a bullet that passed through his shoulder during an operation performed in collaboration with Wehrmacht security patrols in the Klitschev region.[33] At the same time, the unit participated in larger combat formations, again in the sector north of the railroad line. From July 20 to August 7 the unit participated in Operation Adler, near Tschetchezitsch, together with two Wehrmacht security divisions, a police battalion, and a Cossack battalion, an operation supported by significant artillery and two flying squadrons from Mogilev and Babruysk.[34] The operation encircled a partisan group which the Germans invited to surrender and which didn't break up until the very end of the operation, the men attempting to flee individually or in small groups. At the operation's end, 1,381 partisans were killed; 422 individual weapons of all calibers, fourteen cannons, and 36,000 cartridges and shells were seized. In the report by the security division that coordinated the operation, these spoils demonstrated the success of the operation in German eyes. It had cost them only twenty-seven dead or missing and sixty-four wounded.[35]

After a week patrolling around their billet, the men of the unit were committed to the new operation planned by the rear territorial commander, Operation Greif, between Orscha and Vitebsk, together with an SS division, two police regiments, and a battalion of French volunteers. With Operations Adler and Greif, the new policy of anti-partisan combat directly affected the unit's practice: the men of the *Sondereinheit* were now acting within a centralized system whose activity was developing at an increasing rate. The climax of this activity was the "Swamp Fever" action, which involved not just one sector, but the entire commissariat general, and which lasted a full month. The participation of the unit as such in this gigantic sweep is not attested in the sources.[36] Nevertheless, its actions during this period, always along the railroad line between Mogilev and Babruysk, may have been coordinated as part of "Swamp Fever" without that fact being noted in general staff reports. The practice of these hundred men now formed part of a large-scale, systematic, and centralized policy.

The "successes" of the first months of operation had been carefully exploited by Dirlewanger, and supported by von dem Bach's offices, in view of developing the unit, increasing its size, and completing its equipment. Starting in late February, as we have seen, von dem Bach's representative had sent out a report hailing its action and requesting reinforcement to bring it up to 170 men. Unanswered, this was followed by a series of reports and expressions of support by officers close to the unit, such as *Hauptsturmführer* Meyer-Mahrndorff, who commanded it in August, after Dirlewanger was wounded, and praised its action during Operation Greif. This paper flood had a double function. On the one hand, it was meant to influence the outcome of the investigations that had been directed against the unit since Lublin; on the other, it was meant to support the request for reinforcement Dirlewanger had sent to the SSFHA, underlining the experience gained during the first months in Belarus and the first large-scale anti-partisan sweeps.[37]

In the summer of 1942, however, the situation seemed hopeless: Dirlewanger's efforts and the pressure applied by the HSSPF's offices didn't seem to be working, much to the unit leader's exasperation. The latter, under the pretext of treatment for the shoulder wound received in Klitschev in July, went to Berlin with the intention of influencing the commanding authorities and getting the reinforcements he had been requesting since March. These efforts were unsuccessful. When he rejoined the unit in Belarus, he wrote a letter to Berger in which he repeated the points justifying his claims as well as his need for men and materiel.

His efforts were rewarded at last in September 1942. It is hard to tell if the unit reinforcement represented a recognition of the experience acquired by the unit in its first six months of action in Belarus, or simply the automatic consequence of Berger and Dirlewanger's repeated requests. The unit was reinforced by the arrival of a contingent of 115 poachers.[38] It had already undergone profound changes due to the establishment, starting in early summer 1942, of three companies of Russian auxiliaries. The poachers, after the addition of the new contingent, continued as a company, while the Russians were organized in three companies of 150 men each. Thus the unit had gone in a few months from a commando of eighty to a battalion of 750, the four combat companies supported by some forty motorcyclists and by a forty-man artillery unit.[39] The Dirlewanger special battalion had reached the configuration it would maintain until the summer of 1943.[40]

The battalion took part successively in Operations Regatta, Karlsbad, Franz, Erntefest One and Two, Hornung, Zauberflöte, Draufgänger One and Two, Cottbus, and Günther. Eleven operations in a year, one a month on average, most of a duration of over three weeks, constituting the culmination of a campaign by Nazi authorities against Belarusian peasant communities, but also against Jewish communities, which underwent what Raul Hilberg called the "second wave" of genocide.[41] A number of the operations in which the unit participated ended in the destruction under fire of the ghettos that had been set up during the summer and autumn of 1941 throughout Belarus: operation Hornung ended with the liquidation of the Slutsk ghetto;[42] "Swamp Fever" by that of a large part of the Boranowitsche ghetto.[43] The Lida ghetto was liquidated in autumn 1942, and two survivors of the execution affirm that it was the work of a "penal battalion."[44] Nevertheless, the presence of the unit at Lida, a city situated farther west and north on the Lithuanian frontier, is not attested in the sources for this period.[45] At the time of the Lida massacre, the unit doesn't seem to have left central Belarus, notably the region east of Minsk, between Tscherwen, Tschechewitschi, and Beresino, before operating farther south, in the winter of 1942–1943, among Minsk, Slutsk, and, in Volhynia, in the Pripyat marshes.[46]

Von dem Bach wanted to be relieved of his functions as supreme leader of the police and SS for central Russia. This was done as of October 24, 1942, at which time his HSSPF functions were entrusted to Gerret Korsemann. His nomination reflected the desire to export to all of occupied Eastern Europe the techniques perfected in Belarus. Nevertheless Belarus, and more particularly the unit's zone of operations, remained the main theater of war against the partisans, who were now engaging in real organized combat, at least when they were driven to it. On November 12, 1942, for example, the *Sondereinheit*, operating south of Tscherwen, was engaged, according to von dem Bach-Zelewsky's message to Himmler, in "intense fighting against several fortified partisan camps. Enemies killed: 176, including eleven armed women.[47] Spoils: three light machine guns, light arms, hand grenades, 12,250 cartridges. Losses: three dead, seven wounded, five missing."[48]

A war against Russian peasants and Jews: it is in these terms that one may sum up the anti-partisan operations engaged in, starting in early 1942. During these operations, according to Christian Gerlach's calculations, six to ten men were killed for every weapon recovered and confiscated. He concludes that only 15 percent of those killed were real members of armed resistance movements against the Germans.[49] The victims, thus, were primarily peasants and fugitives, notably Jews escaped from the ghettos. More significant still is the amount of food among the spoils collected by the anti-partisan units: potatoes, grain, and cattle appear regularly in the reports of the operations, transforming them, especially after the winter of 1942–1943, into murderous predatory raids against the local peasantry.[50]

The balance sheet of Operation Swamp Fever sums up this situation perfectly. The Germans, by their own admission, had killed only 489 "bandits" in over a month of operation. They had, however, eliminated 8,350 Jews from the Boranowitsche ghetto, as well as 1,274 suspects, and "evacuated" 1,217 other individuals. By "evacuated" we must understand "deported for labor within the Reich." These were persons "fit for labor" found in the villages, while the "executed suspects" were either escapees killed in the forest or those "unfit for labor" from those same villages: women, children, and the aged. The forty-nine camps destroyed during the operation by the reconnaissance and pursuit commandos were merely the tip of the iceberg, concealing a genocidal operation behind the mask of anti-partisan struggle.[51]

Starting in early 1942, German strategy gained a new thrust, still in the context of large-scale sweep operations. These now aimed to empty whole regions of their population. The first half of the year was marked by a test phase, during which the actors of operations, still following the 1942 model, began, in a process of trial and error, to evacuate the populations of villages and to more systematically deport to Germany those persons declared "fit for labor," notably during Operation Sauckel.[52] It appears that this policy, which was accompanied by an intensification of operations, was not new. The great massacres of 1942 pursued a similar objective: to deprive the partisans of an environment that could give them supplies, logistical support, and information. As the year continued, the tribute of men, food, and agricultural produce increased. Starting in late 1942, notably in the Tscherwen region, the men of the unit were accompanied by brown-uniformed officers, members of the local German civil administration reporting to the Ministry of Occupied Territories, who supervised the deportations and confiscation of agricultural produce under the "protection" of the battalion. Von Gottberg's order of August 1, 1943, left no doubt as to the real objective of this type of action:

The entire population (men, women, and children), dead or alive, is to be expelled from the region defined in Article 1. Those men fit for labor will be inventoried by the special staff of the labor action of the *Reg. Rat.* Teschen. The treatment of the rest of the population is the responsibility of local officials. It is not advisable to leave the unfit population in the environs of the designated region. The staff of the *Reg. Rat.* Teschen has organized camps at Stolpce, Iwieniec, Woloczyn, Bohdanov, and Lubcz. [. . .] Agricultural property and cattle must be inventoried by the commandos of Section 3 of the general commissariat assigned to the troop. The villages and all other buildings, bridges, and orchards must be destroyed if they cannot be camouflaged. Forests also must be burned down, insofar as possible. In the future, human beings found in the region will be considered game.

The evacuation day will be determined by radio order after pacification of the area designated.[53]

To create "death zones" (*Tote Zonen*): this was henceforth the new anti-partisan concept. These zones were to be completely emptied of their population, less by massacre, as in 1942, than by mass deportations to the factories of the Reich and, for some, to Lublin and to the Auschwitz labor camp.[54]

In the summer of 1943, *Gruppenführer* von Gottberg, SSPF for Minsk and coordinator of the sweep and agricultural confiscation operations of the combat group bearing his name, to which the Dirlewanger unit was attached, summed up the latter's activity. In proposing a medal for Dirlewanger, von Gottberg stated, based no doubt on the unit's operations journal, that his men had killed nearly 15,000 people in fifteen months of operations, with only ninety-two men dead or missing.[55] Von Gottberg's report stressed the weapons captured by the unit, trying to put the actions of Dirlewanger's men in a strictly martial context. The lists of machine guns, light arms, and light artillery equipment taken from the enemy underlined the bravery of the unit's leader and his men. With this in view, he could make no distinction between true partisans killed in action and Russian peasants or fleeing Jews killed in reprisals and in burned down villages. He had to suppress an entire section of the operations ledger, which nevertheless had become central in 1943: the economic aspect.

The year 1943 saw a change in center of gravity for the unit's activity. The unit was no longer based in Mogilev, but in Lagoisk, 40 kilometers north of Minsk. The operations in which it participated moved to the west and the south, around Slutsk, in Volhynia-Polesia, and to the unit's billeting area in Lepel and Borissov. The latter region was the theater of the largest and most murderous of the unit's actions in Belarus: operation Cottbus. Ten days after it started, the morning of May 30, Oskar

Dirlewanger sent an incident report: in the two preceding hours, the Russian company had lost seven men who had stepped on mines, and Dirlewanger reported several men missing. The German company, the one made up of poachers, had not suffered similar losses, but during the same period two NCOs and two troopers had already been wounded. Two hours later, five additional men were reported hit.[56] Cottbus was the theater of more intense combat than other operations, but above all it was one of the summits of the extreme violence used behind the front lines against Russian civilians and surviving Jews, with more than 12,000 dead. The *Sondereinheit* was only one unit among many, and its reduced numbers apparently kept it from being one of the major actors of the operation. It does seem, however, that it played a central role in the protocols of planned destruction developed by the *Kampfgruppe* von Gottberg, particularly in the consistent practice of sending civilians into mined areas to detonate them, which alone cost the lives of nearly 3,000 people. As von Gottberg noted with satisfaction in his final report: "The mines set on most roads and paths necessitated the use of mine detectors, as per order. The mine detector developed by the Dirlewanger battalion successfully passed the test."[57]

Operation Cottbus and the explosion of paroxysmal violence it represented in an area that had been the continual theater of sweep actions were the occasion for civil authorities to intensify their protests against the scorched earth policy applied by von dem Bach and von Gottberg. At the local level, the commissioner of the Borissow district, to the north of which Operation Cottbus was carried out, sent a report ten days after the beginning of the operation to one of the adjutants of the general commissioner at Minsk, Kube, in which he reported a massacre committed in the village of Vitonitsch. He complained of an influx of bullet-wounded escapees from executions who had managed to climb out of pits and came to seek help in hospitals and care centers. Two days later, Kube sent Rosenberg, the Minister of Occupied Territories, a report based on information collected *in situ*, begging him to intercede with Hitler to put an end to this practice. This intervention at the highest level of the Nazi hierarchy did not mean that Kube preferred to win the hearts and minds of local populations. Christian Gerlach has convincingly demonstrated that Kube subscribed fully to the policy of predation and extermination decided on by Berlin, and that he merely sought to ensure that civil authorities remained dominant at the local level and to retain control of decisions taken in the general commissions. Kube's death at the hand of his Belarusian housekeeper on September 22, 1943,[58] took place, thus, in a context of open crisis between civil and SS authorities. During the period of uncertainty that followed his death, and when his assassination had revealed to Berlin the extent of the partisan problem in Belarus, Kube's department sent to Rosenberg a report summarizing the line defended by civil authorities and the use they made of the "Dirlewanger example":

The situation of the commissariat general of White Ruthenia is clearly dominated by the problem of spreading bands. [. . .] As the general commissioner [Kube—report translator's note] wrote in August, the situation is worsening considerably. He [Kube] added: "Railroad lines formerly considered out of danger are today closed to circulation. Traffic with Vilnius itself is more and more obstructed by acts of terrorism, mines, etc. [. . .] To this may be added the erroneous psychological treatment of the population by units on police operations. Here the name Dirlewanger plays a particularly significant role, for this man, in the war of annihilation he wages pitilessly against an unarmed population, deliberately refuses to consider political necessities. His methods, worthy of the

Thirty Years' War, make a lie of the civil administration's assurances of their wish to work together with the Belarusian people. When women and children are shot en masse or burned alive, there is no longer a semblance of humane conduct of war. The number of villages burned during sweep operations exceeds that of those burned by the Bolsheviks."[59]

Cunningly, the department head of the civil administration quoted from the report sent in August by Kube, a month before his "hero's death," giving it a prophetic tone. The accusations against Dirlewanger constituted, in the eyes of the civil administration, a weapon in the conflict opposing civil administration and security forces. Kube's colleagues did not understand the relative positions in Berlin of Rosenberg, out of favor, and Himmler, virtually at the height of his influence. Kube's rapid replacement, furthermore, left no observer in ignorance of the outcome of the battle between these two pillars of Nazi power, the SS security forces and the civil administration. Von Gottberg combined the position of SSPF for Minsk with that of commissioner for Belarus:[60] he was above all Dirlewanger's direct hierarchical superior and had given the very orders that legitimized the actions of the *Sondereinheit*. His nomination ratified the complete victory of von dem Bach and Himmler, and with it their scorched earth strategy.

In the month following Operation Cottbus, there was a change of personnel that would transform the sociology of the unit's composition. Although it had until that time been made up uniquely of cynegetic delinquents taken from concentration camps, starting in July 1943 the *Sondereinheit* received large contingents of "delinquents" of a different kind. The idea was not new. In early spring, March 28, Himmler had ordered that "Germans of the Reich and all men of the class of 1901 and later living in an irregular situation within the General

27

Government who have no military training or assignment, and who have avoided the draft for years, arrested in a General Government sweep, must be gathered [. . .] and assigned to the penal battalion of the Dirlewanger unit."[61]

This order was coordinated with the commission of General von Unruh,[62] who, charged with recruitment, was launching major campaigns to that effect.[63] He systematically drafted marginal candidates, criminals or not, poachers or not, but he had little effect on the unit's troop strength, as witnessed by the unit's numbers at the beginning of the summer.[64] The new wave of—forced—recruits arriving at Lagoisk around July 7, 1943, was going to transform its composition. Out of the 321 men, 294 came from Dachau, Buchenwald, Mauthausen, and Sachsenhausen.[65] They were managed by a group of NCOs whose incorporation was no doubt unforeseen. Four months after they arrived, Dirlewanger received a stern letter from the WVHA threatening to take the matter to Himmler if he didn't send them back immediately.[66] It was that organization that, probably on Himmler's instructions, had selected the prisoners. Of varying ages, since they were born between 1893 and 1921, they had been imprisoned for the most part as "asocial individuals" or "professional criminals." The latter, constituting half of the contingent, had received long prison sentences for crimes against property (burglary, purse snatching), but more often for crimes against persons (armed robbery, assault, manslaughter, murder). The "asocial individuals," a category including petty criminals but also persons considered misfits—beggars, the unemployed—were grouped with prisoners described as "intellectually inferior," "feeble-minded," or "psychopathic" and having a less extensive criminal record. The atmosphere changed: witness the three summary executions and the extremely high number of punishments occurring in the six following weeks.[67]

No sooner had this contingent arrived than it was put into training and divided into companies within the unit. There was no mixing between the categories of recruits: the "old boys," the poachers, continued to make up the first company, while the new arrivals were incorporated into two new German companies, themselves formed during the transformation of the *Sonderbataillon*—special battalion—into a *Sonderregiment*, a special regiment.[68] The order to form the Dirlewanger regiment stipulated that the armaments required by these reinforcements were to be taken from the enemy, a disappointment for its leader. Dirlewanger had planned to use these reinforcements to justify improved equipment for his unit. Once the WVHA had confirmed that they would be coming, he had turned to Berger to request "600 rifles, 120 sniper rifles, fifty pistols, thirty-six flare guns, six motorized field kitchens [. . .], six radio sets with twelve radios, twenty-four heavy machine guns, thirty-eight light machine guns, twelve small and medium caliber grenade launchers, seventy-two submachine guns, 144 compasses, thirty-six sidecars, forty cars with drivers, [and] six all-terrain vehicles with drivers."[69] Dirlewanger added that Berger's own adjutant had said he could "obtain these arms and equipment if the SSFHA received the necessary instructions from the SS *Reichsführer*." Dirlewanger continued his strategy of incessant lobbying for reinforcements, equipment, and logistical support, and even the camp prisoners were not enough for him. Even as he received these contingents, he also benefited from a new policy automatically sending cynegetic criminals to his unit, thanks to an agreement signed September 3, 1943, between Himmler and the Reich's authority for hunting-related matters—Goering.[70]

Only a week after their arrival, the men taken from the concentration camps were engaged in Operation Günther, which lasted less than three days. On July 14, Dirlewanger made his report. He made much of new instructions he received from Gerret Korsemann, in clear contradiction to the practice established in Operation Cottbus. Korsemann had ordered

to spare a certain number of villages, although
n gathered by SD reconnaissance troops established,
opinion, that these villages were on the side of the
indits," or even active in road mining. Dirlewanger's discontent was all the greater because he felt that such instructions were directly responsible for the unit's losses, and that the operation had been badly planned both in its "military phase" and in the phase of inventory and confiscation of property and displacement of the population.[71] Thus his report specified that it "seemed necessary, therefore, that intervention orders [be] issued by officers having practical anti-partisan experience."[72] In all, however, the handwritten total of combat deaths and "eliminations" seems to indicate that the operation took the lives of 3,484 people for the loss of five German and six "alien" troopers, with seventeen Germans and thirty-one auxiliaries wounded in combat.[73]

The numbers of soldiers in operation reflect at once the chronology of the large-scale sweep operations and the intense rhythm of the unit's activity. Its German company consists of between 212 and 235 men, 150 of whom are in operation at any given time. The only relaxation of this tempo occurs precisely at the beginning of the month of July, when the unit is preparing to receive the reinforcements of criminal and asocial prisoners. During this period, only one hundred men are active. At the same time, fifty others stay in Lagoisk for "internal service" and an average of thirty men perform workshop tasks, such as equipment and vehicle maintenance. Five percent of the troops are on leave, and nearly ten percent are in treatment or convalescing in the hospital or the infirmary. Let us note that there are no close arrests between May and July, and very few in early spring: four men the week of April 26 through May 1, only one the previous week.[74] What is striking is that the number of men in treatment has no relationship to operations: whether these are large-scale operations like

Cottbus or small ones like Günther makes no difference in the number of men unfit for active duty. As in Lublin and also in Belarus during the unit's first period of activity, combat losses remained extremely low for the German company. Nevertheless, despite this relative absence of risk, a week after Operation Günther the Dirlewanger unit experienced two significant losses. On July 19, one of its supply convoys was attacked by partisans. It repelled the attack, but two men were killed. The next day, one of the unit's cars hit a mine, killing two soldiers instantly, mortally wounding two others, and injuring an officer, who survived. Convoy attacks and landmines: these were the principal dangers of the "war" engaged in by the men of the unit.

With the arrival of the prisoners in July 1943, conditions changed. The combats of the first week of August, for instance, are enlightening: during this operation, named Hermann in homage to Goering, then still considered one of the leaders setting the manpower policy,[75] there were four Germans killed and seven wounded, four requiring immediate evacuation by airplane.[76] The combat reports specify that the unit was being used to reduce the encirclement zone and that it was engaging in intense combats there.[77] Its total losses during Operation Hermann were thirteen Germans killed and thirty-five wounded, with eight Ukrainian Hiwis also wounded.[78] The difference is marked in relationship to earlier months, particularly in the spring, when the only losses were in ambushes unrelated to organized combat.

It seems difficult to ascertain with certainty the determinants of the evolution. The change in the unit with the arrival of the criminal and asocial prisoners, for the most part untrained and totally inexperienced in combat, no doubt played a determining role in this evolution. Nevertheless, the wounded include *Obersturmführer* Blessau and Dirlewanger himself, as stated before: two men with the greatest experience in these matters.[79]

Combat conditions were changed as well. The partisans were now better organized and equipped, and the Germans had greater difficulty overcoming these units in a direct encounter. In November 1943, furthermore, Operation Heinrich, in which the unit was engaged, occurred at the very moment the Red Army made a breakthrough in the Vitebsk area, obliging the Dirlewanger unit to act as line troops. Until January 1944, daily reports give a picture closer to what one would have expected of a calm sector of the Western front between 1915 and 1918 than to the rear front in the Second World War. On December 27, 1943, for example, the first company reports two men wounded; two days later, two others wounded and two sick; January 2, two dead and six wounded but "nothing special to report"; January 4, another dead, the company having been the target of forty shells and having itself launched sixty shells and 600 light artillery shots. The following day, an additional man dead and three wounded, and 1,100 heavy machine gun cartridges used; January 9, two more dead and 140 shells received. In addition to this daily report testifying to a very real war of position, let us note the omnipresence in the unit's orders of the daily planting of mines and of instructions concerning earthworks and fortifications. In one week the company dug 650 meters of trenches, despite an intense cold making earthwork extremely difficult, to the point that attacks of frostbite were frequent (even though these were declared acts of self-mutilation, the winter equipment distributed to the unit being considered sufficient).[80]

In December 1943, the *Sonderregiment* had once again changed assignments and was settled in Usda, some 50 kilometers south of Minsk.[81] Operation Frühlingsfest marked a new level of sweep activity. It took place in the region around Polosk and Uschaschy, in the Vitebsk district. The unit was part of one of the four *Einsatzgruppen* put together for the occasion by the *Kampfgruppe* von Gottberg. Even if the format of the operation was in line with the "death zone" strategy, the changed combat conditions were reflected in the orders organizing the attack. The very numerous partisan formations were described as formidable,[82] well armed and well fortified, and it was specified that they could count on Red Army air support during the attack. In response to these changed tactical conditions, von Gottberg had been forced to ask the assistance of the Third Tank Army, and he had been accorded a security regiment, a sapper battalion, four artillery formations, two with anti-tank cannons, two units dedicated to protecting the lines of communication, and one tank unit. This was an operation marked by the breadth of means invested in securing a relatively limited territory, the *Sonderregiment* being only one unit among many others.[83] It lasted three weeks, and there were 7,011 dead, 6,978 prisoners, 11,233 deportees, 1,065 light arms, and 360 heavy arms "taken from the enemy,"[84] against seventeen killed or wounded in the *Sonderregiment*.[85] The practices of the *Sondereinheit*, thus, hardly differed from what they had been since 1942. Reconnaissance missions, supply convoys, and search-and-sweep operations were still its day-to-day business.

The authorities charged with securing the rear of the front were still aware of the failure, in security terms, of the anti-partisan policy. If the latter had been effective in its predatory aspects, it had never managed to neutralize armed groups or even to seriously hinder their increase in numbers and activity. Drawing conclusions from the failure of the sweeps, the security organizations developed a new strategy founded on the distribution of their forces over a grid ensuring permanent coverage of the territory, thanks to the establishment of armed and fortified villages that would eventually cover the commissariat general's entire territory. These "armed villages" (*Wehrdörfer*) had already been tried in the Lublin district, where Odilo Globocnik had tried to set up villages of German settlers to replace expelled Polish and Ukrainian peasants.[86] Our current knowledge does not allow us to prove that there was any circulation of information between the General Government and the commissariat. The new Minsk strategy depended on the same tactical principles, although it was not a question of Germanization: the "candidates" were not *Volksdeutsche*, but Belarusian peasants considered "trustworthy."

The first experiments of this type had been made in the sector of the Second Army—that is to say outside the jurisdiction of the civil authorities—starting in spring 1942. In April–May 1943, twenty support stations with fifty men each were set up south of the commissariat, in Volhynia-Podolia, but the project didn't really achieve credibility and resources until 1944, after von Gottberg announced its establishment, on December 23, 1943, to the "Belarusian National Council," the collaborationist assembly. The idea was to organize not isolated villages, but "installation areas for armed villages" of ten to twenty villages each. After a village had been declared an "armed village," its environment was "pacified." The population considered "untrustworthy" was culled and either shot or deported. After a few days, a little ceremony was organized at the end of which a modicum of food, cigarettes, candy, and jewelry was distributed, and, after an inspection, it was decided what cultural institutions—churches, schools—would be created and what renovations would be undertaken. In the following three weeks, the inhabitants received rudimentary military training and were incited to denounce suspicious movements and to forbid partisans to enter the village, thenceforth armed. Even though there were a hundred villages of this type, with a total of some 20,000 inhabitants, the project never went beyond these preliminary steps. Still the Germans lacked resources; still, above all, they lacked time. This abortive movement was combined with the installation of Armenians, Caucasians, and Azeris.[87]

The arrival of these contingents of aliens was a windfall for Dirlewanger, who, as usual, was constantly trying to obtain reinforcements. He schemed to get certain "Eastern legions" installed in his sector, no doubt intending to take control of them. He wrote relentlessly to Berger to hurry their arrival and to get this projected takeover confirmed. He was defeated by the resistance of the officer commanding the unit, and Dirlewanger tried to have him summoned to Berlin in order to impose on him the assignment of his men to the *Sonderregiment*.[88] Nevertheless, the Dirlewanger unit participated in the *Wehrdörfer* project, supplying protective detachments to the Turkmenian, Tatar, and Azeri units used for the earth- and fortification work constituting the first phase of fitting out the villages.[89]

These efforts were part of an all-out strategy of ceaseless demands to reinforce the regiment's troop strength. In the summer of 1943, as we have seen, Dirlewanger had been assured of the recruitment, after selection by physical criteria, of two types of delinquents: poachers and criminals. In February 1944, the order had been systemized by Himmler himself, who had fixed the number of men to be added to the unit at 800. But this figure was not reached for several months, the prisoners arriving by detachment. The convoys, notably those of May 19, where 182 men set off from Auschwitz and 287 from Sachsenhausen to reach the unit, were the last of the new wave of recruitment. Dirlewanger tried to ensure his recruitment of SS men imprisoned for disciplinary reasons, and he asked that all prisoners of the Black Order's three major close arrest centers, in Prague, Dantzig-Matzkau, and the SS penal labor battalion in Babruysk, be released and transferred to his unit. He thought in this way he could ensure a supply of trained people that, according to him, had always been wanting. He had been asking since March 18, 1944, that all these prisoners be turned over to him to be made useful and be put to the test.[90] Dirlewanger thought he could count on an additional 2,000 men from this. According to Hans Peter Klausch, however, only 200

SS men reached the unit before its retreat from Belarus.[90] At that time, the *Sonderregiment* Dirlewanger seemed at last to have reached a size justifying the unit's name change, which had been in effect for six months. Putting together the 250 or so poachers who formed the original nucleus of the group, the 1,200 criminal and antisocial prisoners added in the summer of 1943, the 200 SS men transferred for disciplinary reasons, and the 500 Russian auxiliaries incorporated in the summer of 1942, the unit had recruited in total some 2,150 members. If we subtract the Russian auxiliaries, who were no longer used in combat after the retreat from Belarus, there were 1,650 men of whom only half—881—could be considered "fighting troops."[92]

The last sweep in which the unit participated was Operation Cormorant. It took place from May 25 through June 17. The next day, in the night of June 19, the partisans against whom the unit had struggled for almost thirty months set off no fewer than 10,500 missiles, paralyzing the communication lines of the German rear troops.[93] Three days later, June 22, 1944, there began the land phase of the great Russian offensive, which ended with the encirclement of nearly 300,000 men in the stronghold of Minsk.[94] The unit beat a retreat and left Belarus by way of Lida and Grodno, where its last combats occurred. It had spent fifty-three months in Belarus and had without a doubt eliminated more than 30,000 people and burned several dozen villages.[95] It had arrived as a small commando of fewer than one hundred men and left as a regiment. A campaign that could, despite the final collapse, appear as a triumph in the eyes of its leader.

From Warsaw to Cottbus, August 1944–May 1945

The unit reached Poland early in July. Its quarters were in Lomza, 100 kilometers west of Bialystok and 150 kilometers to the northeast of Warsaw, and it was originally supposed to leave at the end of the month to be resupplied and refreshed in Eastern Prussia, in the Arys training camp. As it was starting for its new billet, it received the order to change route and to make with all speed to Warsaw where an uprising had just begun. It had nevertheless apparently had the time to reorganize itself in part and to transform itself into a brigade, under the name of *Sturmbrigade* (assault brigade) Dirlewanger, endowed with two combat groups disposing of forces approximately equal to those of battalions without, however, reaching the size of a classic battalion.[96]

The Soviet offensive had been irresistible. The push at the central front had been combined with an attack on the southern flank, equally successful, and a whole swathe of what was supposed to be the Germanized heart of the Nazi Empire had fallen into the hands of the Russians. Galicia, Lvov, and Lublin had been reoccupied in the first days of July, and on July 25 small Soviet advance units had established bridgeheads at Magnuscev and at Pulawy, only a few kilometers from Warsaw. The high command ordered them to encircle what remained of the Army Group Center by converging towards the Polish capital.

A week later, the Armia Krajowa launched the uprising, thinking to precede the arrival of the Soviets by a few days. The directors of the AK, Polish nationalists, wanted above all to avoid having the city "liberated" by the Soviets. The day before the great offensive on the Southern front, a national liberation committee controlled by the Soviets had been created with Stalin's approval, prefiguring, in that dictator's eyes, the advent of a Poland controlled by the USSR. That was precisely what Polish nationalists, both in London and in the underground, as well as the Allies, wanted to avoid. On the morning of August 1, therefore, the AK gave the signal for the uprising. Their forces, some 20,000 men, badly armed, without artillery, didn't even have handguns or minimal reserves of munitions. The rebels managed to take by surprise many central neighborhoods, but they failed in their attempts to capture the central railroad and especially the bridges of the Vistula, which would have allowed them to join with Soviet forces.[97] The situation rapidly became desperate as the Germans reacted with particular speed and brutality.

The brigade arrived in Warsaw on August 4, 1944. It stayed there almost three months. But the most intense combat seems to have taken place during the first days of the troop's engagement. Between August 5 and 7, the two combat groups, *Kampfgruppe* Meyer and Steinhauer (named after the officers commanding them), were engaged in the central quarter, along the axis leading from the eastern suburbs to the central Square, with the Brühl Palace as their objective. The mission of the first group was to break through the line, while the second was to follow, "clearing" the site and cutting down pockets of resistance. The first three days were extremely difficult for *Kampfgruppe* Meyer, made up of 356 combatants who were only able to advance 400 meters in the first two days,[98] and who, when they broke through on the third day, lost 310 men—killed, wounded, or missing.[99] This costly success was made even dearer when the insurgents managed to close the breach, obliging the second combat group, reinforced by two companies from a police reserve battalion and a company of constabulary, to make a second assault August 7 and 8, 1944.

The following week was also spent in intense combat in the city. From August 9 on, the Brühl Palace was the unit's rear base, whose general staff, joined by Dirlewanger the night of August 9, were quartered in Stanislas Hospital, where the unit remained billeted until the end of September 1944.[100] The brigade was then engaged in the reconquest of other central neighborhoods and of the neighborhood along the Vistula, until September 2, 1944. Combat was intense, and the brigade distinguished itself both by its extreme violence and, as we have seen, by very high losses. The unit had 881 men in fighting condition when it entered Warsaw. At the end of its action, it had only 648,[101] despite having received a reinforcement, according to the Flensburg prosecutors, of at least 1,650 soldiers from various army detention centers (Anklam, Glatz, and Torgau in particular), as well as 200 criminal concentration camp prisoners. One may thus calculate that the unit lost at least 2,083 men (killed, wounded, or missing).[102] Losses from the Warsaw population were considerably greater, of course: they amounted to 200,000 dead. On August 5, 1944, on the 400 meters captured under fire by the brigade, there were no fewer than 16 massacres of civilians, with a total of 12,500 victims.[103] We know that, despite the denials of its members during post-war trials, the unit performed numerous liquidations, notably during the day of August 5. It is not unreasonable to think that, from August 5 through the end of September 1944, the brigade put some 30,000 civilians to death: not only AK partisans, but also simply men, women, and children.

Dirlewanger was present at the capitulation of the men of the AK. On October 8, when the uprising was finally crushed, Dirlewanger's hierarchical superior, Reinefarth, got him a Knight's Cross, "for his tactical qualities, his coolness, his courage, to which we owe our ability to begin the offensive in the first days [of the uprising]. Dirlewanger always fought on the front lines, giving an example of personal courage."[104] Ten days later, although the brigade was supposed to go rest in the city of Radom, it was instead sent by railroad to Slovakia to combat a new insurrection.

On August 29, 1944, an uprising orchestrated by elements of the army and the pro-communist Slovakian underground had broken out in the region of Banska Bystrica. The target was the pro-German government led by Msgr. Tiso, a government whose policy was cautious, wait-and-see collaboration, supported as it was from the right by Karmazin's Hlinka Guard, favorable to a more extensive collaboration, and by an army fearful of a confrontation with the Soviets, whose approach, since the summer offensive, had become inevitable.[105] The uprising, thus, aimed at preventing the reversal of the strategic situation and anticipating the arrival of the Russians. The Germans were not yet occupying Slovakian territory. At the approach of Russian troops, however, the question of sending in the Wehrmacht grew ever more acute. It was Tiso's agreement to the intervention by German troops that had triggered the rebellion. On August 29, then, while the first and the fourth Ukrainian fronts were on the eastern frontier of Slovakia, the Slovakian army and the underground movements established that summer by communist partisans from Galicia in 1943 launched the insurrection. The heart of the uprising was Banska Bystrica, in the middle of the country, at the foot of the Low Tatras, in which mountain range groups of communist partisans had taken refuge. From the capital, Pressburg (Bratislava), the German forces—*Einsatzgruppe* H of the SIPO and the armed formations of the Fourteenth Division of SS Grenadiers—commanded first by Gottlob Berger, then, after a few days, by Hermann Höfle, left the south for the center of the country.

The Dirlewanger Brigade attacked from the north. It arrived October 17 and 18 by train in Ruzomberok and Biely Potok, located some 50 kilometers north of Banska Bystrica, and intervened in the final phase of the uprising, as the insurgents, beaten in combat, surrendered en masse or tried to take refuge in the Low Tatras in the hope of the rapid arrival of the Soviets. Nine days after the Soviets arrived, the troops coming from the southwest took Banska Bystrica. The brigade's nine days of combat were intense, the well-entrenched enemy resisting their assault. Nevertheless, even if Hans Peter Klausch attempts to put the effects of the latter in perspective, the insurgents' journal, quoted by him, shows that the brigade pushed them back

19 kilometers over nine days.[106] The Nazi hierarchies in place in Slovakia were not of the same mind as those that had supported the men of the unit in Belarus and Warsaw. Höfle was not von dem Bach-Zelewsky, and he was little inclined to welcome on his territory a unit whose bad reputation, to his eyes as well as to those of the population, had preceded it. The brigade was not alone in this: the Ukrainian and Azeri troops enrolled en masse by the SS also had a well-established reputation for pillaging. It is remarkable, nevertheless, that Höfle and the men of the BdS seem not to have been the only ones to complain: the hierarchy of the Fourteenth Division of SS Grenadiers, the very one, made up of Ukrainian volunteers, that had acquired a lurid reputation and operated in the same sector as the brigade, appears, according to certain statements published after the war, to have deplored the inefficiency of Dirlewanger's command, as well as his propensity for disobedience.[107]

The brigade, in any event, underwent few losses, and the combats in which it engaged were not strategically important: no situation report issued by *Einsatzgruppe* H during the final phase of the uprising mentions their sector as significant. No archive of the repression mentions it at combat points. On the other hand, the unit spent the next six weeks in the same sector, where it distinguished itself—something that is mentioned, this time, in *Einsatzgruppe* H's reports—by its brutality towards the civilian population and its pillaging. It was thus, it seems, with a certain relief that Höfle's men saw the brigade leave for Hungary in December 1944.

Since autumn, after the Warsaw insurrection and the great losses the battalion had undergone, Dirlewanger had continued his search for new recruits. He had managed to get any soldiers and SS men jailed for disciplinary reasons assigned to him, which caused, as we have seen, an influx of more than 1,500 SS prisoners from Dantzig-Matzkau, and surely more than 2,000 Wehrmacht prisoners. By mid-October, the unit had between 4,000 and 4,500 men, of whom only 800 maximum came from the group of concentration camp prisoners and the original nucleus of poachers.[108] A new wave of recruitment was once again about to transform relations within the brigade. On October 7, 1944, Dirlewanger sent a personal letter to Himmler in which he noted the proposal made to him by Glücks, the head of the WVHA's concentration camps.[109] "When I was making my selections in the concentration camps," he wrote, "*Gruppenführer* Glücks and *Standartenführer* Pister advised me to try forming a unit of former political opponents of the Movement. In our camps we have men who in February 1933, and perhaps even after March 5, 1933, remained faithful to their own conception of the world and didn't hide behind an appearance of national socialism. In this they showed character, unlike those thousands who went over to the stronger side and, despite an interior hostility, turned towards us with their right arm high after March 5." Dirlewanger therefore asked the *Reichsführer* to promulgate the following orders: "KL commandants will personally select from each camp 250 former adversaries of the Movement whom they firmly believe have changed inwardly and desire to prove so by participating in the struggle of the Greater German Reich. Age, up to forty-five years. In exceptional cases, fifty years. Strictures must be relaxed in the case of notable military skills."[110]

Dirlewanger got Himmler's agreement the following week.[111] One month later selections were finished in the concentration camps and on November 7 the selected prisoners—essentially communists or socialists—left to join the unit. The directives given by Himmler and the WVHA set the number of political prisoners to be incorporated in the brigade at 2,000. For example, 441 were supposed to come from Auschwitz, 149 from Dachau, and 775 from Sachsenhausen. In reality, only 800 came. Transports joined the brigade progressively starting

November 15, the formalities of incorporation having been performed in Cracow between the prisoners' leaving the camps and their being sent to the unit. From the start, it was understood that the political prisoners would be concentrated in the third battalion of the second regiment of the brigade. Within the brigade, the prisoners from Sachsenhausen were to constitute the ninth and twelfth companies, the two others not being made up of political prisoners. The other political prisoners were incorporated in the second battalion of the same regiment, where they formed the fifth, sixth, seventh, and eighth companies and constituted a minority among the other "populations" represented, while the number of political prisoners in the third battalion allowed them to remain among themselves.[112] This strategy of concentration set by the unit's commanders, curious as it may seem, was traditional: since the summer of 1942, the practice of integrating new populations had always aimed at preserving the cohesion of the groups preceding the new arrivals. Nevertheless, even in the eyes of the unit's commanders, this population could not be compared to those incorporated earlier: the marginality of the preceding arrivals was social and judicial, while this last group consisted of men whose ideological antagonism to Nazism was obvious, as was their political proximity to the Soviet enemy, represented as it was by the Ukrainian partisans infiltrated from Galicia.

In the final analysis, however, these new arrivals represented an upheaval in the atmosphere of the unit, but not, it must be recognized, in its composition. At the very moment the last political prisoners were arriving, the unit was assigned an SS judge, given the responsibility, as we will see in the next chapter, of reintroducing a minimum of procedural regularity in the arbitrary disciplinary practices current in the brigade. Interrogated after the war, this judge gave American investigators a striking picture of the makeup of the Dirlewanger unit in late 1944:

43

The Brigade consisted of 6,500 men and was made up as follows: the old stock of poachers had been promoted over time to the highest NCO posts. A small group, approximately ten to thirteen percent, was SS men or former police officers, punished and expelled, sent to the unit to be put to the test. Thirty percent of the men were former concentration camp prisoners, some political, the others common criminals. The largest group of men— more than fifty percent—were men from the three Wehrmacht corps sent there for disciplinary reasons. There were also two regular artillery batteries from the Police. Besides these batteries, there were a handful of men and officers who had not been condemned.[113]

Even if this inexplicit testimony must be considered with the greatest prudence, it nevertheless puts in proportion, in terms of troop strength, the arrival of the political prisoners. The unit was not now made up of "antifascists in SS uniform," to use the title of Hans Peter Klausch's book. But it was also no longer a unit of "black hunters."

On December 9, 1944, the unit, then billeted in the Slovakian countryside to the rear, received the order to move southeast immediately, towards the Hungarian frontier. The push on the Ukrainian fronts, begun in the summer of 1944, had brought the Soviet troops into the Hungarian Puszta; they were within reach of Budapest, which was defended by the South Army Group and threatened with encirclement. Höfle took the initiative of sending part of the brigade to support the troops of *Heeresgruppe* "South," which held this sector of the front.[114] The men of the unit were entrusted with a sector of capital importance. North of the city, on the left bank of the Danube, the front made a salient before the town of Ypolysag, the block preventing Russian tanks from completing the southwestern turning movement that had encircled the Hungarian capital. On

December 11 and 12, 1944, the combat units of the brigade were charged as follows: the second regiment to occupy the town itself and the first regiment to provide cover and protection outside the town.

The unit's intervention appeared inauspicious, and Dirlewanger, like Himmler and Höfle, was well aware of the brigade's unpreparedness. Dirlewanger even refused, in his own words, to "fight the Russians with communists."[115] In three days, the situation collapsed: the Russians attacked Ypolysag, which was held only by a company although a regiment had been expected. On December 14 the town was in their possession and the two regiments from the unit, while not changing billet, went under the orders of the fourth tank corps of the Wohler Army Group. The town had been taken, according to the general staff themselves, due to a fatal tactical error on Dirlewanger's part. The defense of the Ypolysag salient and of the town itself was a fundamental weak point, given the sparseness of his garrison. But there was worse: the men of the general staff observed that an entire company of the second regiment of the brigade, composed of those recently incorporated political prisoners, had gone over to the enemy. From the following day on, the Soviets exploited the terrain and attacked in force from the town. Dirlewanger counterattacked quickly with five of his battalions, but despite some initial tactical successes, the Army Group was obliged to send in five reserve divisions to attempt to recover the town and to reset the blocking point.[116] It was in vain, though, as the town remained in Russian hands. Ten days later, the encirclement of Budapest was in effect, but the defection of the soldiers and the loss of Ypolysag did not alone explain the fall of the Hungarian capital. The city held out until February 11 and then was occupied by the Soviets, who multiplied their exactions against the civilian population.[117]

On January 12, the first Ukrainian front made a significant offensive attack on the salient of the front on the Vistula,

45

reconquering the Polish cities of Czestochowa, Cracow, and Lodz, and threatening those of Breslau and Poznan, transformed into fortresses; this time, the territory of the Reich itself was threatened with Soviet invasion.[118] Himmler, who had been named head of the Vistula Army Group, hastily brought back the brigade, which, like the Ninth Army, was billeted in Lusatia, near Cottbus. Dirlewanger seems to have been present and to have followed his troops as they settled near Guben in the second week of February 1945. On February 16, however, the brigade was assigned a new commander, *Brigadeführer* Schmedes, who had already served in the unit before as a regimental colonel. Dirlewanger had apparently fallen ill, one of his chest wounds having reopened and become infected. He left to be cared for in Swabia and never returned to Lusatia. The unit was split in two, one of its regiments being entrusted to *Heeresgruppe* Vistula and to the Ninth Army, while the other, together with the rest of the unit, went under the command of *Heeresgruppe* Mitte and was attached to the Fourth Tank Army.

Beginning on February 15, the brigade engaged in intense combat in Nauenfeld and Krossen. This was the beginning of a final engagement of sixty days, marked at once by desertions, in small groups, of a certain number of political prisoners, and by the intensification of violence within the unit itself. On the institutional level, the unit had undergone a last transformation on February 19: by Himmler's order, it had become the Thirty-Sixth Division of SS Grenadiers. A strange division: no sooner had it been established in theory than it was taken apart in practice and its elements dispersed among "various troop corps." The unit was completed by one hundred SS student officers from a nearby *Junkerschule* who were immediately assigned to be section or company leaders, as well as by 400 SS prisoners.

Combat consisted of a very unequal war of position: two million Germans against six million Soviet soldiers. Since the former now lacked munitions, provisions, and air cover, the

Russians could attack daily, engaging companies and regiments in turn, supported by numerous tanks, simply to harass the German troops, while Zhukov prepared the great offensive that was to end in the conquest of Berlin, now less than 100 kilometers away.[119] In this war of position, the combat practices of the division hardly differed from those of the other troop corps, alternating insignificantly successful counteroffensives with limited retreats. Formations of the unit also participated in offensives intended to relieve the city of Küstrin on the Neisse. During this time, north and south of this portion of the front, the Russians had launched operations to reinforce their line and eliminate the last redoubts of resistance, like Posen, Breslau, Pomerania, and Silesia. During these two months, the Soviets concentrated on the center front more than fourteen million soldiers who were to be the spearhead of the future Battle of Berlin.

The great attack took place on April 16, 1945. General Gotthard Heinrici, who a few days before had replaced Himmler at the head of the *Heeresgruppe*, tried to prepare his defense and fortify his positions. But, although he prepared artillery "as never before," the flood of tanks and infantry rapidly submerged the German forces. Two days after the offensive began, the front was broken and the units, despite a desperate defense, fell apart under the Soviet battering ram. The Ninth Army and the Fourth Tank Army, the two formations to which the division's units were attached, were encircled in the Halbe region, less than 100 kilometers from Berlin. The last statistics available to us, even if they aren't totally trustworthy, eloquently express the division's annihilation. On April 25, there remained nothing of the first regiment, only thirty-six men of the second regiment hadn't been disabled, and the artillery and engineering corps had completely gone missing.[120]

It is difficult to give an account of this last offensive. The last figures date, let us recall, from the engagement in Hungary and claim 6,500 men.[121] If we assume that losses in Hungary were only partly replaced by the influx of SS student officers, soldiers from different troop corps, and political prisons between the beginning of February and the end of April, we could estimate 6,000 men in the division, of whom only 250 were political prisoners, and fewer still asocials and criminals. Condemned SS men and soldiers made up the majority of the unit. Of these 6,000 men, only fifty remained on April 25, 1945. The others were killed in action, wounded, or taken prisoner—634 returns from Soviet prison camps were counted.[122] So ended the existence of the Thirty-Sixth SS Grenadier Division, responsible for the death of at least 60,000 individuals, most of them civilians.

Chapter 2

The Dirlewanger Case

The debate over "ordinary Germans" versus "willing executioners" has, beyond the differences opposing partisans of one interpretation or the other, always involved the thorny question of the normal and the pathological.[1] The study of the Dirlewanger unit is no exception. The answer appears simple: the unit was made up of the criminal dregs of the German army and of the concentration camps, with the exception of the political prisoners added near the end of the war, and its leader himself was a criminal whose practices seemed abnormal even by Nazi standards. With reassuring and unanimous agreement these men are viewed as the perverse rejects of a system that itself was perverse. But Dirlewanger was also the product of a society and an era, and thus revelatory of social and cultural mechanisms that played an important part in Germany's destiny. As a Nazi foot soldier, Dirlewanger was at once a man at war, a political militant, and a misfit.

War as Horizon

Oskar Dirlewanger was born September 26, 1895, and died June 7, 1945.[2] He participated in World War I immediately after his military service, begun in 1913, and he continued to fight for at least three years in various armed formations. Thus, his

Great War lasted eight years. Starting in 1936, he was engaged in the Condor Legion and participated for three years in the Spanish Civil War, before coming back to Germany and attempting to join the Waffen-SS. He took part in the war starting in the summer of 1940. His combat activity may be considered to have lasted nine years. Dirlewanger experienced a total of seventeen years of war—a third of his biological life and more than half of his life as an adult. But his childhood and formative years were spent in a world at peace, that of Wilhelm's Germany.[3]

Oskar Dirlewanger was born in Würzburg, Swabia, in the south of Germany, where he spent his childhood and adolescence, moving to Stuttgart in 1900, then to the suburbs of that city, to Esslingen, in 1905.[4] His father was from a middle class family. Of his parents, Dirlewanger wrote that they were "neither poor, nor wealthy," that his father was "calm, intelligent, and frugal," and that their relationship was "peaceful." A family without history, so to speak.

Dirlewanger obtained the German equivalent of the baccalaureate, although his education did not include the humanities. His post-baccalaureate studies in a renovated lyceum destined him for the private sector. Eighteen years old in April 1913, he enlisted without waiting for the October draft, like many young students. Thus, he was at the end of a year of army service when Germany entered the war.[5]

Oskar Dirlewanger's war began on August 2, in a machine gun company of the 123rd regiment of grenadiers, who were heading to France from Ulm by way of Belgium. In the confusion of general mobilization, troops that had already had their basic training were considered as part of the Reich's standing army; thus, they were the spearhead of the Schlieffen Plan, and Dirlewanger was thrust into the battle at a time when losses were at their most nightmarish.[6]

One can but imagine that this experience became the touchstone of his character. Unfortunately, aside from the list of his postings, his wounds, and his decorations,[7] we have little firsthand information and even less personal insight into key elements of his relationship to combat: his first contact with the enemy, his entry into enemy territory, and the threat of snipers that made any Belgian or French civilian a potential suspect and often, at that time, a candidate for the firing squad.[8] Dirlewanger was a machine gunner—he had been trained as one for a year; in other words, he was a prime target and above all, because of his weapon and his early training, a soldier in isolation, exposed.

The machine gun was not new at the time of the war; it had been used, notably, in the Russo-Japanese War, as well as in Africa and in the Balkans. What was new in 1914 was that the two opposing armies had massive supplies of this weapon, considered by the Germans as "indispensible for infantry."[9] At the beginning of the war, machine guns, most of them heavy caliber and neither numerous nor extremely mobile, were not a permanent element of the infantry battalion, oriented as this unit was towards attack by rifle formations in a war of movement. Starting in 1916, trench warfare and the war of position led commanders to favor the light machine gun and to make it a fundamental element of the infantry. In 1914 there were 323 companies with six guns each; in 1918, nearly 2,500 companies with twelve.[10] Thus, the machine gun became the terrible queen of the battlefields of the Great War.

The soldier Dirlewanger was wounded in the foot during the first four months of battle. He seems not to have returned to the front until June 1915, after a long convalescence. In September 1915, he was again wounded, this time in the arm by cold steel, and was incapacitated by 40 percent.[11] He was one of the very rare soldiers of the Great War to have survived this type of wound, representing barely 1 percent of the convalescents counted. This is hardly surprising in light of the panoply available in the trenches—dagger, sharpened shovel, bayonet—and the efficacy of these tools. The blade killed more surely than the bullet: it was the weapon of hand-to-hand combat, of the most transgressive violence, the least spoken of in that war.[12]

Recovered from his wound, Dirlewanger was posted in September 1916 to the general staff of the Württemberg Seventh Defense Division and made instructor in machine gun courses. He had been promoted in the meantime to NCO, according to the practices of the German army—promotion according to behavior under fire, transmission of experience to troops in training within a program of instruction going straight to the essential: assault under fire. Dirlewanger perfectly embodied the profile of a man experienced in combat, risen from the ranks, who would prepare the new generation of soldiers that, building on the experience of their elders, would make Germany's final, decisive effort.[13]

They were trained as riflemen, experts in moving silently, in using the characteristics of the terrain to get as close as possible to enemy positions in order to open fire and profit by the element of surprise. With this in mind, coordination between riflemen and teams of machine gunners was crucial, and the latter needed to be as mobile as shock troops. The course designed by the instructors therefore included physical training—obstacle courses, races with full military kit; technical training—exercises preparing crew members to assume varied duties, simulating the loss of the spotter, of the group leader, or of the dispatch riders; and shooting—by day, by night, with gas mask, and so forth.[14]

But his duties as instructor did not satisfy him. Having received a new posting in November 1916, Dirlewanger again volunteered, in April 1917, for the front lines. Yet, as previously noted, his cutting wound had permanently stiffened his left arm and had even affected the use of that wrist entirely, although the autopsy report identifying him in 1960 does not confirm this.[15] At this autopsy, however, examination of Dirlewanger's skeleton nevertheless showed a complex fracture of the right foot whose seriousness is demonstrated by the formation of a bony callus and a deformed big toe, as well as a slighter deformation of the left shoulder.[16] Both attributed to Dirlewanger's first wounds, they confirm his disability. Despite this handicap, Dirlewanger was thus promoted to the rank of lieutenant, and, still within the Seventh Wurtemberg Division, became responsible for the second company of the 121st infantry battalion. In line with the new tactic in which he himself had trained recruits the preceding year, this company was made up solely of machine gun crews.

This posting marked a second rupture in Dirlewanger's experience of war: he served until November 1918 in the southern part of the Eastern front.[17] We have no information on his experiences during this third and last period. Combat in Russia was already a type of war of movement. And not without reason: when Dirlewanger arrived on the front, the Russian army was collapsing. This situation, of course, had little to do with the war of position on the Western front, but for the first time Dirlewanger came to grips with his founding experience: the confrontation with unknown populations in a space imagined as infinite.[18] If there were ever a laboratory for the ethnic fear of the enemy during the Great War, it was the Eastern front. Over and over, soldiers' letters spoke of the dirtiness, the inferiority, the primitive nature of the population,[19] and this observation reinforced a social Darwinism and an essentialist view of the Eastern populations. Dirlewanger stayed in Russia until November 1918 as company leader and lieutenant.

One of the men of his regiment had this to say about the end of his war: "When the revolution broke out, our battalion was on the road leading from southern Russia to the Fatherland, and was supposed to be interned in Romania. Lieutenant Dirlewanger decided to push through and go back to the Fatherland. The other companies' troops, some of whom weren't happy with their officers, voluntarily put themselves under Lieutenant D.'s orders. He brought them back home, through monstrous efforts and dangers, keeping them to the old discipline. It is rare for an officer to be honored as our comrade Dirlewanger was after his successful return, a return that the soldiers owed to him alone. He kept 600 men from being interned as so many were before and after us. [. . .]"[20]

This text is surely not free from ideological complicity between the "hero" of its war saga and the journalist, both Nazis and members of the SA when the article was written. Nevertheless, the narrator does seem to have been a direct observer of the machine gunners' odyssey. And it must be recognized that nothing invalidates this odyssey, nor the charismatic dimension assumed—we will come back to this point— by a Dirlewanger refusing to be sidelined or to let his unit be abandoned.

Dirlewanger was at once a survivor and an expert. Familiar with the new usages of grenades, blades, rifles, and repeating artillery, he was selected to transmit these procedures to new recruits. In many ways, Dirlewanger's experience lays out the paradigm of the early twentieth-century warrior. Nevertheless, we must not accept this as an exact portrait: if the majority of the men who fought could recognize themselves in the Dirlewanger case, there were elements in his character less widely shared. His volunteering reveals a troubling hunger for military action. His attitude under fire, often evoked among the justifications for decorating him, was characterized by great bravery, personal excellence, and a "desire to achieve" expressing both a conformity to the norm—developed by training that aimed to make troopers both disciplined and autonomous—and a much less widespread attraction to combat. Dirlewanger, without a doubt, fell in love with war almost immediately, to the point of not being able to accept being kept away from it by a disabling wound.

If combat had a primary fascination for him, the other dimension of his experience, its cultural dimension, is less easy to evaluate. Dirlewanger left no writing, no letters, providing us with a little more knowledge of how he perceived the conflict into which he was projected. He clung, no doubt, to that vision of a "world of enemies" allied against Germany. His presence in an invading army, in Belgium (in which he quickly lost the ability to distinguish between civilians and soldiers), his passage into the army of the East (marked by colonial references), the memory of the crusades, and the ethnic perception of an adversary stigmatized as savage and backward, no doubt also led him to live in that vision of a besieged citadel through which German society represented itself in war.

His demobilization could have been a new point of departure, a reintegration into a society attempting to disassociate itself from war. But his demobilization was no demobilization, and his course describes perfectly Germany's difficulty in returning to stability. Dirlewanger belonged to three army units: the Twenty-first *Reichswehr* Protection Brigade, the Thirteenth Wurtemberg Brigade of the Reichswehr, and General Sprösser's Wurtemberg volunteer section, all three derived from the *Freikorps*. In this context, Dirlewanger fought, at first, against communist insurrectionary general strikes in the Württemberg region, plunging through the little towns around Stuttgart in an armored train under his command and filled, originally, with men from his machine gun company. After having fought in the area where he was born, Dirlewanger left Württemberg to take part in actions against communist movements in the Ruhr in

March 1920, and then, in 1921, in the Central German insurrection in Saxony and Thüringen, where events culminated in confrontation with armed groups led by Max Hoelz.[21]

On Wednesday, March 26, 1921, the armed communist groups, some three hundred strong, burst into the little city of Sangerhausen, situated on the northwestern edge of the terrain of the uprising, after the local section of the KPD had two days earlier called for a general strike and the active support of the uprising begun a few days before in the neighboring city of Mansfeld. The communist militants occupied public places and official buildings, and began to extort money, clothes, and food from the city's elites. Hoelz and his men attacked property in the main, destroying the telegraph service and taking a number of patricians hostage, all with the avowed goal of confiscating large sums of money, necessary in their eyes to finance the general strike and insurrection. The same day, the armored train commanded by Dirlewanger entered the Sangerhausen station and confronted Hoelz's men. More heavily armed and better trained than the communist militants, Dirlewanger's men rapidly gained the upper hand, and their adversaries were forced to leave the city that very evening. In the exchange of fire, seven soldiers, three insurgents, and three city inhabitants lost their lives.[22] According to Dirk Schumann, the events of Sangerhausen had a traumatic effect on the population of Thüringen, not so much because of the exchange of fire between the insurgents and the armed men but because of the use of explosives, which caused significant damage in the city. Interestingly, non-communist newspapers described Hoelz's action as a "bandit war."[23] In our view, this semantic shift indicates how the enemy was transferred from one "war" to another: for the first time, Dirlewanger was making war against an enemy marked as communist, whom it was unthinkable to recognize as a legitimate combatant.

If the general population viewed these civil upheavals as war psychosis, if counterrevolutionary activists viewed them as combat, it is not surprising that Dirlewanger integrated them into a continuation of the Great War against a "world of enemies."[24] During the fighting at Sangerhausen he received his fourth wound, this time to the head.[25] His later autopsy report shows that it was a slicing wound that opened the parietal bone, reaching the brain without actually touching it, but putting his life at great risk.[26]

The "liberation" of Sangerhausen was different from the previous combat, and the actors were fully conscious of that. Society was no longer the same as it had been before the war, and while the national sanctuary might be menaced by internal enemy action, norms of behavior were no longer what they had been during that conflict. The regime considered certain of Dirlewanger's actions illegal, and twice, in 1920 and 1921, he was condemned to short prison terms for participation in concealing weapons. The next condemnation occurred only a few weeks after the Sangerhausen episode. He spent two weeks in prison, and two days after his release again joined a *Freikorps* and left to fight in Upper Silesia.[27] Oskar Dirlewanger, thus, belonged until 1924 to the paramilitary formation movement that descended directly from the combats of the Great War.

Doubtless, as we will later see, combat wasn't Dirlewanger's whole life; but it drew his horizon, structured his expectations, and determined his movements. Certainly, this "war" didn't have the same intensity as the great conflagration whose end, signed at Versailles, he refused to accept; but it succeeded it, though without providing the resolution of a clear continuity. The last noteworthy episodes of Dirlewanger's engagement, in any event, lost their warlike character, demonstrating at once a certain normalization of political life in Weimar and a growing fusion between political engagement and military or paramilitary activity. The last action of this type in which Dirlewanger participated was a fruitless attempt to support the NSDAP putsch in Munich in 1923 by sending in the Stuttgart police forces' armored vehicles.

So ended the first period of military activity in which Dirlewanger participated. He was now a twenty-nine-year-old activist, his body and soul irrevocably marked by the experience of war and its prolongation. A period of twelve years would follow during which time war would recede from his horizon, before invading it once again, this time permanently, in 1936, when he joined the Condor Legion in Spain, an engagement of which we know little.

The continuation of his military life then merges with the fate of the unit he founded, which bore his name and which he led, practically, until the end. A unit in which he reinvested the knowledge accumulated during the Great War and its prolongations. Having extensive experience of combat and unit leadership, with a solid training in assault techniques and trench warfare and with a history as an instructor in these techniques, he could pick and choose from these skills in the creation and organization of the unit he led. In doing so, he reinvested the experience of the Great War, a fund of memory completed by combat in revolutionary Germany where Dirlewanger and the *Freikorps* fought against an enemy without a uniform, badly armed, disappearing into the civilian population, and organized in bands rather than in regular military formations. This last experience led him to confront an atypical type of war, prelude to the partisan war he led for three years in Belarus, Poland, and Slovakia. As in the city streets of Thüringen and Württemberg, the adversaries of the Belarusian forests and the Warsaw streets were political adversaries; as in the counter-revolutionary battles, it was difficult to distinguish between civilians and soldiers.[28]

Militancy as Substitution

Dirlewanger enrolled at the Technical University of Mannheim as soon as he was demobilized. The student world of that time was subject to several phenomena linked to the demobilization, material or cultural, of the young German elite. They had paid a heavy tribute to war. Losses among the volunteer battalions in 1914 and the high percentage of officers killed at the front had thinned their ranks. Aside from the difficult integration of students returning from the front, there was also the problem of incorporating new generations of university students who had experienced war behind the front lines, with its food scarcities, its mourning, and its cultural mobilization, whose importance is still not fully measured. Be that as it may, student associations were going through a period of upheaval, a fact worth noting even before examining more closely the career of the student Oskar Dirlewanger himself. The years 1920–1921 were thus marked by new representatives in the general student councils, the *Allgemeine Studentische Ausschüsse* (AStA), which directed student life in the universities. The evolution of student life was based on a strong associative tradition that, since the beginning of the century, was more and more concerned with political problems going beyond the university itself. The appearance of youth movements, of opinion-based associations, the participation of student groups in the "war of words," and finally their function as a mourning community during the war put all associations—athletic, cultural, corporatist—in a position of engagement with the problems stirring Germany in its time of trouble. Richard Bessel and George Mosse, for example, have shown that students were disproportionately represented in *Freikorps*, defensive militias, and movements of resistance to the consequences of the war and the defeat.[29] In the 1920–1921 elections, the politicization of students increased to general surprise given their pre-war pluralism—although there was a leaning to the right at that time.[30]

The main German student organization was the *Deutsche Hochschulring*, which as of 1919 fell under the direction of *völkisch* students. In 1921, the *Deutsche Studentenschaft*, an authority representing students in the governing bodies of the university, also seemed to be turning towards an elitist revolutionary ethno-nationalism through the action of radical student organizations. The movement, common to all German universities, has been admirably summarized for the case of Berlin by the great German historian Friedrich Meinecke: "Out of 10,000 students, 9,400 simply went to their lecture halls, seminars, or laboratories and cared only for their studies and exams. Some 600 were enthusiasts, of whom 400 were hyper-nationalist and '*völkische*,' while the 200 remaining students were divided among communists, social democrats, and democrats."[31]

This description does not take into account the strong support of the silent majority for *völkisch* ideas. Starting in 1921, nationalist groups began their assault, thanks to the elections, on the AStA and the *Deutsche Studentenschaft*.[32] Among these groups, naturally, was the *Deutsche Hochschulring*. Against the background of the occupation of the Rhineland and of the uprisings in Silesia, at the moment when large numbers of students, like Dirlewanger, were joining *Freikorps* such as the Ehrard Brigade or the Orgesch, a debate broke out in the German student congress meeting in Erlangen on the subject of conditions for joining the association. The *völkisch* radicals raised the question of "German lineage" as a criterion, as well as that of the future status of Jewish members of the association.[33] In 1922, at the fourth student congress, the *Deutsche Hochschulring*, already a majority party in the *Studentenschaft*, imposed, by eliminating the leaders elected in 1921 at Erlangen, its racist and anti-Semitic position, voted in then and there with a two-thirds majority.[34] It designated leadership in conformity with the new line at the following congress, held at Würzburg—Dirlewanger's birthplace. Since the Erlangen congress, a pan-German congress, these principles had been inscribed in statutes of the Austrian and Sudeten *Studentenschaften*, forbidding access to students who could not prove their "German bloodlines." The German case was more complex due to the institution's relationship to public powers: the *Deutsche Studentenschaft* was financed and recognized by the state and thus could not legally inscribe exclusion of Jews and foreigners in its statutes. In 1921, however, despite pressure from the Prussian Ministry of Religion and Instruction, successive student votes approved by very large majorities— between 66 percent and 90 percent of the votes—the *völkisch* and anti-Semitic line. Student participation, amounting to around 70 percent of total registered students, is the most definite indication of general consent to the "biological" projects of the activist far right:[35] the silent majority described by Meinecke expresses itself here without ambiguity.

Oskar Dirlewanger had thus begun in 1919 an intermittent course of study at the technical university of Mannheim, interrupted by his periods of service in the Württemberg armed forces. He distinguished himself very early by his *völkisch* convictions and expressed them with unusual violence. The University threatened him with disciplinary proceedings for "avowed anti-Semitic agitation." This fact merely reflects Dirlewanger's political involvement. Since 1919 he had been a member of the *Deutsch völkisch Schutzund Trutzbund*, one of the most virulent organizations in terms both of anti-Semitic hatred and of revolutionary nationalist feeling. It counted in its ranks future leaders of Nazi repression, such as Reinhard Heydrich and Reinhard Höhn.[36] Dirlewanger belonged to a nebula of parties and associations linked by the feeling that Germany was in imminent danger of disappearing, diminished as it was by territorial losses, the rulings of the treaty of Versailles, and internal and external enemies who, despite the peace treaty, had not disarmed. All believed that the world of enemies that Germany had fought for four years continued its work even within the frontiers of the Reich, beneath the mask of communist activists or in the form of Jews, to whom Germans attributed the main responsibility for the revolutionary troubles that had forced Germany (unvanquished, to their mind, on the battlefield) to sign an infamous pact.

Oskar Dirlewanger left the University of Mannheim for Frankfurt, studied economics and law for six semesters in all, and finished his scholastic career with a doctorate in "political science."[37] His studies having been oriented towards professional practice, he became an accountant and occupied a certain number of positions of responsibility in various businesses. At that point, his political activity diminished. He had certainly become a member of the NSDAP in 1923, on the occasion of gymnastics meetings in Munich, but his involvement slowed considerably after the failure of Hitler's putsch. Like all members of the party, he submitted to the latter's interdiction after the putsch and rejoined in 1926, when its existence again became legal. The contrast between the period preceding the putsch and its political activity is symptomatic of the change undergone by far right revolutionary militancy. Until 1923, it was a substitute for war: Dirlewanger, as we have seen, alternated periods of service in the *Freikorps*, of study, and of militancy, all in a defensive mode in perfect continuity with the culture developed during 1914–1918.

After 1926, militants engaged in electoral activism, exactly as did NSDAP organizations themselves. This activism was certainly not free of violence, but it did not use the representation and experience of war in the same way. Dirlewanger was only marginally involved in this evolution: he had again been obliged to renounce the Nazi party, for reasons that his NSDAP evaluators judged with an extremely peculiar indulgence. From 1928 to 1931, as it happened, Dirlewanger was the executive director of a textile factory owned by a Jewish family in Erfurt. If Dirlewanger renounced active service in the "Nazi cause," he nevertheless remained—the SD report claims in his defense—a benefactor of the SA.[38]

He again joined the SA and the NSDAP in 1932, under radically different conditions: the party he had known in its larval stage from 1923–1926 was about to become one of the three main German parties, brilliantly confirming the success of the strategy of legal conquest of power inaugurated after the failure of the putsch. However, militancy in the SA was still experienced as belonging to the world of combat, with a direct linear relation to the warrior imagination. One of Dirlewanger's old companions in Russia expressed it clearly in the article he devoted to him in the *Sangerhausener Zeitung*:

> During the world war, Dr. Dirlewanger was my company leader and, as a member of the armored train [that he directed] I wish to report the following facts to you:
>
> The leader of the armored train that liberated Sangerhausen in 1921 was wounded thrice during the war and was the only officer of our regiment who volunteered, despite a debilitating war handicap (stiffened left wrist) to command a machine gun company at the front. [. . .] He saved 600 men from internment [. . .]. A few weeks after the battle of Sangerhausen, our comrade Dirlewanger was arrested at his home and incarcerated for fourteen days in Mosbach prison for breaking the law against possession or use of weapons. This sentence clearly did not "reform" him, for two days after his release he rushed to Upper Silesia to fulfill his duty as a soldier.

Today, comrade Dirlewanger is serving as a simple SA in Adolf Hitler's brown army. Let his example inspire many other veterans to join the SA![39]

Dirlewanger's SA officer's dossier shows his ascension to have been rapid. He served a year as a simple trooper, then was swiftly promoted to the rank of *Truppführer* and, in three months, received the temporary command of a *Sturmbann*, before being named *Obertruppenführer* fifteen days later, then *Sturmführer* with a permanent *Sturmbann* command. Dirlewanger participated, at the very moment the *Sangerhausener Zeitung* was publishing his praises, in the assault on the Union House of Esslingen with his *Sturmbann*. This brawl made a certain impression in the region, for it recalled in many ways the confrontations of the times of troubles. Dirlewanger was wounded once again and identified by the police, which brought him another condemnation for disturbing the peace. This was his last condemnation for political reasons by Weimar justice. The episode, as far as one can judge, confirms that the SA was a sort of conservatory of the activist practices of the years of trouble, the prolongation, even on the semantic level, of the affective universe, and the social bonds formed on the battlefields of the Great War and perpetuated in the *Freikorps*. It was at once an example of the use of violence and a framework of socialization, whose fundamental role in the structuring of the Nazi movement contemporary historians are at pains to point out.

We have said that Oskar Dirlewanger combined militant commitment, paramilitary activities, university study, and professional practice. Should we conclude that he considered his extra-political activities at the university and in the professional world as separate from his Nazi commitment? The content of his thesis left no doubt as to his political opinions. This work of a hundred pages, slightly more than the average for this period, was accepted for his doctorate on condition that its thesis be modified—a modification he still had not performed in 1925, the year the University threatened to invalidate his diploma if he did not comply.[40] His work was entitled, "Towards a critique of the theory of planned control of the economy." From the introduction, Dirlewanger began by summarizing the economic and political history of the Reich since 1871 and the birth of that central European "economic entity" arising from the creation of the German state and growing, according to him, from thirty million inhabitants to seventy million between 1870 and 1914 thanks to the improvement in subsistence methods due to an economic development brutally ended by the Great War. For Dirlewanger, this developing economy "transformed itself into an economy of scarcity which demanded a sudden change of the state's economic policy. The latter had recourse to authoritarian organization, to requisitions, to price restrictions and control, in other words to a system of state intervention synonymous with centralization and bureaucratization."[41] From the start, Dirlewanger gave his work a political connotation, perceptible from the title onwards, from which the rest of the work would not deviate. The representation of the Great War, of that "enemy full of hate and desire [for destruction]," of Germany the victim of iniquitous and harmful peace conditions, conformed at every point with that crystallized by the German culture of war, a very common image shared by men all along the political spectrum, from the liberal historian Gerhard Ritter to avowed *völkischer* like Werner Best.[42] But Dirlewanger went further: after describing the economic consequences of the war and its aftermath, then analyzing them in terms of inflation and the pauperization of the property-owning middle classes, he insisted on the perception of these mechanisms by entire sectors of the population, convinced of the failure of capitalism. For him, it was because "the theory of socialism and the aspiration towards socialization live[d] today in millions of heads that it is urgent to examine them critically."[43]

Dirlewanger conceived his work as an academic contribution in response to this invasion of the popular mind by revolutionary socialism described at the end of his introduction. The memory of war, economic anxiety, and anticommunist feeling mingled in a work whose political message was clear. What is surprising is that this political message is expressed in a doctoral thesis, a work traditionally colorless in the fields of law and political economy, if we are to judge by the theses of the jurists of future institutions of repression of the Third Reich, themselves *völkisch* activists at that period.[44] Dirlewanger, on the contrary, chose to orient his doctoral work resolutely towards militancy, seeing therein a way of opposing on a theoretical level the advance of the leftist enemy. A weapon in the battle of ideas, so to speak, if this term could be said to have a meaning for him, who wrote between the Thüringen uprisings and his passage to Upper Silesia.

He meant not only to criticize the project of communist collectivization, but also to contribute to a *völkisch* theory of economic planning. And after some preliminary remarks, Dirlewanger dealt immediately with the only case in which, for him, it was legitimate to introduce economic planning: the state of war. For him, "it is profitable to study a planned control of the economy if it is intended to be implemented when a vital need of the nation (for example, the defense of its territory) requires a planned organization and a centralized direction of the economy. If the appearance of such a phenomenon has for condition an attitude of the people similar to that of 1914, a spirit full of a pure and true love of country, then the ethical conditions for a planned economy would be partly fulfilled."[45] After having dismissed socialist and liberal theorists, he continued by stressing the practical dimension of his work, thus revealing another objective of his text: "In a future war, because of the geographic situation of our country, we must deal with an economy of scarcity despite all possible preparations. And all objections to a planned control of the economy must be put aside before the national objective of creating, by means of a planned control of the economy, the economic conditions favorable to the conduct of war."[46] Thus, for Dirlewanger, centralization and economic planning were one of the indispensable conditions of victory. His statement was based on reference to the previous war, which had been lost, according to him, because of the weakening of the country due to scarcity, before the final "knife in the back." Beyond even the question of theoretical struggle against socialist theories, Dirlewanger prepared here, in his discourse, the renewal of a combat that for him had never been interrupted.

In the beginning was the war, the war that Germany had temporarily lost and that had cast it into a dire fate. The revolutionary episodes and the communist threat seemed to hold the front of the stage, in his life as in his thesis. But the paramilitary, militant, and academic combat that preoccupied him were all oriented toward that Great War whose final issue, for him, had not yet been decided.

Marginality and Tenacity

Was Dirlewanger seen as a marginal man, an "outcast," to use the expression of Ernst von Salomon, like him a *Freikorps* fighter and a *völkisch* sympathizer? We must observe, before even attempting to answer this question, that Dirlewanger was embroiled regularly with the civil authorities, starting as soon as he returned from the front. His troubles began in 1921, at the University of Mannheim, when he was threatened with disciplinary action for "avowed anti-Semitic agitation." The accusation did not specify if the problem lay in the content—the anti-Semitism—or in the form taken by this agitation. If one remembers that the student corporations were at this very moment adopting the statutes allowing them to request certificates of nationality and to exclude Jewish students, one is inclined to believe that it was the form of Dirlewanger's action that called down on him the wrath of university authorities.

Dirlewanger was then twice sanctioned, but that by no means indicated marginality: for post-war German prosecutors, little inclined to pro-Nazi sympathies or unwarranted indulgence towards crimes or misdemeanors, these two condemnations were pronounced for "far from dishonorable political reasons."[47]

For all his legal liabilities, his contemporaries did not consider Dirlewanger socially inadmissible. We can thus better understand his singular judicial history. We have seen that the SD's report on his morality and his ideological reliability specified that he had had to leave the SA between 1928 and 1931 because he had then been employed as the executive director by what the men of the SD called a "Jewish business." "As such, he remained a constant financial benefactor of the SA," the report continued.[48] We infer that Dirlewanger continued to give money to his *Sturmbann*. But where did the money come from? The "As such" of the SD men strongly suggests that Dirlewanger got it from the cashbox of the textile business that employed him. It was surely a militant gesture, for the SS men of the SD, but it was also an act of embezzlement, a crime that, to the German prosecutors, was far from the ideal and heroic political engagement that haloed his two previous condemnations. If he doesn't seem to have had any trouble with justice or the police in this business at the time— he will not be condemned for these acts until 1936[49]—it provides a precedent for the condemnations to which Dirlewanger was subject starting in 1933. Even before then, he was again condemned for disturbing the peace, due to his SA activism. It was unclear whether it was a case of political offense, personal attack, or attack on property. It is perhaps this liminal aspect of Dirlewanger's attitude that explains that Nazi dignitaries did not see in him, until 1933–1934, a misfit who might prove awkward for the "cause," but a committed militant who did not hesitate to risk his personal security either on the physical or the penal level.

In 1933 Dirlewanger was named director of the Heilbronn Employment Agency, a strategic post for the local leaders of the NSDAP and the SA. Unemployment was high in those times of economic crisis, and Party authorities counted on partisan solidarity to provide jobs for the troops first of all. Did Dirlewanger become a more exposed figure at this time? Did he think he had been given certain impunity? It is difficult to answer these questions for lack of sources. Nevertheless, from the day he took office, complaints against him multiplied. The textile company that had employed him as director took action against him for embezzlement. He was also the object of two actions for traffic accidents and was, finally, found guilty and condemned for statutory rape.

On July 22, 1934, he was put in preventive detention after having had sexual relations several times with a Red Cross volunteer less than fourteen years old at the time. Dirlewanger's only defense was that the young girl had deceived him as to her real age and that he had believed in good faith that she was not a minor. The medical testimony requested by the court was a stinging refutation, and he was condemned to two years in prison.[50] This time the punishment, like the crime, was infamous. Dirlewanger was now excluded from the social framework that was familiar to him, and even stripped of his doctoral title. As an aggravating circumstance, he was then condemned for acts of embezzlement in the Erfurt textile factory.[51] Only a few weeks before director of the Heilbronn Employment Agency and a respected SA leader, Dirlewanger was now a criminal among criminals in the Ludwigsburg prison.

The mechanism excluding Dirlewanger from partisan and social life is interesting: what sets it in motion is not the attack on property—the embezzlement—nor the attack on persons, but the morals charge. In the summer of 1934, the prisoner Dirlewanger had thus become a marginal man. Was it indeed due to his actions? The question is worth asking, given that it constitutes the spine of his defense system. Dirlewanger always fiercely denied that it was he who committed the acts of embezzlement; he swept aside the accusations involving traffic accidents. He attributed his judicial troubles in regard to these two affairs to political intrigues led against him by the *Gauleiter* of Württemberg, Wilhelm Murr,[52] with whom he claimed he had had a disagreement of a political nature. We have no information on this disagreement, even if several witnesses—all linked with Dirlewanger—attest to this hostility between the two men. It is thus impossible to draw a conclusion as to the reality of this explicatory factor. Later, Dirlewanger was constantly the object of complaints concerning thefts of supplies and clashes mingling verbal and physical aggression, and he was thus subject to reprobation from his superiors. He was investigated for having misappropriated food, poultry in particular, and for having organized banquets with these misappropriated goods on various leaves in 1941. He was also the object of complaints for having insulted an officer of the Ministry of Occupied Territories during a party in the home of Kurt von Gottberg, then commissioner of the White Ruthenia district.[53] Finally, in June 1944, he received a warning letter signed by Himmler for not having followed an order to return immediately to his unit.[54]

All his life, Dirlewanger found himself periodically at odds with the authorities. His marginality consisted of conflict-seeking behavior, a propensity to verbal as well as physical violence, and a sort of incapacity to readapt to civilian life on the part of a man who placed his entire life under the seal of war. This did not prevent him from mixing militancy and personal interest.

He was continually under scrutiny in Poland, where the numerous misdeeds committed by the men of his unit with his consent earned him at once the reprobation of certain among them, who denounced him by anonymous letters, and an inquest led by both SS justice and the staff of HSSPF Globocnik.[55]

But Dirlewanger benefited from certain impunity, stretching from the indulgence of Himmler, who blocked all inquiries against him, to the almost unconditional support of other Nazi dignitaries like Victor Brack, and above all Gottlob Berger, whom Dirlewanger had known in time of war. This is why, despite the reprobation that generally surrounded him, Dirlewanger was not a true misfit in the Third Reich. Criminal, prisoner, stripped of the honorific titles that had been bestowed on him, SS officer accused of theft and—worse still—of racial crime, Dirlewanger always benefited from relationships that allowed him not only to get out of the sticky situations in which he found himself, but also to make a successful career. And he applied a tenacity to them that distinguished his whole life-course.

At thirty-nine, Oskar Dirlewanger found himself behind bars, a petty local official of the NSDAP struck down for embezzlement and sex crime. No sooner was he out of prison than he sought to obtain his reintegration in the military and militant structures of the Third Reich, as well as his symbolic reintegration in society, by the annulment of his condemnation and of the loss of his doctoral title. He created such a disturbance demanding the reversal of his condemnation, appearing before the court as well as in the Chancellery, that he was arrested and sent to a concentration camp, emerging only with the understanding that he was forbidden to write again to the Chancellery.

He then left for Spain, where, according to the SD men later responsible for ruling on his ideological trustworthiness, he was given the opportunity to rehabilitate himself through a trial by combat. He began by a period in the Spanish Foreign Legion, before joining the Condor Legion; then he was put under arrest and sent back to Germany, his criminal past having become known in the formation. Thanks to another intervention by Victor Brack, he was returned to Spain, where he remained, as noted, until 1939.

As soon as he returned, he resumed his efforts to be cleared of his convictions and restored to his university title.[56] After a first unsuccessful attempt in the Heilbronn court, which considered that there was no new evidence requiring another ruling,[57] the courts cleared him, on April 30, 1940, of the morals charge. On September 9, the second conviction was annulled by the equivalent of the court of appeal of Stuttgart, and Dirlewanger could at last ask Frankfurt University to restore him to the ranks of doctorate holders. This was done on April 4, 1941, after the Chancellery applied pressure on the university's deanship, which had initially refused to readmit him despite the judgments annulling his conviction. Seven years had passed between his first conviction and the annulling of the last.[58]

His tenacity had exasperated certain dignitaries, as witnessed by his "protective detention" in a concentration camp in 1937. He confirmed this tenacity by the incessant "lobbying" he performed to equip his unit as soon as he arrived in Belarus, as well as in his skirmishes in the General Government with occupation authorities and the police. He made an extraordinary effort to free a Jewish woman—an interpreter employed by him at Stary Dzikówand arrested by the Lublin Gestapo, and suspected of complicity in crime and of illicit sexual relations with Dirlewanger. He even managed to undermine the loyalty, until then unshaken, of Gottlob Berger, the author of an exasperated letter giving him the order to create no more upheaval and to organize his unit's departure for Belarus.[59] Dirlewanger spared no effort, mustering travel, correspondence, and personal interviews to acquire reinforcements, arms, and equipment. It's in part thanks to this incessant activity that Oskar Dirlewanger transformed into an SS division the little commando of poachers he was given in July 1940, and that he himself went from the rank of lieutenant to that of SS general.[60]

In 1944–1945, at the height of his career, Dirlewanger managed to combine marginality and social power. Hated and scorned by many SS men who found him unworthy of the black uniform, he was nevertheless a general officer with powerful support in the highest ranks, notably the HSSPF for Belarus, the supply and equipment corps of the Waffen-SS, and even of Himmler himself. He had also been a leader of men of recognized qualities, who had succeeded in maintaining discipline; even his subordinates admitted this to be a supreme triumph.

Chapter 3

Consent and Constraint

Oskar Dirlewanger put his mark on the special unit to which he was assigned leadership in the summer of 1940, so much so that this unit bore his own name almost until the end of its existence. The behavior of the unit's members and the social relationships within it, often analyzed together by historians, have frequently been attributed to the personal action of the Swabian *reiter*. At the head of a band of some few dozen violent misfits, over whom his power was extraordinary, was Dirlewanger an all-powerful and feared leader? If we examine the unit carefully, its situation calls for a more nuanced answer than interpretations that are based on systematic repression.

A Charismatic "Bandit Leader"?

It would have been a helpful strategy in their post-war trials for the veterans of the unit to have described it as a hell of repression into which they had been plunged against their will. They could thus have invoked, as a defense against the multiple charges presented by the judges, constraint as the single motive underlying their actions. But they did not. Only a few veterans evoked violence by their superiors. Even more surprising, despite Dirlewanger's disciplinary practices, which were, as we will see, brutal, the majority of the veterans expressed their fascination with the leader. Guided by our sources, we must start with their fascination as an attempt to understand how Dirlewanger was perceived and how he constructed his authority over the group.

For a unit whose commander had the power of life and death over its members, post-war investigations reveal a surprising image of Oskar Dirlewanger: he is described as a man of integrity, even by the least enthusiastic of his men.[1] The first testimony of those mentioned is laconic: the man questioned says only that he has no fault to find with his former leader. Others are more forthcoming as to his personality.

This is the case for Paul Dorn, a former criminal prisoner not belonging to the original group of poachers. Condemned in 1941, he was sent first to Neuengamme, then to the Oranienburg concentration camp, and then directly to Minsk to join the unit. He testifies with much detail and doesn't disguise the great brutality of the discipline. Nevertheless, he attributes it not to Dirlewanger but to his adjutant, *Sturmbannführer* Weisse, and he describes Dirlewanger as a leader often absent, but unquestionably courageous. Unlike his adjutant, described as both a tyrant and a coward, Dirlewanger appears as a leader always at the forefront of the attack, fearless, and wounded several times. Dorn's testimony is in perfect conformity with history in terms of the wounds and the position at the head of his troops, and is presented in such a way that it highlights the image of the dazzling leader.

But Dirlewanger exerted a fascination for his former subordinate that went beyond respect and beyond authority. After the war, the latter Paul Dorn searched long and hard for his commander, and with unshakable faith refused to believe the official report of Dirlewanger's death as a French prisoner—a death confirmed by exhumation and an autopsy report.[2] Rejecting these findings, Dorn pursued his search in Italy, where a Jesuit told him that he had helped former Nazis escape to Egypt and that among them was the leader of the black hunters.[3] A strange quest, this: a criminal sent to a penal unit where terror reigned—Dorn himself describes soldiers' summary executions—but who nevertheless persists in seeking his old leader. This fascination, however, is far from being an isolated case. Some twenty veterans express the same feelings for their officer during the course of their questioning on the Warsaw uprising.[4]

This feeling is not limited to Dirlewanger's former subordinates. When historians from the *Institut für Zeitgeschichte* decided in 1962 to take oral histories from SS leaders, Helmut Heiber, a historian specializing in Nazism,[5] went to Swabia to question Gottlob Berger, the former head of the SS general staff. Heiber describes Berger in a report as a "typical Swabian," superficially pleasant, and he discusses many subjects with him, among them what became of Dirlewanger. Berger confesses that he, too, cannot believe in his friend's death. He imagines that Dirlewanger is in Syria or Egypt, a power behind some throne. Like Dorn, he has not lost his fascination, which, however, does not prevent him from seeing Dirlewanger with a critical eye, particularly his immoderate appetite for drink and women.[6] We must now attempt to understand how this image of Dirlewanger was constructed, as well as the messages conveyed by it and the common values shared by the members of this very particular social group, the *Sondereinheit* Dirlewanger.

The *Sangerhausener Zeitung* article quoted earlier offers the first clue. A Nazi militant describes Dirlewanger's activity at the head of his company of machine gunners, as well as the odyssey of the unit's return to Germany. He shows, above all, the tie that bound him to his company leader who, by his magnetism and gift of leadership, succeeded in sparing his men the shame of internment in enemy territory. Vanquished but not defeated, force do cease combat but not prisoners, the men followed Dirlewanger in his refusal. And it was by his talent, his fearlessness, and his warrior virtues that he won their loyalty and their obedience. These are the same virtues that assured him the support of the men of his SA *Standarte*.

In the Great War, during time of troubles, Oskar Dirlewanger's charisma was firmly established. One might think the transition from one conflict to another would be simple. However, biographical documents and observations made in prison describe him as a "cretin," incapable of any outstanding action.[7] His conviction on a morals charge as well as for embezzlement gravely damaged his aura. Nevertheless, a few men never ceased believing in Dirlewanger's charismatic virtues. Notably, Gottlob Berger made extraordinary efforts to send Dirlewanger to a place where his charisma could be fully utilized: at the front. Our analysis can go no further. For lack of sources, we know almost nothing about the first weeks of the unit's existence; we may simply suppose that the poachers, almost to a man, absorbed the charisma of their unit leader and that later members did the same in their turn. The first expressions of that authority date back to the summer of 1942, during the time in which the first anti-partisan actions took place in Belarus.

The first tangible trace of the attachment Dirlewanger's men had to their leader, and of his capacity to lead them into combat despite their inherent lack of trustworthiness, is a report in the form of a testimony written by an SS economic manager, temporary unit commander during Operation Greif. This report certifies that the men spoke with the greatest deference of their absent leader, that they gave him the nickname "Gandhi," and that they felt great admiration for him.[8] This early report proves similar in sentiment to the post-war testimonies.

Some of the twenty testimonies evoked three major traits of Dirlewanger's "character." All insisted on their leader's great courage—the key of the magnetism he exerted. This is the great constant, transmitted from one war to another, of Dirle-wanger's power over his men. Furthermore, all stress Dirle-wanger's "great dedication" to his men. Reinhold Vieregge insists on the unquestioning support Dirlewanger gave his unit: the solidarities created there were unconditional.[9] Other witnesses add that this dedication represented a kind of fellow-feeling. Dirlewanger knew, according to Gustav Strumpf, what life in a camp or a prison was like, and he tried to get his men the best provisions possible.[10] If we add the testimony of Adal-bert Deschner who, years after Dirlewanger's death, still repre-sented him as a kind of living god and evoked the fact that Dirlewanger had interceded in writing to Deschner's mother so that she wouldn't disinherit him, we see how significant this paternal dimension of Dirlewanger remained in the memory of the men of the unit.[11] Was he then at once a brave warrior and a father to his men? Such is the portrait drawn for the investiga-tors by former poachers and prisoners.

Another dimension of this fascination with Dirlewanger's character was tied to elements of his daily behavior. Many testi-monies insist on his fondness for drink, but add that he turned his drinking into an occasion for festivity, bringing his men and officers together in a certain fraternity. There was one drawback to this, however: testimonies agree that Dirlewanger became quarrelsome as he drank,[12] a fact that, apparently, did not affect his charismatic image. The men, certainly, associated their chief to a historic, even a mythological, model of the warrior. Once one of the men, Franz Beuser, dared to make a personal remark to Dirlewanger, stating that he had been born in the wrong era. Beuser was very different from the typical veteran under the sway of Dirlewanger's charismatic image: he was an SS militant sent to the unit for disciplinary reasons in 1944. He was speak-ing, too, at a time marked by far greater repression than in the years 1941–1943. Violence, as we will see, was a daily occur-rence, and the slightest fault was mercilessly punished. Thus, it

78

was a risky remark, and an astonishing liberty, that Beuser permitted himself when he told his leader that he saw him as a *Landsknecht* in the Thirty Years' War. Dirlewanger's reaction suggests that he was not surprised by such a remark and far from being offended, he nodded and silently accepted it as a good analogy.[13]

Inveterate drinker, frenetic smoker, and quarrelsome drunk; ruling his men, by general agreement, "with an iron hand"; indefatigable and intrepid warrior, risking his all and wearing his wounds as a testimony to his bravery: Dirlewanger represented, for his men, a sort of reincarnated myth, that of the soldier who sacked Rome in 1527 and made all Europe tremble.[14]

On the other hand, the political prisoners that were added to the unit at the end of the conflict did not accept this charismatic dimension to their leader. There were multiple explanations for this: they came late to a unit in which the leader's presence had become more distant and more episodic; above all, Dirlewagner was, to their eyes, the incarnation of the "political soldier" and of the oppressor, and their ideological choices put them in opposition to the warrior imagination required to accept charismatic domination. Dirlewanger, finally, seems to have lost a part of his military credit at the end of the conflict, multiplying tactical errors, losing more and more men to unrealistic offensive choices, and suffering so much from his wounds and his massive intake of alcohol that he no longer headed his troops' assaults.[15]

Between Orgy and Brutality

The subject of many historical studies and a few novels in the Germany of 1950–1970, Dirlewanger's unit is commonly described as the locus of arbitrary Nazi discipline. No observer, whether an SS judge, American investigator, German or Anglo-Saxon historian, or federal prosecutor, has failed to insist on this point. According to these observers, Dirlewanger, a unique case, had the right to decree life or death for his men. To understand how this arbitrary discipline worked—to develop a detailed picture of its practice—we must break down the construction of this egregious power.

Let us go back to the testimony of those who experienced it, notably to that of Bruno Wille. Wille was an SS judge, assigned to the unit in late 1944. No sooner had he arrived than he became aware of this judicial exception and was required to come to an arrangement with it. His testimony before American investigators speaks volumes, both as to his difficulties in adapting himself and as to the emphasis his interrogators put on the question:

I met Dirlewanger in the neighboring town and introduced myself to him. But I quickly came into conflict with him, because the *Reichsführer* had given him the right of life and death over his men. Thus, there was no tribunal. There was a secret order allowing Dirlewanger to decide on the life or death of his men without a tribunal.

Q. Do you have this decree?

A. Yes, it was addressed to all formations. So I asked what my assignment was. I was told that I wasn't a judge, because Dirlewanger didn't have a tribunal. There were a certain number of SS members in the unit whom the general tribunal of the SS had selected for a rehabilitation procedure. That did not happen because Dirlewanger refused. He tried to get a SS judge to manage and draw up rehabilitation requests. The SS tribunal accepted and ordered the SSHA to transfer a judge to the unit. That man was I. I got angry with Dirlewanger because I was supposed to handle the rehabilitation dossiers and to send them to the SSHA. But Dirlewanger wanted nothing

to do with the SSHA and wanted me to rule on the reha-
bilitations myself. I told him I couldn't, that what he was
doing went well beyond the *Reichsführer*'s decree, and
that as far as I was concerned it was simply murder. I
made an official complaint and left soon thereafter.[16]

It took only a few weeks for Bruno Wille to observe the very
particular inquisitorial practices developed by Dirlewanger:

Q. What penal matters were addressed during your
stay?

A. Concerning the men? Dirlewanger gave all the
defendants he could identify to a *Sturmmann* for interrogation and then had them beaten, or simply shot.

Q. Do you have any specific cases you can describe
for us?

A. No.

Q. In what cases were the defendants killed?

A. For instance, in cases of desertion, looting, or theft.
The men were interrogated by this corporal, who wrote
in a note, for instance: "I propose twenty-five strokes for
this man," or "he should be shot." The man who did this
was a certain Corporal Glück, Oskar Glück.

[. . .]

Q. How many men do you estimate were shot during
your stay in the unit?

A. While I was in the unit, there were twenty deaths in
a month, between mid-December and mid-January.[17]

In all, if we trust the figures of the SS judge,[18] the death rate
by disciplinary punishment was .03 percent per month.[19] A
death rate not to be compared with that indicating mass death—
a rate that, for human communities, could approach
1 percent per day[20]—but whose impact is far from negligible in

terms of representation for two reasons. In the first place, these deaths include a unique factor, a judgment almost arbitrary or, in any case, were represented as such. In the second place, we must remember how these sentences were applied to the men in the unit. They seem to have assumed a very particular semiotic function. A description of one of these executions may help us to grasp its principal characteristics. Karl Richard Engel is not one of the founding members of the unit. If his declarations are to be believed, Engel arrived in Belarus only at the beginning of 1943, a common criminal transferred there against his will. On November 23, 1960, he wrote a letter to the public prosecutor of Pforzheim, his city of residence, to inform him of crimes committed in the Dirlewanger unit. Following that letter, Engel gave testimony on the execution without trial of three of his comrades after the retreat from Belarus, at Katny. Member of the first company of the first regiment of the unit, Engel identified, with certainty, the three individuals as belonging to the same company, although he was unable to give their names.

Engel began by specifying the circumstances leading to the arrest. The flight from Minsk to Grodno through Lida was disorderly, and only eighteen men of the first company presented themselves on the first day at the unit's assembly point. During the following days, latecomers arrived alone or in small groups. The three victims, however, were the only men to be pointed out as latecomers by the company's NCO, Jakob Dett, who, according to Engel, had a personal grudge against them. After being accused, the three men were put under arrest the following morning, although the conditions of their arrest were not severe; several hours later they were taken to the cookhouse, unsecured, to have their meal. They were then put under closer detention and shackled. Around two o'clock in the afternoon, the order was given for the company to assemble at four o'clock in full uniform on the "parade grounds," in this instance the playground of the school being used as a barracks. There, the

men of the troop, unarmed but wearing their dress uniforms—
if this could be said to mean anything in a unit that had lived
through days of panicked flight—saw an execution squadron
of nine men assemble before them. The three prisoners were
brought out of the cellar and Dirlewanger's adjutant arrived in
a car, together with his orderly. He then made this speech,
recalled eighteen years later by Engel: "These three men are in
breach of troop discipline. As we are in a critical situation, it is
out of the question for us to expend even a drop of gasoline on
a trip to a military court. Therefore the death sentence will be
executed here and now." The execution squad then fired a
volley, at the company leader's order. They aimed for the men's
chests, and the NCO stood by to give the *coup de grâce* to the
wounded. Before they died, the three men, according to Engel,
bore themselves like heroes. They made a speech wishing their
comrades luck and accusing their company leader.[21]

Execution, here, is language. What is the message to the
soldiers of the unit—what is the message to us—of these
uniforms attempting ceremonial formality, this volley, these
orders, and this officer's speech, in a unit that so often had
recourse to a hasty bullet to the back of the head to eliminate
the "uncooperative"?[22] Weiss, Dirlewanger's adjutant, was careful to explain to the men about the absence of normal procedure. Ritual, here, held the function of producing a fictitious
reinsertion of the act of killing in a judicial and military framework; the execution, with its uniformed riflemen, its *coup de
grâce*, and the presiding authorities looking on, extended this
logic. It was, nonetheless, totally contrary to the military code
of penal procedure: the sentence was executed in public, a
proof of its discursive function, but also of its intimidating character. The execution demonstrated the arbitrary power of the
officers over the men of the unit, but, at the same time, it was
an avowal of the authorities' malaise, of how vulnerable they
must have felt themselves to have organized such a ceremony!

Finally, a word of context. This execution took place in June 1944. From this date on, the phenomenon of increased troop numbers in the unit, the integration of new types of soldier, and the context of defeat accentuated the atmosphere of repression and arbitrariness. It was as if these two elements were inversely proportional to the power exercised by the leader.

To better understand this phenomenon, we must go back to the origins of the unit, and notably its time in the Lublin district. Dirlewanger already had the right of life and death over his men at that time. We would expect discipline among the newcomers, trained "briefly but vigorously" by experienced SS NCOs. But we find, reading a directive published by Dirlewanger, that the authorities were far from mastering the situation:

I am responsible to the SSPF for military discipline in the house at 19 Chopin Street. The stairways and the alleys are full of garbage. Drunken men often break windows and furniture, causing willful damage. In the early hours of the morning not only are songs and music heard, but also shouts, brawls, dancing. Men returning to barracks have gotten in the habit of shouting and singing.

Visits by wives and other women have increased to a point unacceptable for a military facility. The courtyard and the garden are treated as a garbage dump, although I have had a bin set out.

After the failure of all attempts to put an end to this gypsyish behavior through argument and upbraiding, I order the following:

1. Any man responsible for nocturnal disturbance (unwarranted gunplay, deliberate damage to facilities, lights shot out) will be immediately placed under close arrest and handed over to the appropriate

authorities for punishment. This ruling applies from ten o'clock in the evening onwards.

2. The NCO on duty in my commando is ordered to check and to put out the troop's lights. I will have the lamps removed if lights are still on after ten o'clock.[23]

Such a text is surprising in a unit known for its rigorous discipline: the arbitrary power of its authorities seems to have accompanied an extraordinarily relaxed discipline. To better understand this paradox, we must put these two elements, in theory incompatible, into context. These disciplinary problems were acknowledged by all, starting with Dirlewanger himself in several letters to Berger on the occasion of conflicts he had with the Lublin KdS. He pointed out that his being suspected of racial crime and the judicial adventures of the unit were undermining his authority. He deduced that a "sort of mutiny" was affecting the unit.[24]

But Dirlewanger's text omits one important detail: the leader was behaving in the same way as his men. We have already mentioned his taste for alcohol and drinking sessions with his men. Other reports cite the "fondness" of Dirlewanger and his officers for women, the organization of evenings combining gang rapes, torture, and drink, both in Poland and in Belarus. It was in the Lublin district that Judge Konrad Morgan carried out an investigation on these abuses and collected the testimony of the head of the Lublin Gestapo, Johannes Mueller, who evoked this collective violence of a sexual nature.[25]

Let us also remember the special relationship between Dirlewanger and his men. A former poacher cited the fact that "Dirlewanger addressed [them] with the familiar '*du*' constantly, called [them] by [their] first names, and arranged parties (*Kameradschaftliche Abend*) for [them]."[26] The officer cultivated too friendly a relationship with them for the order cited above not to have contained an implicit normative statement. Dirlewanger wasn't really trying to forbid his men to womanize, to riot, or to drink, but merely to keep them from doing so openly. This analysis is supported by the date of the order, which corresponds to the beginning of his troubles with the KdS. Dirlewanger wasn't recalling his men to military discipline, but simply to the discretion necessary to its permanent transgression. He behaved thus, objectively, as an accomplice, covering himself in the eyes of his superiors while continuing his habitual behavior.

Dirlewanger's mixture of brutality and friendliness, of complicity in the orgy, combined with the fascination he aroused among the poachers, creates a kind of internal portrait of the charisma exerted by Dirlewanger. An ambiguous, changing domination, nevertheless, during the four years in the East; we have only to compare the Lublin episode with the execution of the three soldiers in Kradny.

The unit's brutal relationships, charismatic domination, and orgiastic practices were present in Lublin as soon as it was free of a strong SS supervisory presence. At the same time, Berlin imposed few punishments, and Dirlewanger used the exorbitant power Himmler conferred on him more to protect his men from local authorities than to punish them. The only men sent back to concentration camps during that period were the twenty-five physically unfit prisoners.[27] For the period of the unit's stay in Galicia and the beginning of its Belarusian campaign, we have no source confirming that Dirlewanger used his discretionary power to send a significant number of men to the camps, nor to have them executed. We may hypothesize that the effective use of the charismatic model, with small troop numbers, a leader close to his men on a daily basis, and a life of pillaging, drinking, and leisure, created a cohesive group, despite the denunciation of Dirlewanger by one of his men.[28]

Did the unit indeed follow a charismatic model? Perhaps, but we must in this case remember Ian Kershaw's conclusions on the case of Hitler, showing a weak dictator—a dictator careful of his image and unwilling to intervene in the routine exercise of power[29]—which is far from the case for Dirlewanger. There is one point, however, on which the image of the weak dictator parallels that of the bandit leader in Galicia: the latter was well aware of the weakness of his position. At the time of his judicial troubles with the Lublin KdS, Dirlewanger wrote to Berger that "the fact that [his] men are taking part in a case [directed] against [him] whose issue is clear to [him] will permanently destroy [his] authority."[30] The SS investigators were also aware of his fragile position, but their analysis was completely different. For them, the fact that Dirlewanger had become involved with a Jewish prisoner, that he had made her his "favorite," and that she had assumed an important role in the interrogation process was the cause of the "alienation between Dirlewanger and his men."[31] Was this a condemnation in the name of the SS's racial morality? Was there tension linked to a surreptitious struggle for the leader's favor? It is difficult to decide between these two explanations, and one may reasonably believe that the two were combined. Once this affair was ended by the unit's posting to Belarus, Dirlewanger's authority over his men was reestablished until at least the summer of 1943. Except for four cases, he did not use his right to impose punishment at his own discretion on his men.[32]

The first break eventually came, due in essence to the change in recruitment for the unit and to its change in scale. Dirlewanger had established himself as the charismatic leader of a band of eighty to two hundred poachers, carousing pillagers. But in the summer of 1943, 321 professional criminals arrived in Belarus. In the first days, three of them were executed with a bullet to the back of the head before their comrades' eyes. In the following months, close arrests and men returned to the concentration camp were common.[33] This outburst of disciplinary violence was still limited in duration and intensity; it ceased once the newcomers had been absorbed, some months later. Nevertheless, Dirlewanger's charismatic domination had temporarily been interrupted. The commanding officer of a troop as large as a regiment could no longer maintain a personal relationship with each of his recruits. Dirlewanger could no longer keep intact the proximity and familiarity that constituted one of the essential components, together with bravery in combat, of his charisma.

This outbreak of violence left its mark on the unit. Officers turned to punishment more often, creating an atmosphere of increased repression in parallel with the Russian advance, even if the unit's original model was partially retained, as suggested by the above-cited testimony of Paul Dorn, a criminal whose enrollment occurred at that time. The decisive break occurred after the retreat from Russia. At this time, the firing squad was used more often; the practice of shooting deserters under fire was instigated by Dirlewanger's adjutant during the repression of the Warsaw uprising.[34] Once again the unit was joined by new contingents, this time from Wehrmacht and SS prisons. And again, certainly, this further step into violence—demonstratively performed under combat conditions—aimed to intimidate the newcomers and impress them that they must immediately integrate themselves into the unit and abandon any ideas of rebellion from the start. The instigator of the battlefield shootings, *Haupsturmführer* Weisse, had told new recruits several days earlier that "those who didn't fall into rank would be liquidated."[35] If discipline had been more rigorous in word than in deed in Poland and in Belarus, practice was now in line with discourse. The orgiastic dimension of the unit, present in all ranks in the first three years of its existence, was now restricted to officers and company leaders. Only brutality now remained for the men of the unit.

There were about ten executions of soldiers during the period between summer 1943 and autumn 1944. The most reliable source for the number of executions, SS Judge Bruno Wille, attests, for the following quarter, to a new intensity: in the month of December 1944 alone, twenty soldiers were executed for various reasons, ranging from theft to rebellion.[36] The last six months of the unit's existence, during which the political prisoners arrived from the concentration camps, marked the highest point of violence inflicted upon the troop. Violent acts became an everyday matter, and no one was safe from it any longer.

One of the most telling testimonies is that of a former civil prisoner who joined the unit in Saxon Lusatia. Some of his contingent had been sent to the Lieberose area, where there was a small concentration camp that had become an important detention center due to the influx of prisoners abandoned on the road in the course of SS-led death marches. On January 6, 1967, Oskar Blöhmer told investigators about the terrible time spent there by the men of what had become the Thirty-Sixth Division of SS Grenadiers. Penned up near an annex of the camp, they were present at the last gassings of Jews, in boarded-up sheds, while SS men newly assigned to the unit—arriving pell-mell from a *Junkerschule*, from SS disciplinary detention centers, and from concentration camps—had been assembled in an area surrounded by barbed wire. Every day new members of the division, accused of rape, pillage, or desertion, were taken out of the camp for summary execution, usually by a bullet to the back of the head after digging their own graves. This was a treatment that hardly differed from those of their neighbors, and Blöhmer's testimony, which betrayed a complete incomprehension, was closer in its narrative structure to that of a camp inmate than that of a former member of the SS.[37]

In the winter of 1944–1945, the unit's plunge into systematic violence coincided with a wave of desertions that revealed to those responsible for the unit—the Ninth Army, South Army Group—that discipline was a central problem and that Dirlewanger was no longer in full control of his troops.[38] The unit was now a division, and Dirlewanger was often away due to his constant trips to Berlin and to Swabia, where he had his reopened wounds tended. Dirlewanger was now a commander less present on the ground (thus less charismatic), dealing with men of whom at least a contingent now professed a declared ideological hostility to Nazism and the SS, although they were, finally, its representatives; this was cause enough to weaken the confidence of the officers towards their men. And this mistrust, in a context marked by a defeat that became more probable every day and a military repression that was increasingly intense and blind, focused on social groups the soldiers and the officers of the unit saw more readily behind the barbed wire of a concentration camp than in a barracks. Thus, the men of the unit's first contingents, or those transferred in for disciplinary reasons, deployed against the new arrivals a violence unequalled even during the Nazi army's defeat, so harsh was it in its reprisals against "cowards" and "deserters."[39]

A last incident demonstrates part of the unit's mechanism and its originality. One of the highest ranking disciplinary transfers was Harald Momm, former director of the Potsdam cavalry school, sent to the unit after Stauffenberg's attempt against Hitler. Momm said after the war that two or three NCOs of the division's general staff meted out the punishment—generally twenty-five blows—with a rubber truncheon, to a prisoner/soldier who often fainted from pain. Momm's story resembles what French prisoners called a "passage à la schlague."[2,40] Everything started in autumn 1944, as if the brutality of relations between camp inmates and guards had been transposed to the division, between soldiers and their leaders. Although

---

2   In English, roughly, "getting the schlag treatment." –Trans.

the radicalization of repression was a general phenomenon few Wehrmacht units escaped towards the end of the war, this "carceralization" of hierarchical violence was certainly peculiar to the Dirlewanger division.

Resistance and Desertion in the Dirlewanger Division

The reaction of the prisoner soldiers to the outbreak of increased hierarchical violence and to an egregious system of constraint constitutes the central interrogation of Hans Peter Klausch's book. When did "resistance"—to adopt the term used by Klausch—begin in the Dirlewanger division? Without reopening a familiar debate on the practices of dissidence and resistance,[41] we must go back to the first disagreements expressed by the soldiers on various aspects of their life in the unit. The SS judges were the first to discern discontent in the troop, on the occasion of its troubles during its time in Lublin. This was neither a revolt against arbitrary discipline nor political resistance as Hans Peter Klausch defines it, but irritation aroused by Sarah Bergmann, the young Jewish woman who acted as Dirlewanger's interpreter and housekeeper—either because she had become his official mistress or simply because she had become the key player in the extortion of funds from the Jews of the ghetto. Whatever the reason, the unit's discontent was far from a show of resistance to repressive discipline.

In the summer of 1943, the first desertion attempts took place. Four soldiers of the unit tried their luck on June 25.[42] At least one of the deserters was a political prisoner from Dachau, enrolled as a survivor of medical experimentation, which leads Hans Peter Klausch to believe that his desertion was an act of antifascist resistance, the first of a long series in his opinion.[43] If Klausch shows convincing evidence of these men's previous enrollment in partisan detachments, although their identity is not definitely proved, it is equally possible to see in the first desertions a reaction to the wave of repression that struck the unit with the arrival of the common law prisoners. According to Klausch, partisans welcomed deserters with open arms;[44] but why, then, were they so few? In fact, deserting was extremely risky, even if the men successfully reached the partisans. Three such attempts ended with public executions, one by hanging, in the camp at Sachsenhausen.[45]

Besides the risk, we must remember that the men of the unit were, as we have seen, engaged in military operations that, for all their violence, were relatively undangerous.[46] They were also subject to relatively loose discipline, since women had access to the billet and the number of soldiers under arrest remained low during the periods for which we have information.[47] The unit's provisions were more than satisfactory, with varied food, quantities of alcohol, and a ration of six cigarettes per day.[48] To these official provisions were added immeasurable goods obtained through plunder and pillage. This relative comfort and physical security was combined with an experience of social domination—shared by all the members of the occupying forces during the war[49]—and a practice of command, as we have said, that was favorable. In a sense, there was established, between the men of the troop and the officers—Dirlewanger foremost—a contractual relation: the men agreed to operations against an enemy whom, in any event, they scorned and hated, in return for the officers' guarantee of relative physical security, relaxed discipline on a daily basis, and a maximum of comfort.[50] To break this contract and to throw oneself into the arms of an enemy marked, furthermore, by the stigma of bestiality, would have been, in this light, an aberration, even if it meant removing oneself from an environment marked by omnipresent and extreme violence.

From Lublin to Belarus, we count seven desertion attempts,[51] all occurring in Belarus. Only one can be said with certainty to have succeeded, since its actor survived the Second World War. The last of the unit's seven deserters was taken by the men of the Minsk KdS during Operation Cormorant, just before the great Soviet offensive that brought on the collapse of the Center Army Group. He was no doubt executed when the German forces retreated.[52] Refusal and "resistance," as envisaged by Klausch, were thus the behavior of the smallest minority, the men of the unit overall aligning themselves with this contractual relationship.

For Hans Peter Klausch, a break occurs during the unit's time in Slovakia, and even more so in Hungary and Lusatia. There begins what he calls the antifascist activity of certain contingents of the unit. The arrival of political prisoners marked the definitive entry of violence into social relations within the unit. The contractual relationship between men and officers was thus completely broken, having already been strained during the Warsaw uprising. Growing losses were the main reason for this surge in violence within the unit. If the unit's first significant losses, seventy-seven men between August and September 1943,[53] could be accounted for by the inexperience of the newly enrolled civil prisoners, those of the following period were not of the same type: of the 481 Germans in the unit as of September 1943, only 330 were still in fighting form by April 1, 1944.[54] In six months, 31.4 percent of the troops had been killed or wounded, a clear proof that the men's physical security was no longer guaranteed. This observation was reinforced by the substantial losses undergone during the Warsaw siege: the unit's troop size had swelled to 2,680 men before the siege but it had lost nearly 2,083 in the uprising,[55] three-quarters of the force. If there is a case where the expression "cannon fodder," used by Klausch, can be justified, it is certainly the Warsaw uprising, especially since most of the losses seem to have been among the new arrivals—criminals and condemned soldiers. For them, the tacit contract between men and officers never existed, and therefore there was nothing to induce their

93

consent to enter the lines in Slovakia and Hungary. This observation is truer still once we realize that discipline, as we have seen previously, was contaminated by practices current in the concentration camps. Henceforth, commanding authorities would opt for a strategy of maximal constraint with the troop. For the soldiers, desertion, under these circumstances, probably seemed a worthwhile survival strategy.

If we believe the figures cited by Klausch, there were around fifty desertions in Slovakia,[56] then a movement of 480 men between December 13 and 18, 1944, around Budapest,[57] followed by a few in Lusatia. Based on the statements of anti-fascist German veterans within the unit, Klausch estimates the number of deserters who went to the Soviet side at one hundred.[58] At a maximum, 630 recruits—between 5 percent and 9 percent of the unit—chose to desert.

The most remarkable case, beyond a doubt, was the massive desertion at Ypolysag, during the Budapest siege. It might seem easier to organize a mass desertion in a war of partisans, where frontiers are mobile, the front undefined, the environment favorable to camouflage and clandestine movement; or in a Saxon countryside completely disorganized by the Russian advance when all might have fled to escape a battle whose loss was a foregone conclusion. Why, then, did they decide to desert in Hungary, rather than Lusatia or Slovakia?

In Slovakia, the Dirlewanger unit entered the campaign at a moment when the uprising was certain to be defeated: Banska Bystrica, its "capital," had already been retaken by German troops, and the men of the *Sonderbrigade* were used only to clean up a few isolated units. Going over to the enemy would have meant putting oneself in great danger with the slimmest chance of success. For political prisoners as for older members of the unit, the situation was the same as in Belarus. The question is more complex in the case of Lusatia. There, the conditions prevalent in the units—the imbalance between well-rested, well-equipped Soviet troops and the shadow of what was once the German army—might confirm the absurdity of continued combat. Nevertheless, the conditions of the conflict seem, according to surviving German antifascists, to have restricted opportunities to cross over to the enemy. There remains the case of Hungary.

Between December 12–18, 1944, four companies of the third battalion of the second regiment of the unit had been billeted in the Ypolysag sector. The companies took their position in ragged order, isolated from each other by wooded hills that made communication difficult and that weakened the control exercised by the regiment commander and the brigade general staff. The four companies of this regiment were made up of political prisoners from Dachau and Buchenwald, integrated according to geographical logic, contingent by contingent. The necessary conditions for attempting a coordinated desertion were thus united: weakened hierarchical control, political networks established in the concentration camps left intact by the method of incorporation in the unit, and topography favorable to discreet departure for the Russian lines. The result was immediate: four hundred prisoners made their way, some in small groups, others in section-size detachments, towards Red Army lines.[59] However, even in such a favorable context, the enterprise remained extremely dangerous: one of the antifascist veterans of the unit, Bruno Meyer, maintained, with documentary evidence, that in his own company one hundred men managed to reach the Soviet lines, while thirty were killed or wounded and fifty did not make the attempt.[60] That is to say that, even when desertion was the choice of a local majority, only a minority of men—25 percent in this case, or close to 45 percent if we count only the political prisoners in the unit— despite their political "motivation," made the decision to desert.

The Ypolysag desertion is a textbook case, for two diametrically opposed reasons. Never in the history of the Second

World War were there conditions so favorable for mass desertion; and never did the German army employ such an array of constraints to force a group of men to fight. And yet the commanding authority was unable to prevent the desertion. At least it was aware of the facts: a few days earlier, Dirlewanger himself refused to "fight the Soviets with communists."[61] This extreme case illustrates the illusory nature of a command system attempting to force soldiers to fight through terror. At the same time, despite the avowed "political motivation" of the antifascist prisoners, barely half went over to the enemy.

Is it possible to speak of mass desertions in general? In absolute numbers, the only significant case was that of the Russian soldiers of the Great War in 1917,[62] when gigantic armed bands of deserters besieged certain cities of western Russia, assembling in railway stations or in front of public buildings.[63] There was nothing comparable to this phenomenon, in form or in scale, in the Hungary of 1945. It would be more worthwhile to explore the motivations of the recruits who chose not to desert, if we want to expose the workings of their behavior. These veterans of the SS, Wehrmacht, or prison could hardly be said to have thought of their relationship to their commanders or to the unit in terms of faithfulness or loyalty. But, on the other hand, they had no political motivation to join the ranks of the Red Army or to accept a captivity in the USSR that they must have sensed would be long and painful, even fatal: the belief in the automatic execution of anyone wearing an SS uniform was widespread, and it was far from being completely unfounded.[64] Those who made the attempt had developed a network of solidarity in the concentration camps and shared a common ideological culture close, at first glance, to that of the Soviet enemy. These were the two necessary preconditions for a desertion that was both a collective action and a political gesture. Thus, it seems that different groups' internal social practices, combined with these groups' representations and political culture, constituted the differentiating factors of their combat behavior. Therefore, to get to the heart of this behavior we must consider not external institutional constraints, such as discipline, blows, and executions, but rather solidarity and the consent or refusal to fight.

Chapter 4

Poachers in the Polis

Here, then, is a unit whose hierarchical and disciplinary environment makes it unique. Led by a misfit and made up of misfits, it seems almost accidental. And yet its creation and the choice of Dirlewanger as its leader are due neither to chance nor to error. The decision, taken at the highest level of the Nazi state, to mobilize cynegetic criminals in the struggle against partisans throws a harsh light on those who took that decision, on those who were its object, and on the type of activity to which these men and their unit were destined.

Between Function and Symbol

On March 23,1940, around 4:00 PM, Ministerial Director Sommer, department chief in the Ministry of Justice, received a telephone call from SS *Gruppenführer* Wolff, head of Himmler's general staff, informing him of Hitler's decision to give "suspended sentences to so-called 'honorable poachers' and, depending on their behavior at the front, pardon."[1] The call was unusual, to say the least. Hence the rapid reaction of the judicial administration, which sent a telephone order five days later to all the public prosecutors of the Reich requesting a report on persons convicted of crimes or misdemeanors according to paragraphs 292 of the penal code and 60 of the legislative code. They were to be divided into three categories: those who had been sentenced and/or were serving their sentence;

those who had been sentenced but were not, or not yet, serving; and finally those liable to sentencing, distinguishing between those remaining at liberty and those under arrest.[2] A week later, twenty-two reports had been delivered to the Ministry. One thousand two-hundred and thirty-one cases met the conditions of the telephone order sent to the public prosecutors: 220 persons were in prison for such crimes, 225 had been sentenced but were not yet serving, and 735 others were liable to sentencing, among whom 103 were under arrest.[3] In the meantime, the *Reichsführer* had sent the Ministry of Justice a letter confirming Hitler's order and specifying the search criteria: the poachers should insofar as possible be Bavarian or Austrian, not be guilty of crimes involving trap-setting, and were to be enrolled in marksmen's rifle corps.[4]

We will return to this last directive, which was not particularly noted at the time by the RJM staff, for whom the salient element of this letter was that dossier selection had been entrusted to Himmler and his staff by Hitler. On May 4, the staffer responsible for creating a dossier on the matter for Secretary of State Freisler pointed out the lack of clarity, to his eyes, in Himmler's order.

For the Ministry director—a law specialist—the suggested procedure was both vague and arbitrary. He requested a meeting with the SS men responsible for the business, and it took place on April 4. But the Ministry directors present had not been informed of Himmler's letter to Thierach, Minister of Justice, in which the former, despite his desire to make things clear, had raised more problems than he had solved, and the civil servants were not in a position to establish a definitive procedure with the officers of the criminal police representing Himmler. They could only consult their offices to supply further details to the police. The following day, however, answers became clearer: the selection procedure remained Himmler's responsibility, the crimes of the men concerned could include

99

violent crimes, particularly attacks on gamekeepers, as well as property crimes. "Professional criminals" were nevertheless to be excluded.[5]

A week sufficed to finalize the procedure. At this point there had been only one awkward moment: the meeting between police officers and civil servants, which had been cut short. This was due to a decision taken at the highest ranks of the Nazi hierarchy, the confusion stemming from the fact that the Ministry's officials had not been informed of Himmler's letter, sent directly to the Minister of Justice. While it is difficult to determine if Hitler really gave the order, Himmler involved himself directly in the procedure: the letters, although handled by the bureaucracy of the criminal police, are nonetheless addressed to him directly, without passing through the relevant organizations. The letters have no heading and—remarkably— the salutation does not include Himmler's title. The letter heading used by criminal police staffers normally carried the acronym of the *Reichssicherheitshauptamt* and the number of the office (here *Amt* V) concerned. The heading of the letters now available to us shows clearly that they came from the *Reichsführer*'s personal staff. Starting on June 14, 1940, the affair was handled on the general staff level, and Wolff regularly corresponded with the employees of the RJM or with Thierach himself: for example, submitting lists of poachers selected for the Oranienburg concentration camp.[6] While the procedure found a more regular bureaucratic level within the Ministry of Justice in autumn 1940, Himmler and Wolff retained responsibility for the affair throughout the initial phase. Starting in the summer of 1941, the procedure was transferred partially to the *Reichssicherheitshauptamt*, which took over the selection of the poachers, and partially to the SS Equipment Office (SSFHA) directed by Berger,[7] according to more ordinary institutional procedure. A final indication confirms the interest of the leaders of the Third Reich in this very specific type of "soldier": by creating what was to become the Dirlewanger Special Unit, Himmler was a few months ahead of Hermann Goering, who, in 1941, expressed the desire to create a special unit made up exclusively of poachers.[8] The latter, naturally, gave up his project, but there too the intervention of the highest Nazi authorities with the Ministry of Justice left an archival document trail.

Even if the procedure chosen to select the "candidates" was based on an arbitrary administrative and judicial decision, the military calculation involved was age-old and classic. Since the military revolution of the eighteenth century, the strategists of all the great European powers had tried to create special contingents using poachers' skills.[9] In France, as in the Anglo-Saxon and Germanic monarchies, "hunters' companies" had been created, uniting poachers and hunters. There was no question of commandos, which came into existence only with the Great War, but already there was a strategy of mobilizing the special categories of hunters and their illegal doubles, poachers.

Frederick II of Prussia created the first units, which served at once as military police, reconnaissance groups on hostile territory, and marksmen. These hunter units were maintained throughout the nineteenth century and, in Austria-Hungary, served in peacetime as frontier guards, fighting smugglers and bandits in the mountains.[10] In all cases, the calculation by military authorities was to take possession of the hunters' and poachers' skills developed in peacetime and to remobilize them within the units. This choice was based on the principle that the experience of the hunt and of clandestinity provided a practical training for wartime activity at its most specialized. On the symbolic level, the status of the units thus created is most interesting: they were *Strafuni* (penal units), both elitist and disciplinary in nature, which suggests that the ambiguity present at the creation of the Dirlewanger special unit, mingling recognized expertise and negative social marking, was not specifically Nazi or, perhaps, even specifically German.

Speaking of the special units operating in the mountains of the Alps and the Carpathians, incorporating Hungarian, Bosnian, and Croatian poachers, an officer was pleased and astonished to see them "change into faithful protectors of the law by joining the *Strafuni*."[11] It is tempting to examine both history and cultural anthropology for the place of the hunter and his black double, the poacher, in the European imagination. We must first understand how such a model was spread among Nazi leaders. The decision having been made by Hitler and the directors of the SS, and envisaged by Goering, it is they who interest us. Hitler's position was certainly the least enthusiastic. We know of his refusal to eat meat, and he expressed several times, in his table talk and in *Mein Kampf*, his position on hunting. For him, "the most honorable element of the hunt is the quarry; the poacher, who doesn't put his life at stake, comes well behind."[12] And elsewhere he had specified:

> I have no particular fondness for poachers: I am a vegetarian myself, but I see in them the romantic dimension of the hunt [. . .] Personally, I don't understand how one can go shooting for pleasure . . . To make such a fuss about killing a deer! To shoot a hare not when it's sitting, but when it's running, in order to wound it more gravely! Associations for the protection of animals should look more closely into hunting. Jokingly: when I speak for poachers, I'm not preaching to the choir. I can swear that never in my life have I hurt a rabbit. I have never been either a hunter or a poacher.[13]

An unshared aversion; Himmler and Goering were devoted hunters. Goering's passion for the hunt even inspired the background of Michel Tournier's novel, *Le Roi des aulnes* (translated as *The Ogre*).[14] Having assumed the leadership of the institutions ruling over hunting rights in Germany, Goering intervened regularly in the legislation.[15] Less well known is the fact that Himmler himself was a hunter and that he had great estates allowing him to pursue that activity. He had an appointed administrator, at once gamekeeper and hunt master, and he invited a carefully selected guest list to sumptuous hunting parties.[16] Those permitted or forbidden to hunt, as decreed by the *Reichsführer*, outline a hierarchy that, while not deviating from that established by the SS, emphasizes the existence of special relationships created by Himmler with some of his colleagues and other members of the SS around cynegetic activity. The tone of the invitations and the guest lists gives us an idea of the degree of intimacy between the guests and Himmler.

On September 4, 1942, for instance, Himmler asked his officer for cynegetic affairs, *Standartenführer* Mueller, to invite Oswald Pohl, head of the *Wirtschafts-Verwaltungshauptamt*, concentration camp administrator Erich von dem Bach-Zelewsky, and also Eberhard von Eberstein or Gottlob Berger. There were also Erich Koch, *Gauleiter* of East Prussia and *Reichskommissar* for the Ukraine, and Karl Kaufmann, *Gauleiter* of Hamburg. With Himmler, Wolff, Berger, and von dem Bach, almost all the protagonists of the creation process for the *Sondereinheit* Dirlewanger were mentioned in the list sent by the *Reichsführer*. If we add that Odilo Globocnik was also invited to a hunt and that he in turn invited Wolff and Himmler to another hunt in Lublin, in January 1941,[17] all of Dirlewanger's hierarchical superiors appear in Himmler's hunting circle. The creation of the poachers' unit to hunt down partisans was decided upon and managed from start to finish by hunters and among hunters.

Wild Men in the Polis?

The protagonists' discourse around hunters and poachers was consistent. Hitler himself, while denying poachers any nobility, recognized their romantic aspect, and it was this aspect, to which we will return, that the actors highlighted to legitimize the creation of this very particular unit. But Hitler insisted, as we have seen, on yet another aspect: these men took pleasure from inflicting pain. Their cruelty, to his eyes, was undoubted. To create such a unit amounted to reintroducing the Wild Man in the military polis. This statement may seem banal, so inherent to the image of the hunter does cruelty seem. Saint Hubert, great hunter and miracle-working saint of the Ardennes, healer—interestingly—of rabies, was converted by a white stag that enjoined him to contain his passion, addressing him in these words: "Believe me, hunter, stop. [. . .] I am come to convert you. Cease the hunt and banish pleasure." [18] The passion of the chase, the pleasure of the kill: the image of the hunt and of Black Blood are summed up in that eighteenth century folksong of the Ardennes, widely known in the Germanic world and appearing in the dictator's table talk.[19]

The cruelty Hitler ascribed to hunters, and particularly to poachers, was not an isolated theme in Nazi discourse. Even then it was of burning current interest: by invading the USSR in June 1941, the Nazis had set in motion a dynamic diffusion of extraordinary violence that overtook most of their combat units. There was nonetheless a type of unit in which cruelty posed, to Nazi eyes, a particularly acute problem: the *Einsatzgruppen*, the units responsible for "maintaining order" in the wake of the frontline troops.[20] The rhythm of killings established by these units rose strikingly between June 22, 1941, and the months of September and October: each man, on average, killed one person a day for six months.[21] Needless to say, acts of cruelty multiplied during this genocidal sequence. But this was never considered normal: group leaders perceived the accusations of cruelty to which they were sometimes subject as insults.[22] Some commando chiefs, like Walter Blume, the leader of *Sonderkommando* 7b, warned their men, telling them that any act of cruelty would expose the culprit to heavy punishment.[23] Of course, these barriers did not hold before their daily confrontation with extreme violence, but cruelty was unanimously stigmatized.[24] Hitler's rejection of the supposed and specific cruelty of poachers was thus shared by the Nazis, and the age-old stigma against that group was reinforced.

If not all Nazi dignitaries evoked so clearly the cruelty of hunters and poachers, many stressed the passion to which hunters were subject. Hitler himself, while speaking of their cruelty, recognized that their behavior was under the influence of passion: "In the mountains, there is passion. A young man climbs them ten times to get his chamois. Then there is the roe deer he offers to his *Zenzl* or his *Marei*. It gives him glory in the eyes of the young woman."[25] But Hitler was not alone in using the term "passion." When Goering decided to organize his own unit of poachers, an official of the Ministry of Justice described, in these terms, the *Reichsmarschall*'s project: "He [Goering] wants to bring together the passionate members of the smugglers' bands who make their way over the border by firepower and whose passion is to stake their lives to evade the watch of the customs men."[26] They were to be brought together "in bands to serve in the East. In the territories given over to them, these bands, whose primary mission would be to annihilate the leadership of enemy partisan groups, could kill, burn, rape, and profane, and would return to strict surveillance [once back] in their homeland."[27] The terms chosen by the official express perfectly an idea of passion and unbridled violence confined to very particular spaces. Did they refer to a specific discourse of violence and passion?

The anthropologist Bertrand Hell has shown that, in an area going from the Mediterranean to the Ural-Siberian steppes, hunters and poachers are locked in a social discourse interpreting violence in terms of humors, of heat. It is due to an excess of Black Blood that must be shed during the hunting season, in the gesture of violence uniting animal to man.[28] When the latter is too "possessed" by black humor, he transgresses the established laws of the hunt, begins hunting secretly out of season, becomes a poacher, and thenceforth eats only red or black meat, with its intense heat. Then, if the passion is too strong, he ends by becoming a man of the woods, a wild man, closer to the game he hunts than to the domestic world—the world of men that he has left to slake his passion.[29] Bertrand Hell shows, furthermore, that this discourse was embodied not only in the figure of the man of the woods, but also in that of the possessed warrior, prey to accesses of blind destructive rage—notably in that of Orion—of the maenads or of the Nordic Berserker.[30] From the Nazi point of view, to invoke cynegetic passion and cruelty was to reintroduce the Wild Man into the polis at war.

But this does not occur under just any condition or in just any place. Ministerial counselor Joel, repeating Goering's words, authorized, as we have seen, the unit in question to "kill, burn, mutilate/violate/profane [*schänden*]" in the territories confided to it, but once returned from the arena of operations it would remain "under close surveillance."[31] What was permitted in the wooded, liminal, and disputed margins of the thousand-year empire being built was not permitted within the Nazi Polis. The function of constraint was expressed here according to a discourse in line with the vitalist analysis of the impulse towards violence attributed to poachers. This would have free rein in sectors whose marginality was threefold. They were marginal because topographically they were situated at the eastern extremity of the empire; then because they were the theater of a war that did not follow the rules of classic conflict, against an enemy without uniforms, hidden in the midst of a civilian population indistinguishable from the partisans.[32] They were marginal, finally, because they acted in wild spaces where the "German civilizing mission" had not yet been able to accomplish its "work."[33]

In practice, this theory encountered strong resistance on the ground. If the behavior of the *Sondereinheit* was authorized, even welcomed, in certain regions where it was sent, local authorities nevertheless wanted to distance themselves from it. The case of the SS administration of the Lublin district and that of the civil administration of Belarus are characteristic examples of this. We've already noted that the Dirlewanger unit had serious problems in Galicia. These were due essentially to a series of investigations performed by security services at the local level and to complaints received by the central justice organizations of the SS. While we must not analyze the adventures of the *Sondereinheit* in Lublin exclusively in light of the expressed desire of local authorities to rid themselves of an anthropologically marginal troop, to deprive ourselves of this key to understanding the unit's troubles would be to lose sight of an important part of their significance.

In early September 1941, the Lublin KdS arrested four young Jewish women, among them Sarah Bergmann. Accused of theft, she was detained in the criminal police's jail, while her three companions were freed. A month after this arrest, Oskar Dirlewanger began to take steps to have her freed. The affair, however, quickly took an unexpected turn. The intervention of the police owed nothing to chance: they had been alerted by anonymous letters sent directly to Himmler and copied to Globocnik. On September 6, Globocnik passed the matter on to the KdS, who hastened to have one of its staffers investigate, leading to the translator's arrest some days later.[34] The investigation lasted more than a year and was closed only after the unit left for Belarus.

There were several reasons for this: first, relations between the unit and the institutions surrounding it, particularly the police, had become dire. The investigation became extremely complex, due to the multiple charges against Dirlewanger and his men. If we are to believe the final investigative reports, there were eleven counts in the accusation, involving at least thirty separate incidents. Such a profusion constitutes a good demonstration of the fundamental irregularity of the behavior of the men of *Sonderkommando* Dirlewanger, who looted, stole, trafficked, extorted, abused, and raped well beyond the norm—if such a term could be said to have had a meaning in occupied Galicia.[35] We may thus analyze it as the reflection of tensions between the different Occupation authorities, and specifically between the KdS and the former convicts making up the *Sonderkommando*. It would also be possible to see in it the complex game of protection and accusation opposing the central authorities—Berger's SSFHA, which consistently covered for Dirlewanger—and also the regional authorities—the Lublin KdS, Globocnik's SSPF, and Krüger's HSSPF—who insisted that the investigation be allowed to reach its conclusion.

All these analytical keys are useful in understanding the procedure; all hold their part of the truth. Nevertheless, a letter from Dirlewanger draws our attention to another possible interpretation. This letter, the last document in the voluminous dossier, is addressed to the investigating judge dispatched by Berger to exonerate Oskar Dirlewanger. In his conclusion, the latter brought to light one of the most troubling aspects of the series of affairs from which he had just escaped on arrival in Belarus:

> It appears that *Brigadeführer* G[lobocnik] made the matter of my poisoning Jews in Lublin the object of his investigation, in his typical way of presenting things exactly as they are not. All to be able, just for once, to make me look bad. But there again luck was against him. It's true I had Jews (fifty-seven in number) poisoned by

the Lublin doctor, rather than having them shot. I did it to save their clothing (coats, etc.) which I subsequently gave to *Haupsturmführer* Streibel for his forced laborers. The dead Jews' gold teeth were removed by the director of the Lublin SSPF infirmary to supply dental fillings for the SS. All that was done with the approval of *Brigadeführer* G[lobocnik], who nevertheless denied having known anything about it, after the SD got involved.

My word, things are comic in Lublin; in one case, I have a [sexual] relationship with a Jewess, I drink schnapps with Jews, and then again I'm merciless [*herzlos*: heartless] and I poison men and women. In one case, I'm supposed to have the wrong attitude towards this people, and I must have thrown my firm ideological convictions overboard for a Jewess; when this turns out not to be true, I'm accused of exactly the opposite.[36]

Beyond a defense strategy based on the idea of a conspiracy, did Oskar Dirlewanger not dimly sense, writing these lines, that the accusations addressed to his unit expressed a contradiction too deep not to be significant? What motivated Globocnik to support the men of the KdS despite Berger was doubtless expressed in this letter. It didn't matter whether Dirlewanger was philo-Semitic or merciless; what mattered was his relationship to his victims. He is depicted here, in light of the double ambiguity of the wild man, closer to his quarry than to the world of man, and of the man of definitive cruelty.[37]

Dirlewanger, at heart, was disturbing, and it was difficult for Globocnik to express his reasons for opposing the poachers. The latter brought down on their unit an impressive number of complaints and denunciations. Bribery, poaching, violence, and even—to a lesser extent, perhaps—*Rassenschande* were nonetheless common in the district;[38] and Globocnik himself had not escaped the accusation of bribery. It is the intersection of the image of poaching misfits and the crimes described that made the SSPF react.

Was Globocnik maneuvering to expel to the margins of the Nazi Empire a unit he felt belonged there? It did not matter to him whether it was marginalized in the USSR or in Yugoslavia. The important thing was that it go fast and far. For him, the Lublin district was not one of those badlands requiring the presence of units with "appropriate" behavior—territories to be Germanized immediately;[39] it was a potential center of the Nazi Empire, and the presence of the Dirlewanger unit represented a stain thereon.

But in Belarus, on the disputed margins of the empire, the men of the unit were not left in peace either. Christian Gerlach has shown convincingly that a wide consensus existed among civil administrations, armed forces, and security organisms to make large-scale sweeps a weapon against Russian peasants at least as much as against partisan groups. With this in mind, the creation of "death zones," including the massacre of civilians, the burning of villages, and blind reprisals, posed no problem for civil authorities. Institutionally motivated, seeking to ensure their supremacy over security organizations, Belarusian civil authorities declared a covert war against the anti-partisan combat forces during 1943.[40] And while their attacks remained mostly rhetorical, it was nevertheless the Dirlewanger unit that they targeted above all.

In a report referring back in large part to an earlier document sent by Kube to Berlin nearly one year earlier, one of his adjutants described in outraged terms the consequences of Operation Cottbus, the largest and most murderous of the anti-partisan operations, and cited the Dirlewanger unit as having lamentably distinguished itself by its policy of destruction. From the point of view of the civil authority, stigmatization was in order: the author insisted on the brutality and the behavior worthy of a "*Landsknecht* of the Thirty Years' War" displayed by the unit.[41] There again, the denounced practices supplied merely the background of the report. In fact, the latter expressed the desire to establish an administration that would be just as predatory, but more polished; an administration in which the cynegetic practices of the *Sondereinheit* would have no place.

What was true in Galicia and in Belarus was even more so in the territories to the west. One could add to these two examples that of Slovakia, where HSSPF Höfle did all he could to distance the unit's battalions and to send them to the Budapest front.[42] Everywhere the unit passed, it spread disorder and violence, but it was preceded, above all, by a reputation mingling truth and legend, and reinforcing the rhetoric that had presided at its creation. Its men were considered savages by those who had created the unit as well as by those who had coexisted with it in the occupied territories, and if the authorities accepted their violence, represented as irrepressible, they universally did their best to distance themselves. The poachers, despite the fiction of their being "tried by combat," seem to have remained prisoners of the image projected on them by Nazi society—an image in conformity with German society's image of the Wild Man.

Wild Men and Warriors

The unit was quickly brought into contact with formations of the same type, and soon became an object of observation by the latter. As mentioned previously, in autumn 1941 the unit was investigated by the Lublin KdS. This investigation was instigated by the denunciation of an SS NCO billeted with his group in the same building as the *Sonderkommando*.[43] This first example shows how negatively the men of the unit were often viewed. Nevertheless, this was not always the case. Documents from neighboring institutions and testimony given in post-war trials reveal two images, one of courage and efficiency, and another, perhaps complementary, of great brutality.

During the Belarusian campaign, the appreciation "in combat" of Dirlewanger's men was unequivocal. While unanimously against them in town and in the pacified regions, higher ranks and fighting units recognized their efficiency and bravery in the Belarusian woods and the Pripyat marshes. The HSSPF for Central Russia thus stated that the "commando had been engaged wherever the situation required especially intrepid plungers (*Draufgänger*) caring nothing for danger."[44] In other circumstances, at the beginning of their action in Belarus, it was noted in HSSPF correspondence that "the unit proved itself superbly. It [was] better adapted than any other troop to anti-partisan action in a hostile environment."[45] The commander of the 286th Wehrmacht Division also expressed his satisfaction, addressing his special congratulations to the unit before the HSSPF for Central Russia, Erich von dem Bach-Zelewsky.[46] And rightly so: Dirlewanger had collaborated closely with the division during Operation Adler, and one of its reports gives an idea of the intensity of the combat and the prevailing conditions: "[The enemy] tried to evade capture by hiding neck-deep in the marshes or perched high in trees. Its attempts to break through were fierce. In several cases, the officers and political commissioners escaped capture at the last minute by killing themselves."[47] For their military observers, the men of the *Sondereinheit* had performed marvelously because anti-partisan operations called upon their "natural qualities"[48]; in other words, their poachers' qualities. Certainly, these victory announcements or proposals for decoration emphasize the operations' difficulty, the better to grant heroic status to their participants and to support their requests for decoration.

One example, however, shows to what extent the unit was considered one of the best adapted to the type of war waged by the Germans in Belarus. During all their operations in this theater, the Germans were confronted with the knotty problem of anti-personnel mines. One of the partisans' practices consisted of mining the roads and the edges of the forest, which acted at once as an alarm system and an easy way to destroy the occupiers' communication infrastructures. The *Sonderein-heit* established, in the summer of 1943, a "method" that was widely copied. Here is how Dirlewanger's hierarchical superior presented it in the final report on Operation Cottbus: "The mining of most of the roads and paths made the use of mine detectors necessary, as per order. The mine detector developed by the Dirlewanger Battalion successfully passed the test."[49] What von Gottberg meant by "mine detector" was to round up the Russian inhabitants of local villages and make them walk in close order in front of the troops in order to detonate any mines, the justification being the presumed complicity of these populations with the partisans.[50] Beyond the "procedure," to which we will return, the Dirlewanger unit appeared as "inno-vative" in the eyes of their superiors. The unit had developed the procedure, and the officers found it so successful that they began using it elsewhere.[51]

The unit's brutality was never doubted by its contemporaries, whether German or Russian. Innumerable atrocities are attrib-uted to it. In February 1943, for example, it burned no fewer than ten villages. The exhumation report of the Soviet investi-gating commission mentions, besides the number of villages and the number killed in each, that neither cartridges nor projectiles were found, and it concluded that the two thousand victims had been burned alive in barns.[52] A witness to the massacres, Alexander Mironov, saw a man, laughing, throw a fourteen-year-old child into a bonfire and identified his Łahojsk-based unit.[53] A Russian former auxiliary trooper, ques-tioned by the commission investigating Nazi crimes in the Mogilev region, declared for his part, "What I understood from my direct experience was that the Dirlewanger special unit had been created specifically to undertake reprisal operations against the partisans and the peaceful population of Belarus. During more than two years, this unit, under the command of Dirlewanger, of the Zalski brothers, of Zimmermann, of Ted Jakob, and of other Nazis, systematically took reprisal actions around Mogilev, Minsk, Vitebsk, and other areas. During these actions, the peaceful inhabitants of towns, villages, and hamlets were shot, burned alive, hanged. Houses, schools, hospitals, clubs, churches, and other public buildings were burned. [. . .] If my memory is correct, more than a hundred inhabited areas were destroyed, together with their inhabitants."[54]

It is unusual to find a killer speaking so clearly during German trials. No doubt the fact that he was questioned by Belarusians had something to do with this volubility. These declarations were corroborated by the unit's archives and by the Soviet commissions' investigative reports. Other documents specify the characteristics of this violence. The examination quoted here reveals an essentially collective operation, and one might well be curious as to the chain of command justifying—or demanding—such behavior. Alexander Mironov's testimony also shows its interpersonal dimension, sometimes arbitrary even to the killers, noted by a member of the unit in regard to one of the NCOs: "Feiertag [the NCO] is a swine. I remember exactly how he killed a Polish woman for nothing, absolutely nothing. The old woman was driving an old cart, drawn by a little horse, with a bit of hay in it. She was sitting on the hay, and was literally shot down for no reason. I believe this happened near Minsk."[55]

The utter arbitrariness of individual exercises of violence appears fully here, even in the eyes of a man suspected of having himself participated in the massacres committed by the *Sondereinheit*. And if we add the laugh of the killer mentioned in Mironov's testimony, cruelty is added to arbitrariness. It is not merely a passing detail in the stories of a few victims or non-members of the unit. Fire, rape, multiple fusillades, and interrogations under torture are repeatedly evoked—but not always with great accuracy—by witnesses.

This violence, obviously, was not limited to Belarus. During the Warsaw uprising, the unit was again noted for its great brutality, occurring, furthermore, before the eyes of troops who had never before participated in anti-partisan combat and who were thus not used to it.

A former sapper gave the most striking testimony. His unit seems to have been integrated with the combat units formed to take the Okhota and Wola neighborhoods by assault, and he gives a glimpse of the behavior of the men of the Dirlewanger, notably during the assault on a hospital and a convent:

> I would now like to describe the assault on the hospital. As usual, rush to the objective, grenades, and, after they exploded, we went in. I was about to fire, but I heard: "Don't shoot!" from the inside. What to do? I signaled to my comrades twenty meters away to cover me. I ordered the Poles to open the door and come out with their hands up. Inside, I heard snatches of conversation, some in Polish, some in German. The door opened slowly and a Red Cross nurse stuck out a white flag. My comrades came up and we went in, bayonets fixed. [. . .] A Polish officer, a doctor, and fifteen Polish Red Cross nurses surrendered the hospital. The Germans asked us not to hurt the Poles. Then the SS arrived. They immediately executed all the Polish wounded, and attacked the nurses, who were soon stripped and raped. We were pushed out the other door of the hospital. When we could come back that night—the SS had relieved us—there was tumult on the execution grounds. Soldiers from all the units, SS, Ukrainians, were playing flutes and singing, and there I saw something so frightening and horrible I can hardly describe it, fifty years later. The SS were pushing

the nurses, naked, their hands on their heads, to the gallows. They had cut a short tunic for the doctor, had put a rope around his neck; and pushed him towards a gallows where some ten civilians were already hanging. The crowd laughed and shouted. Some soldiers were protesting, but they were drowned out. I saw we could do nothing, so I kept my remarks for our headquarters.[56]

The SS who relieved his unit are of course the men of the *Sonderbrigade*. Schenk describes the abuses they committed, which correspond perfectly to the terms used two years earlier by *Ministerialrat* Joel when he authorized the unit to "pillage, burn, rape" in its zones of operation. Wasn't that precisely what the brigade was doing in Warsaw? Schenk, however, combined this description of their profanatory violence with that of their combat practices:

Then the reinforcements arrived—the SS. It was the Dirle-wanger penal battalion. Its soldiers wore no marks of rank. They had drunk a lot and weren't sober. They immediately attacked the Polish positions. They charged the houses, yelling: "Hurrah!" Just in front of the houses, they fell under Polish fire. They died by dozens. Many were wounded.

They didn't gain a meter of ground. Their leader was frenzied.[57] We then advanced together with the SS under tank protection. A few meters in front of the buildings, the tank was hit and exploded. A soldier's helmet flew into the air.[58]

The former sapper describes the unit's behavior under fire in a fundamentally ambiguous manner.

On the one hand, he sees them as a band of drunkards, acting under the influence of alcohol. On the other, he insists

116

on their nerveless courage and on the rage, the possession, that overtakes them at the charge, giving them an inhuman courage. Can one be separated from the other, in his eyes? For the narrator, it is also because the men are under the influence of alcohol that they can advance under Polish fire. Courage, alcohol, cruelty, rage, and possession went together.[59]

"Cruel hunters,"[60] the men of the unit were also, in the eyes of the former sapper, possessed warriors. Like Bertrand Hell's *Berserker* and werewolves, the unit's men discharged, for Schenk, a blind, destructive rage as they spilled the enemy's blood.[61] To him, these soldiers seemed to obey a symbolic order invoking the vital forces of the non-domestic world in the warrior's domain. Should we take this rage as a prerequisite condition explaining the behavior of the men of the *Sonderbrigade?* Were these men the prisoners of this condition, to the point of having no other choice but to "burn, pillage, and rape"? Certainly, by deciding to create a unit of poachers, and by sending it to the Eastern fronts, the leaders of the Third Reich participated in a collective imagination widely present in German society, and this imagination created in advance the conditions making paroxysmal violence possible. This discourse described the poachers as violent and cruel even before they were so, and, thus, made it possible for them to become so.

There is nevertheless a second element to be considered. Matthias Schenk's report and the judgments of many actors of the *Partisanenbekämpfung* are post-war testimonies. As such, they were no doubt subject to certain considerations. All describe the unit as particularly cruel, but the instances of violence described and attributed to it have a rhetorical function. It may be useful to examine one of them in an attempt to understand. The case is the attack on a priest by the men of the unit:

The cloister: it was an enormous building, already badly damaged by bombs and shells. We were to take it by assault. There was a heavy door behind which were cellars. While the third man of my squad stayed twenty meters behind—partly to cover us, partly to signal the SS to advance as soon as we'd made the assault—we broke down the door and went inside. The cellar was full of people praying aloud. In front of us was a priest, who was giving communion. Perhaps by reflex, we knelt and took communion. My third comrade entered in turn, and he too knelt and took communion. Then the SS arrived. Shots, groans, screams. Many nuns were there, in their habits. But we had to go on. Hours later, that evening, I saw the priest again. The SS, drunk, were tormenting him; his face was bloody, his cassock was torn. The SS were drinking the wine from the communion vessel, the communion wafers were scattered and trampled. A crucifix had fallen from the wall, and the SS were urinating on it. Without dealing with them, I picked up the Cross, took hold of the priest, and took him to our quarters. My two comrades went with me. The SS were surprised; before they could react we were far away.[62]

Schenk, a Christian faithful to his convictions, reticent before "useless violence," describes himself as an honorable soldier in a dishonorable war, the black hunters serving to set his singular attitude in relief. Without commenting on the reality of the latter, we will simply mention that Schenk was consistently used as a point man in an assault squadron, and that he thus was part of the contingents most confronted with combat violence, particularly during the Warsaw siege. Must we conclude that this story was part of a strategy of exoneration? This question opens the problem of the image of the hunt and of the Wild Man in post-war discourse, and its instrumentalization—conscious or unconscious—in the judicial defense strategies of former Nazis.

The investigation of the *Kampfgruppe* von Gottberg by the Hamburg prosecutor's office constitutes a typical example in this respect. This group, made up of several units, including the *Sonderbrigade*, became, as we have seen, the principal actor of the *Partisanenbekämpfung* in Belarus starting in summer 1942, and it played an important role in large-scale sweep operations, particularly in the "death zone" strategy. The principal commanding officers were absent: Kurt von Gottberg had committed suicide at the end of the war; the Minsk KdS, Strauch, had gone mad and died in a Belgian prison in 1946. The suspects thus adopted an ambiguous position: they presented the events in Belarus as the result of orders given by a centralized chain of command over which they had little control, but they also sought not to be accused of having carried out murderous orders. It was essential for them to present aggressions in the field from a position of variability.

They delivered a softened version of the actions of the Wehrmacht and of security forces, while explaining plausibly the facts observed in the field by the Belarusian investigative commissions, by systematically incriminating the Dirlewanger unit in the abuses described by witnesses and suspects. The examination of Paul Rumschewitsch, a Russian-speaking German from the Volga, employed by the Minsk KdS before being sent to the Vlassov Army, gives a minimum of concrete information to the investigators: no names, no places, no dates. However, as though to compensate, he describes in detail the drinking of the Dirlewanger unit and notes the systematic nature of the fires set. He thus delivers what could be thought of as the *leitmotiv* of the German testimony: "We generally said that the unit was wrong to ravage the villages so horribly."[63] Rumschewitsch suggests that the matter was proverbial among

Partisanenbekämpfung members: "Where there's fire, there's Dirlewanger."[64] Rumschewitsch wasn't the only one to incriminate the unit. Most of the investigation's protagonists—except for the black hunters themselves—imitated him.

The accusation against the unit was systematic. It was in perfect continuity with that image of the hunt and of the Wild Man that had been the precondition of its creation and had accompanied its existence. Furthermore, this discourse around cruelty and unbridled violence was now instrumentalized in the service of the exonerative strategies of the protagonists of the *Partisanenbekämpfung*, who found therein a convenient scapegoat allowing them to turn the attention of the investigators away from their own abuses. But this behavior went so far as to find its place in the construction of memory in the new West German society. In the wake of Adenauer-period amnesia and the unspoken amnesty from which those implicated in Nazi abuses benefited until 1955 or 1960, there begin to appear articles and pamphlets spreading a specific image of the Dirlewanger unit. If this image was intended to normalize and to play down the abuses, it nevertheless involved some interesting passages on the unit's cynegetic element.

Thus the interview with Heinz Feiertag, a former NCO of the *Leibstandarte* transferred to the unit in 1941 and implicated in numerous investigations thereof. On May 22, 1960, he gave an interview to a journalist named Fritz Langour, in which he spoke both of "the origins of the unit and combat conditions it had experienced in Russia." Picking up the legend of its founding after a poaching case had brought it to Hitler's attention, Feiertag began to describe the training received by the recruits at Oranienburg before recounting the unit's first actions in Belarus:

It was a summer action, at the beginning of the year. It was a difficult action because anti-partisan combat is difficult in itself, but the whole business was made still more difficult by the marshy terrain. Since they were well trained and equipped, the partisans had taken up their positions in the marsh. Some of them were even hidden there up to their necks, camouflaged by plants and green clothing. They let us come in and as soon as we were in the middle [of their positions] shots rang out from everywhere. The surprise worked wonderfully for them. We were dazed for a moment, but we got hold of ourselves quickly.

Q. Did you have many losses?

A. Yes, there were lots.

[. . .]

A. In this action the poachers showed what they could do. The training they'd gotten on the terrain was useless to them, because they already knew it instinctively.

This remark was followed by a confirmation of their great aptitude for combat, Feiertag explaining that the mission he spoke of was merely a reconnaissance by the group as an assault troop, in the context of a big operation that cost the lives of five thousand. Without pausing over the number of victims, the journalist continues to question him on the relationship between the troop and the officers, as well as the harshness of their training. This is how Feiertag takes the reader into the heart of the poachers' relationship to violence, while whitewashing completely their violence against civilians:

Due to [the presence of] convicts and criminals, it had to be that way [Feiertag is speaking of the harshness of their training], to give the commando a disciplined appearance externally and to reinforce it internally. But there's a difference to be noted. The seventy poachers, you could really tell very quickly, in a few weeks, who was really a poacher and who was only secondarily so, that is to say, someone who had been a criminal and stolen and had, then, done something else, and poached as well.

Q. Were there any who had only poached and nothing else?

A. There were a few like that, who had only poached. In hunters' language, we say: he stole, and he stole game, because he's not a real poacher, but just a meat dealer. And the other, who was a real poacher, didn't see the meat, just the trophy. There were fellows who would sit in the cellar at night, because they couldn't hang up the trophy, they would turn on the light, they would sit for hours just looking at it. It's clear, of course, that when you've got men from East Prussia who shot a King Stag there that was meant for Goering, you've got something special. Such a man is neither a meat dealer nor a bandit nor a thief, but a real poacher.

They were described as a legion of honorable poachers, the only ones capable of taking the measure of combat. Only poachers could surmount the disadvantage of not knowing the terrain; only poachers could use sniper rifles and submachine guns and triumph with reduced firepower in anti-partisan combat. The harshness of battle demanded the harsh instruction meted out to other categories of recruits. Feiertag, with the journalist's complicity, skillfully avoided mentioning the systematic aggressivity towards civilians, the burning of villages, and the pillaging of resources. In his discourse, one element strangely recalls Hitler's words and those of Ministry Counselor Joel. The romantic dimension of the hunt, its connection with risk, the passion for trophies—so many obligatory figures in an anthropological reflection on the hunt and the Wild Man. Concession to the times, cruelty is muted, both to normalize the memory of Nazism in the Germany of the 1960s and, more concretely, to give no grounds for investigation by those magistrates who were beginning to look into what had gone on in the East.

Post-war Germany analyzed the unit's violence in terms comparable to those of the Nazis, always returning to the pregnant imagery of the hunt and of Black Blood. The poachers, here mingled indiscriminately with types of recruits with whom they had nothing in common, continued to generate ambiguous representations, going from criminalization and social exclusion to a real fascination. We see here the mixture of functional calculation and a symbolism of unbridled violence that had presided over the creation of the unit, as well as that social marginality that had struck the poachers at the moment of their joining it. A new element is the doubling of social analysis with strategies of exoneration, or rather of dilution of responsibility in the vast totality of crimes committed in the East.

In a sense, these soldiers had confirmed the discourse that gave them—as "wild men"—a specific place in the world of men at war and accepted in advance that their savagery be mobilized against an adversary that had been animalized from the start. The proposal was not an injunction: when, in 1939, Hitler spoke of the cruelty of the black hunters, he didn't order them to burn villages and their inhabitants in Belarus, but he accepted in advance that it might come to that. He accepted the violence assumed to be inseparable from savagery, established it as a "necessary evil," dictated by "circumstances" and by an adversary that had lost all humanity, if he had ever had any. For an inhuman adversary, necessary cruelty.

Later, fire and massacre became the norm on the Eastern front, and the men of the Dirlewanger were perceived, in continuity with this discourse marked by excellence in combat and by cruelty, as warriors possessed by an extraordinary violence, convenient release valves allowing the Nazis to consider themselves as human, unlike the Soviets who were supposed to take a perverse pleasure in annihilating their adversaries. The presence of men like Dirlewanger allowed the "ordinary soldiers" of the war against the partisans to think of themselves as incendiaries and mass murderers by necessity alone, without taking pleasure in it, unlike the black hunters who were so close to their prey that they could not help absorbing some of its qualities.

It was these "ordinary Germans," however, who spread this unprecedented violence on the Eastern front. Very reduced in number, the *Sondereinheit* Dirlewanger wasn't capable alone of doing the dirty work of village burning, mass shooting, and deportation, any more than anti-partisan combat itself. Its presence alone is thus far from providing a plausible explanation for the whirlwind that fell upon Belarus. These practices, always presented as typical of the black hunters, although they weren't always the first to use them, became the norm. The massive involvement of German society explains why the protagonists of the post-war trials fell back once more on the discourse of the Wild Man. On the one hand, this usage belonged to the unconscious translation of a discourse immortalizing a specific image beyond the end of the war and that of the Third Reich. On the other, it supplied a ready-made interpretation of German atrocities in Russia. Combined with a strategy of criminalization of the men of the unit, this discourse allowed factual elements of guilt to be cast aside with ease. But in so doing, it also cast responsibility for Nazi violence upon the Wild Man and marginality, conveniently exonerating a German nation then undergoing full political and economic reconstruction. The nation not only condemned itself to the loss and incomprehension of its past; it restored archaic cultural structures from which it had never fundamentally departed since the time of Wilhelm.

Chapter 5

A Hunters' War?

How shall we go about establishing with certainty that the war of annihilation had this cynegetic dimension? We cannot count too much on the testimony of unit veterans; in general, a soldier is reluctant to speak of the "hunting" element in war. The nature of the war the *Sondereinheit* waged in the east, in light of the fact that involvement in Nazi criminal policies was still liable to prosecution (not to mention the sociological marginality of the "black hunters"), restrained what those questioned told judges and a few rare interviewers. Using the reflections of anthropologists and prehistorians,[1] let us try to recover the points of contact in the Nazi imagination and practice between cynegetic and military activity.

The first Dirlewanger mission independent of other units stationed in the sector was reconnaissance in the form of *Spähtruppen*. These units penetrated the woods to detect partisan groups, to detail their camps, their manpower, and their weapons, and to identify their leaders. The following report is an example of this:

A 1/20 hunting commando from Sabalotje going through Novij Sabalotje, Gutschin by the north entry of Swilotka and by Kasenje Bortoschky, Petuschowka up to the railroad going from Sloboda to Pyraschewo.

According to civilians' statements, small and medium-sized enemy troops went through the village on June 2. In all the villages were enemy posts that had to be avoided to accomplish our mission. [. . .]

Two hundred meters before the railroad line, vehicles and riders turn towards Sloboda. The hunting commando arrived approximately five minutes late to the lookout post, nevertheless taking its position at the place described by the deserter. However, the enemy did not appear on the road before the commando's retreat at five o'clock. [. . .] At five fifteen, the commando left the lookout position and began reconnaissance on Sloboda and Pyraschewo. It had to make a one-kilometer detour before the village because of unmistakable bunkers and rifle positions there. There were no skirmishes with the enemy during the expedition and the hunting commando's lookout wasn't observed by the enemy.[2]

The second Dirlewanger mission, following the model of the SS and the Wehrmacht, was to perform sweep operations, particularly in 1943. There is nothing astonishing in that: it was at this time, let us recall, that the coordination of anti-partisan forces reached its point of optimal efficiency through the formation of the *Kampfgruppe* von Gottberg, in which the Dirlewanger brigade became a key element. The unit was integrated for the first time in a much larger formation; there it took part in some of the most important and most murderous anti-partisan operations, such as Hornung and Cottbus.

Strategically coordinated several months in advance, Operation Cottbus lasted four weeks, the *Sondereinheit* being responsible for the southern sector of Lake Palik.[3] Two police regiments, seven Wehrmacht battalions, and eight battalions of Schumas and auxiliaries were engaged—16,662 men in all, forming a net closed by a cordon of units that combed the

Borissow sector, burning villages and pushing the surviving, panicked populations ahead of them.[4] The goal was to capture everything living in the sector and to force the cornered partisans to fight. Fifteen thousand people died in this trap.[5]

On one hand, then, they served as small lookout groups, seeking to identify and evaluate the enemy—engaging in a war closely resembling the *Pirsch* practiced by individual hunters, tracking and following the deer, identifying it, reading in earth and vegetation, in its track and fumets, its size, sex, and age, before bringing it down with a single rifle shot, face to face, as close as possible. In this elitist hunt par excellence—the *Pirsch*—the hunter's joy lies as much in tracking the animal and in sizing up the prey as in the final confrontation with the quarry.[6] This type of hunt was favored by Himmler, Pohl, and Berger, in a sense all the dignitaries who had participated in the unit's creation. The hunting permits issued by Himmler always mentioned a single quarry and were very specific as to the age and sex of the animal to be shot.[7]

On the other hand, the large-scale sweep operations were, inversely, the equivalent of the battue, or hunt with beaters. The latter consists of disturbing the living space of the game by noise, blows, and fires, causing them to flee towards the cordon of shooters. The sweeps performed in Belarus functioned along exactly the same model. The first hunt, elitist and individual, is set against the second, collective and egalitarian, but far more murderous.[8] Consciously or not, the Germans had based their anti-partisan actions on immemorial woodcraft.[9]

It remains to be understood how this cynegetic impregnation modeled the representation of the enemy and of war itself. On November 27, 1942, during Operation Nuremberg, Kurt von Gottberg, Dirlewanger's hierarchic superior, writes to Gottlob Berger about one of the group's actions. Rather proud of his successes and alluding to the additional heavy artillery recently received, whose effect is presented as decisive, von Gottberg writes: "The IG6 were enough to make those rascals [*Lumpe*] run. Nevertheless, they sometimes let themselves be killed or burned on the spot. We had fine weather, with a slight frost. Ideal weather to send the beaters out."[10] The SS general could not be clearer: the enemy was prompt to flee, but let itself be killed on the spot, facing its killers courageously when flight was in vain, like the Bavarian mountain boar (the archetypal black animal).[11] The mention of the weather—clear and frosty—is a commonplace of the cynegetic literature, as in Ernst Jünger's story of a boar hunt, in which the description of nature has an important place, more important even than the description of the cynegetic baptism supposed to constitute the narrative.[12] The experience of a forest environment becoming a cathedral of ice through the action of an eastern winter,[13] assimilation of the enemy to the blackest game on the scale of wildness, and explicit comparison between sweeps and beaters' drives all indicate that von Gottberg experienced this war as a hunt. Everything leads us to believe, furthermore, that he was completely representative of his men in this matter: his descriptions of enemy, missions, and representation of danger may be studied as so many hunters' tales.

Thus it is for the partisans' cruelty: it is regularly mentioned by the German protagonists of the *Partisanenbekämpfung*, and the members of the *Sondereinheit* who felt they had experienced it frequently and early, as soon as they arrived.[14] After the war, one of the closest battle companions of the *Sondereinheit*, the commander of the fifty-seventh *Schutzmannschaften* battalion,[15] described that particular cruelty through a series of set expressions not exempt from exonerative insinuations:

> I myself, in three years of anti-partisan action in Russia, saw—or saw described in reliable reports—thousands of soldiers, *Nachrichtenmädel*, and Red Cross nurses hung head downwards, alive, whose eyes had been torn out or

whose genitals had been severed. I remember one case in particular, because it involved soldiers I myself knew; the attack on the Horodysche police commando and a detachment of my own company. The Horodysche police commando was buried alive, and the dead and wounded of Lieutenant Jonath's detachment were bestially mutilated. While they were still alive, their eyes were torn out and their genitals cut off. That was the substance of the report by a wounded man who had survived this butchery by playing dead.[16]

Images of mutilation arose from the savagery attributed to the partisans. We will not discuss here the truth of these reported incidents, even though the numbers cited must be examined with caution. The belief in the existence of these mutilations and of their systematic character served as proof of enemy savagery. Thus the story, whether personally witnessed or recounted in "reliable reports," followed its unquestioned course: a discourse of the same type as those stories of old stags' charges or the attacks of adult male boars bringing down unfortunate hunters.[17] For if the savagery of the boar and the wolf justifies the hunt and the kill, stories of partisan atrocities legitimize the abuses of sweep operations.[18] For Siegling, the story has the function of "contextualizing" the facts at the heart of the investigation: townsmen massacred, Jewish communities fusilladed, and villages burned.[19]

A second analogy between cynegetic discourse and soldiers' testimony is the dangers confronted and losses. One of the first to evoke this aspect was Dirlewanger himself, together with his hierarchy. In August 1942, correspondence from the HSSPF evoked the "numerous members of the SS falling daily, victims of the partisans,"[20] and Dirlewanger spoke of the "significant losses continually experienced" by the unit.[21] These letters had the object of requesting reinforcements, in men or in materiel.

As already noted by Hans Peter Klausch, the belief in the high mortality rate among the men of the unit does not stand up to analysis. Only nineteen poachers were listed as "killed in battle" until the summer of 1943.[22] Nevertheless, for Himmler the *Partisanenbekämpfung* remained something of a trial by ordeal. Whoever had transgressed SS norms could redeem himself by joining the unit and undergoing its trial. It was necessary to believe that the stakes were high—were life itself.

This firm and widespread belief in the danger inherent in anti-partisan action—and, more generally, in the territories "infested by bandits"[23]—had its parallel in cynegetic discourse. The theme of the danger of the hunt—not in terms of accidents among hunters but of attack by the quarry—took on a central importance in the economy of the hunters' discourse. Hunters insist that the conflict is not as unequal as it appears. Even though the prey is an herbivore like the stag or the boar, even if the hunter kills from afar, he is never totally safe from the charge of a rutting stag or a mother boar protecting her young. This danger—heightened, in the case of the *Pirsch*, by the final face-to-face encounter between animal and hunter—gives nobility to cynegetic activity in the eyes of those who practice it. Without certifying that it is exactly the same for the *Partisanenbekämpfung*, the aspiration to be respected by the world of combat is generally found in the men who are actors therein. The idea of danger is capital in the analogy between anti-partisan action and frontline service, as witnessed by the criteria for *Nahkampfspangen*, those decorations awarded upon completion of a certain number of duel-like close combats or after a certain number of days under close, direct enemy fire. The parallel, in these cases, between service on the front in a situation of immediate danger and sweep operations considered as analogous explains why the *Nahkampfspangen* were among the decorations most prized by the men of the unit, who received a not inconsiderable number of them.[24]

The killers themselves were not alone in making use of the analogy between war and the hunt to account for the violence of their struggle. German prosecutors in 1960 persevered in an investigation against the leader of the Minsk KdS's Wilejka outpost. They called for testimony from Russian survivors, Jewish and non-Jewish. Fifty of these were translated into German and included in the dossier. Practically all the witnesses questioned used the verb "*jagen*," "to hunt," to designate the action of assembling people by force and with violence in order to execute them on the edge of pits or inside barns to which the Germans set fire.[25] Certainly, this systematic use of the term seems strange. Aside from the term having been translated from Russian into German, the interrogation procedures developed by Soviet investigators led to a standardization of the victims' replies. One thing at least is certain: victims, Russian investigators, German translators—one of these categories or the three together—adopted and generalized this analogy. The cynegetic imagination worked for the killers and for their adversaries, whether wartime foes or postwar judges.

If we look for the origin of the cynegetic model in the East, it coincides with the situation during the first months of 1942. At that time, groups of Soviet soldiers overtaken by the German advance organized and structured themselves, occupying the countryside and especially the forests, far from communication lines.[26] Against an enemy whose presence was at the very least making itself felt, when it wasn't actually disruptive on the strategic or economic level, German authorities reacted by turning to the German culture of the hunt. Although, during the year 1941, "partisans" had been intercepted and shot along communication lines, the Germans subsequently established operational methods congruent with the *Pirsch* and the battue. It was also at this time that there developed a new series of rumors about Soviet atrocities, which had been frequent in the first weeks of the invasion, then disappeared from unit reports for several months.[27] Now essentially forest-based, practiced through battue and from blinds, against an enemy whose violence again left physical traces on the bodies of Germans fallen into their hands, anti-partisan combat constituted a wartime parallel to hunting, offering a coherent behavioral model to the Germans taking part in it.

Quarry and Spoils

These poachers, waging war as though they were hunting, carefully noted the number of their victims and detailed the spoils collected, an accounting at first glance inconsistent with the cynegetic model, beginning with the question of the treatment of women by the men of the unit. Bertrand Hell has shown that the gendered dimension of cynegetic activity was central in the European imagination of the Wild Man. The *Pirsch* is an exclusively masculine activity and tends to take as its target only the ten-pronged King Stag, dominant and at full sexual maturity. At the belling hour, two virilities confront each other, and if the tracking and traces to which the hunter devotes himself constitute the essence of selecting a hunt-worthy beast, calling the stag is at least as important as analyzing his spoor. The hunter must challenge his future victim by counterfeiting his belling, but he must do so with discernment: the imitation of too young a stag will evoke only the scornful silence of a dominant male; that of too powerful a stag will intimidate the younger specimen. Thus, everything depends on the hunter's evaluation of the age and sexual power of the quarry. A successful *Pirsch* compels the stag to come forth to the forest's edge at dawn, prepares him to confront a potential rival, and allows the hunter to bring him down at that very moment.

Female game, however, arouses only contempt. Never shot face-to-face, does are called "cows" or "mares" by the hunters, who meet their hunting plan by killing a set number of them before the hunt every year. They complete this task grudgingly, fulfilling their social responsibility as hunters by organizing battues. In Germanic countries, a battue is used only to fulfill a hunting plan and is devoid of any social prestige.[28] It is the only space in which the hunter consents to kill females.

What of the *Partisanenbekämpfung*? The situation was much less simple. Certainly the *Spähtruppen*, who practiced the "man-*Pirsch*," almost never killed women, which would tend to support the coherence of the cynegetic view. But in large-scale operations, women were treated in radically different ways, depending on context. In the case of assault on partisan camps, during major sweep operations, women were shot exactly like men who possessed weapons. On September 9, 1942, the *Sonderkommando* Dirlewanger reported: "A newly built camp two kilometers south [of the operation area] was attacked by *Hauptsturmführer* Weber on his own initiative and taken by assault, with the guard remaining inside the camp. There were four enemy dead, and four women found in the camp were also shot."[29] We do not know if these women were interrogated before being shot, but their chance of survival in this situation was almost nil.[30] In such a case, in which death is the logical outcome of the battue and where the analogy between battue and sweep operation is in full effect, the coherence of the cynegetic model is preserved.

However, few women were captured in assaults on entrenched camps. Most of the thousands of women who fell into the *Sondereinheit*'s hands did so during the village encirclements during the last phase of sweep operations. This phase consisted of returning to the units' starting point after having reached the determined topographic objective, systematically searching the villages passed during the advance. It was during this phase, as Christian Gerlach noted, that civilian massacres were the most frequent[31] and that deportations were performed. This last phase, however, had no equivalent in the battue. Doesn't this represent a limit to the cynegetic model? Two possible configurations suggest themselves. In the unit's operations reports, women, rarely separated from children in the unit's statistics, are mentioned under two headings: those "suspected of belonging to a partisan band" (*Bandenverdächtige*), executed en masse; and those *Erfassung*, inventory for removal, or, in other words, deportation. In the first case, unit practices aimed to kill all members of the category. In the second case, they were to be removed, with two distinct objectives: either they were to be relocated in sectors beyond partisan reach, or they were to be sent to forced labor.

If we examine the case in which the victims were kept alive, we see the recurrence of a new category of violence. It is in this case, and we are tempted to say in this case only, that violence of a sexual nature appears in the written sources. The testimony of unit veterans reveals that members of the unit, notably officers, selected from these human spoils a certain number of women who were separated from the rest of the group and taken to the barracks for orgies during which they were collectively raped. A unit veteran, Waldemar B., civil prisoner convicted for homosexuality, certified that the officers, during their stay, shut up eight women, confiscated their clothing, and in the evening took them to the castle, where they whipped them.[32] Albin V. gave similar testimony. Other stories indicated that this practice, widespread in the *Sondereinheit* Dirlewanger, was not restricted to that unit alone; officers of von Gottberg's general staff themselves adopted it, at least from time to time.[33]

Our sources seem to indicate that the women were systematically put to death after this torture.[34] We will return to the meaning of this gestural language of violence soon. Let us note, however, that none of the witnesses attributed any special function to it.[35] Let us also note that these tortures seemed to occur only when the women belonged to populations having undergone operations of concentration and displacement. While the killing of women during sweep operations was in perfect conformity with the cynegetic mode, the practice discussed above indicates that the cynegetic model had been abandoned. European hunters do not concentrate their prey, do not displace it, and they kill it but do not torture it. The treatment of women in these cases defines a sort of cynegetic frontier, revealing what remains within the model as well as what does not belong to it. It also suggests that we must find an alternative interpretation to account for the treatment of those populations so concentrated and displaced.

The second test of the war/hunt analogy is constituted by the treatment of the young. In European hunting, the latter are excluded from the kill, a cynegetic taboo whose strength may be measured by the duration of its observance.[36] In contemporary Europe, all forms of the hunt respect the obligation to spare the young. The hunt for "stinking beasts"—foxes, badgers, polecats—traditionally by gassing them certainly transgresses this taboo; its exterminatory nature spares neither the young nor pregnant females, but this is an extremely marginal form of hunting, now banned. Generally, and since the dawn of time, hunters avoid interfering with their quarry's offsping.[37]

The *Partisanenbekämpfung* did not respect the cynegetic analogy in this matter. The men of the *Sondereinheit* and the other combat troops killed more children than any other unit during the war in the East, the *Einsatzgruppen* excepted. In early September 1942, however, Erich von dem Bach-Zelewsky sent a note to all units under his command that was transmitted from General von Schenckendorff, commander of the security troops of the Center Army Group. This note stipulated the rule to be followed in the treatment of local populations, and legitimized putting them to death if they belonged to or had collaborated with a partisan group.[38] As for children, however, von Schenckendorff ordered that they be shot only "if they [were] aware of the consequences of their actions. This is not the case for children younger than ten; they [were] to be punished, but not shot."[39] The transmission of this note to the soldiers and commanders most involved in anti-partisan actions raises certain questions. On the functional level, Christian Gerlach perceptively analyses the moral duplicity of its author, General von Schenckendorff, who, according to Gerlach, "posed as a humanist" while inditing orders generating ever-greater violence.[40] On the symbolic level, however, this note restored the analogy between *Partisanenbekämpfung* and hunt, resetting the taboo on killing the young.

To go further, we must distinguish between instances and examine, first, the children found by the *Sondereinheit* during assaults on partisan camps. No combat report mentions the presence of children. The only indication, very sketchy and to be taken with the greatest precautions, is the fact that, in 1944, children from territories considered as controlled by the partisans were kidnapped and sent to Germany together with children from cities or villages destroyed in the creation of "death zones," some to work in the fields, the others enrolled in anti-aircraft units.[41] How many of these children were captured in partisan camps, though? It is impossible to know, and probably only the tiniest minority of the 35,000 or so children kidnapped in the USSR during the war belonged in this category. Nevertheless, these kidnappings were performed by men close to the *Sondereinheit* Dirlewanger: the action was controlled from beginning to end by the Ministry of Occupied Territories, and the two officers who supervised the process, Siegfried Nickel and Walter Brandenburg, were subordinates of Gottlob Berger. Dirlewanger's protector and main provider of men and materiel for the unit was, furthermore, a direct participant in the program, being a liaison officer between Himmler and the Minister of Occupied Territories, Alfred Rosenberg. The officers involved quickly came to know Dirlewanger, though not always in the most favorable circumstances. Walter Brandenburg spent an evening at SSPF von Gottberg's home together with Dirlewanger, who, somewhat intoxicated, insulted Brandenburg, calling him a son-of-a-bitch and a coward.[42] This child-capturing program seems to indicate that, in 1944 at least, children taken during anti-partisan actions were less likely to be massacred than during earlier years. An instruction as to counting and gathering inhabitants and their property during operations Regenschauer[43] and Frühlingsfest[44] also confirms this impression: the memo is careful to recommend that women and children be allowed to collect baggage and food before being taken to the assembly areas at the rear.[45] But this conclusion does not merely concern children captured during combat. Above all, it applies to those who were victims of the *Erfassung*.

We must turn now to this second case. Most children were killed en masse during the large-scale sweep operations and they were victims of gestures of an extraordinary cruelty: raped, thrown living onto bonfires,[46] or beaten to death,[47] when they were not executed by firearm.[48] Starting in late 1943, however, an adolescent's chance of survival, and that of certain women, increased. The census, concentration, and displacement of populations, with the goal of putting them to work, became more important in the choices made by those responsible for security policy in Belarus. More than economic choices, the criterion of selection between "fit for labor"— adult men and single women—and "unfit for labor" determined the likelihood of survival. Children and their mothers were excluded therefrom.

Zinajda Piluj was among those Russian peasant women who were captured during one of the *Sondereinheit*'s village-burnings near Tscherwen in late 1942. She tells of the displacement and concentration of the villagers of the district and of their review by the Germans before their temporary return. During this concentration phase, men "fit for labor" were separated from their families and usually sent to Germany. Several days later, the Germans reappeared on the outskirts of the village. They performed a new selection, this time taking only young single women. Once this was done, the men of the unit split the remaining group, consisting, according to Piluj, "essentially of children, women, and old men," into three. Each of these groups was then shut in a house, on which the men of the unit fired with automatic weapons before systematically burning the village. Piluj managed to get out of the house in which she had been shut, but without being able to save her child.[49]

In any event, these practices are not analogous to battue operations, even if they occur in this context. The treatment of children does not follow any cynegetic logic. We must, then, find an alternative model to understand them.

And the third and final test of the cynegetic model: spoils. In principle, hunters pursue a quarry, not spoils. The German term used in the reports, "*Beute*," introduces an ambiguity, however: it means both a pillager's spoils and a predator's prey. It suggests, then, a strong analogy with the hunt, or rather with predation. In the reports, we find notes of spoils taken during sweep operations. The first category consists of weapons taken from the enemy, by far the least important component. Operation reports list the different types of weapons and the quantities of munitions and explosives found. In the combat report of Operation Draufgänger Two, which was a precursor of Operation Cottbus, the *Sonderbataillon* took "a heavy machine gun, 110 Russian guns, sixteen explosive mines (dynamite and Ekrasite), one complete printing press, one complete transmitter, one Polish radio, one card file as well as the full archives of the partisan group, prospectuses, one box of detonators, mine detonators, explosive devices as well as a new type of silent munitions, one Russian voltmeter."[50] We may thus follow, through these reports, the progress of the partisan movement, the growing presence of light or heavy machine guns, and also, occasionally, small cannons.[51] These captures were significant enough that the weapons not brought back by the commandos were systematically mentioned in the reports. The men of the unit never displayed the weapons captured from the enemy, nor did they attribute the demonstrative character that would elevate them to the rank of trophy to them; nevertheless, the reports did not omit this aspect of the spoils collected, whose presence confirmed the warlike character of the operations, even though the ratio between captured weapons and human losses clearly showed, as we have seen, that nearly 90 percent of the dead were civilians with no relationship to the armed resistance.

The second type of spoils cited in the reports is that of confiscated agricultural products. The economic dimension of the *Partisanenbekämpfung* has been thoroughly studied by Christian Gerlach, who saw in it one of the factors determining the evolution of the policy of occupation in Belarus.[52] We are less interested in this aspect than in the use and perception of such spoils among officers and troops. In the first place, the unit established, starting in Galicia, a solid reputation for pillaging. Property and food confiscated irregularly were, of course, impossible to quantify, and we are further almost equally unable to specify the methods of confiscation. Nevertheless, different battalion orders given by Dirlewanger repeatedly forbid individual confiscations, an indubitable sign that this prohibition was constantly transgressed. One example, dating from autumn 1943 was Battalion Order Forty of October 4, 1943, forbidding any unit to have more than a single cow for daily milk supplies. On September 23, Order Thirty-Seven had already deplored that "companies continually procure, on their own initiative, horses, cows, etc., which turn out later to belong to relatives of auxiliary members of the unit."[53]

Most of the spoils, however, fell into the unit's hands during sweep operations, transforming the latter into harvesting campaigns. The men were perfectly well aware of this;[54] grain was counted in tonnes, cattle by hundreds—sometimes by thousands. Operation Hornung brought in 16,122 head of cattle and 222.8 tonnes of grain.[55] During Operation Günther, the men of the unit complained of having been held up by the lack of preparation of the civil administration responsible for holding cattle and—note the juxtaposition—civilians deported for labor in the Reich.[56] Certain operations were simply confiscation campaigns, the Dirlewanger unit being present only to protect civil servants responsible for requisitions. On May 23, 1944, a few weeks prior to the liberation of Belarus, the unit performed such a function at Senkowitsch. Cavalry troops were accompanied by a motorcycle squadron, as well as by trucks to encircle the village and transport confiscated goods.[57] The document doesn't say what became of the civilian population of the village, agricultural products being the mission's aim and determining its form: the weaponry borne by the unit is sparse, nothing like that carried during sweep operations, during which the unit anticipated skirmishes with the enemy. After the trophy-hunt or the gathering-hunt represented by spoils of weaponry, spoils of agricultural products suggest the hunt as harvest.[58]

A final type of spoils consisted of prisoners taken by the unit, which seems a strange way of considering persons taken to be used as forced labor. An order, previously cited, by von Gottberg, describing the modalities of intervention and coordination between civil administration and security forces during operations of economic predation, helps us to better understand this distinction:

The entire population (men, women, and children) and property, dead or alive, are to be expelled from the region defined in Article One. Men fit for labor will be collected by the *Reg. Rat.* Teschen's general staff for labor. The treatment of the rest of the population is the responsibility of local commissioners. It is not recommended to leave unfit population in the area around the designated region. *Reg. Rat.* Teschen's staff has organized receiving camps at Stolpce, Iwieniec, Woloczyn, Bohdanov, and Lubcz. [. . .] Agricultural goods and cattle must be inventoried by the commandos of Section Three of the General Commissariat assigned to the troop. Villages and all other construction, bridges, and orchards must be destroyed if they cannot be camouflaged.[59]

From the first lines of the text, the writer juxtaposes "property dead or alive" and population to be deported. The objective of the mission is a twofold predation, material and human, leading us to believe that for the Nazis the deported Russian population could be considered spoils. Did not the war against the partisans become at this moment the "man-hunt" of which Pierre Clastres speaks?[60] Von Gottberg believes so when he says that, "in the future, human beings found in the region will be considered game."[61] However, this war, aimed at capturing specified categories of the population, cannot be considered a hunt. This war cannot be considered a hunt for it aims not at a kill but a harvest. The populations so captured were not game, and that is precisely what von Gottberg said: only those who remained were considered as such. Only the men and women of the camps deep in the forests and marshes were game. The others have another status in the black hunters' imagery. This is what we must now attempt to understand.

The Origins of Violence

What happened when the black hunters took over a Russian village? The villagers who were not considered partisan accomplices—we will return to the fate of "bandit villages" later—were assembled in the center or on the edge of the village and sent to transit camps. Selections were, as we have said, performed sometimes on the spot (generally followed by the execution of women, children, and the aged) and sometimes, starting in the summer of 1943, in transit camps organized by civil administrators. The Senkowitsch mission mentioned previously suggests the distance between such operations and the practice of war as hunt: the villagers, if they survived the operation, were no doubt taken to the transit camps by the unit's mounted contingent. Thus herded and penned up, the populations in question were put to work within the Reich or on the spot. The collected workforce was also traded, especially in the case of women: Dirlewanger pointed out a company of policemen operating with the unit for its habit of capturing women around Lake Palik during Operation Cottbus. Taken prisoner, these women were collectively raped, then sold. The report detailing these facts stated that, upon investigation, four of these women had been hanged, while the others had been sent to Germany as forced labor.[62] A radio message sent by Dirlewanger on March 11, 1944, confirmed this practice of sale or barter: "The Russian [women] requested by Stubaf. Otto will be captured Monday and delivered [*Versand*] with the next men to go on leave. The price is the same as that fixed by Ostuf. Ingruber in the Lake Palik woods. Price per Russian woman: two bottles of schnaps."[63] Captured, penned, put to labor, or sold, the populations in question were subjected to a kind of domestication process that reduced them to the level of sexual livestock.

We may suppose that this was not an unfamiliar experience for the men of the unit. In Galicia, they had been confronted with populations submitted to a similar process, more sophisticated and far-reaching. The men of the unit had been in proximity with Jewish communities marked by the yellow star, penned in labor camps, and forced into hard labor. Certainly, arriving in Lublin in autumn 1940, the men of the Dirlewanger unit weren't responsible for the control of the Jewish population; they didn't carry out that symbolic domestication that saw the Germans turning their victims into human cattle. But never before were the men of the unit confronted with so advanced a process of symbolic domestication,[64] for never was a population so radically reduced to the rank of cattle as that of the Jews of the General Government. And, in fact, the men of the unit were mobilized on missions consisting almost entirely of guarding and watching over these animalized beings. Three labor camps were managed by the unit between October 1940 and February 1942. If we have little information on Stary Dzikow, managed by Dirlewanger himself, and on the Lublin-Janowska camp,[65] documents are more numerous for Krasne, near Lutsk, in Volhynia. There are striking similarities with Belarus: the same unpredictable, individualized violence, characterized by the desire to mark the body of the victim by blows, the whip, or cigarette burns, all to inscribe and make permanent the domination of the torturer over the victim. In Galicia as in Belarus, everything suggests that the men of the unit were transformed from hunters of men to herders of men.[66]

We have already mentioned the fact that the *Sondereinheit* developed a widespread "anti-mine procedure," to use the euphemism from von Gottberg's report. A veteran recounted in these terms how the unit proceeded with this human livestock:

> After several accidents occurred from mine explosions during the Budnicki attack, Dirlewanger personally went in front of the unit with his car. He ordered that we round up and gather together all the inhabitants of the neighboring villages. These people had to walk in close ranks on the paths, and a second row followed, walking exactly in the spaces left open, so that every bit of the terrain was

trodden by these people. They went forward in rows
[. . .] and these rows got blown to pieces. Those who
were still alive were executed with a bullet in the back of
the head by SD men. At Budnicki, there were only
women, children, and old folk.[67]

Dirlewanger had formalized this practice several days earlier,
during Operation Cottbus, in an order specifying, "Roadblocks
and ruts are systematically mined. Therefore you must make it
a rule not to clear them yourselves, but always to have it done
by the locals. The blood saved justifies any time lost."[68]

Erich von dem Bach-Zelewsky, HSSPF for Central Russia,
confirmed the extent of this practice during Operation Cottbus:
"Mining of the entire field of operations to an extent heretofore
unknown necessitated the use of special measures to protect
soldiers' lives. Mine clearing operations sent two to three thousand villagers flying."[69] Dirlewanger and his men had certainly
initiated the practice during sweep operations in the summer of
1943. It spread very rapidly among other units, but the "innova-
tion" had had a partial precedent in the same sector. A year
earlier, in August 1942, the commander of the 403rd infantry
division had given an order specifying that mine clearing
should be performed by troops "exclusively made up of prisoners of war and Jews."[70] Russian peasants from forest villages,
ghetto Jews, and prisoners of war from the camps were the
three categories of population suitable, in the eyes of the actors
in the *Partisanenbekämpfung*, to "clear" the territories of mines;
all three categories were subject to processes of corralling, of
marking, and of forced labor.

The analogy of domestication becomes clearer, even deliberate, if we think that the Second SS Police Regiment, a unit
that operated just to the north of the *Sondereinheit* during
Operation Cottbus, performed "mine clearing" by herding
before itself the cattle confiscated during the operation.[71] Cattle,

Jews, Soviet prisoners of war, and country folk unfit for labor became interchangeable before the mines to the eyes of the black hunters and their tracking companions. "Mine clearing" also reveals an analogy between certain categories of people and cattle. It is, itself, a ritual of domestication. We must nevertheless think of the connection between the killers' system of representations and the practices of violence as a dynamic and syllogistic link. The system of representations makes the practice of violence imaginable and thus possible, and the experience of that practice confirms, in the eyes of its performers, the status of the victim. We now have a convincing illustration that the practice of violence constituted a language by which the system of representations was expressed and revealed.[72]

The *Sondereinheit* Dirlewanger used two distinct gestural systems of violence. On the one hand, the unit pursued partisans in limited number, deploying a military violence, expressed through killing in combat, that was occasional, sporadic, though at times extreme. In these operations, skirmishes and exchanges of fire rarely involved large units, and even if partisan formations sometimes included thousands of persons, those who accepted combat—willingly or by necessity—never exceeded a hundred.[73] On the other hand, large-scale sweep operations generated a mass violence, close to massacre: hundreds of unarmed persons were killed by small groups of soldiers.[74]

This first opposition was matched by a second, related to the conception of observed violent strategies. In one case, abundantly shown in written communications, the essential component was perfecting the tracking system, not optimizing skirmishing techniques. What counted was taking the enemy. The elimination of groups was left entirely up to the initiative of small, tactically insignificant combat units. Neither von Gottberg nor Dirlewanger communicated with their men during combat. This part of the operation was empirical, immediate, and spontaneous. Conversely, the massacres of village civilians followed a standardized procedure. It had three phases. The first was the concentration of the victims-to-be; the second was their confinement. The third phase was the least formalized: the victims, once confined, were burned alive, either in barns or in public places to which the men of the unit set fire, after surrounding them with a ring of machine guns meant to prevent the victims from escaping; or, alternatively, they were killed by machine gun fire in the same public places, then incinerated.[75] The schema was simply that of a trap, from which it was impossible for the victims to escape, since the village had been encircled by the black hunters and the killing spots had been surrounded by a second cordon of guards. Sometimes the men of the unit kept order by subterfuge, making their victims believe, for instance, that they were to be deported to Germany to work.[76] In any event, victims were rarely killed individually and face-to-face.

The collective dimension of this tactic was essential. Its constructed nature differentiated it from the violence of skirmishes during commando sweeps or reconnaissance. The second distinguishing element was the use of firearms in killing partisans, but not villagers. Testimony gathered and autopsies performed by Belarusian authorities are unambiguous: the scarcity of cartridges and projectiles found in the burial pits bespeaks death by fire.[77] It is easy to extend this fact to the unit's Galician experience: the whip is omnipresent, and if rifle and pistol are not immaterial—far from it—to the execution of Jews,[78] we see a range of practices absent from operations against armed Belarusian formations. Dirlewanger, for example, had women beaten to death and executed contingents of women and men by lethal injection.

We may conclude that the men of the unit rationalized their killing methods: burning their victims alive rather than shooting them to economize on bullets, or administering lethal

146

injections in order to recover clothing in Lublin.[79] This last hypothesis does not stand up to analysis, however. The preliminary stripping of victims destined for the firing squad was a widespread practice and it seems likely that it came to Dirlewanger's mind in Lublin.[80] We thus can see the limits of this type of interpretation to the violence of the brigade: besides its inability to satisfactorily explain the poisonings of Jews in Galicia—which is unusual but verifiable—it does not take into account certain specific practices of the unit, such as beating people to death.[81]

Therefore, we come to an analysis of the unit's practices in terms of domestication. The desire of a herder to mark his domination over his livestock appears clearly enough in the practices observed among the unit's officers, in regards to cigarette burns and whip slashes[82] generally reserved for animals. In this perspective, the practice of lethal injection could also— even if it is impossible to prove that the actors were themselves aware of the analogy—be assimilated to ranching practices requiring livestock to be put to death before being skinned.

Here we must address the problem of the unit's cruelty. We have seen that cruelty was a distinguishing characteristic of the social discourse surrounding its creation and its evolution. However, nowhere does cynegetic discourse—meaning, in this case, the discourse of hunters about the hunt—celebrate cruelty. Never do hunters mention inflicting pain on their quarry. In the *Pirsch*, the hunter must instantaneously kill, with a single shot, an old stag attracted by the decoy belling.[83] Now, it seems that if the unit used certain practices of extreme violence—close combat with knives, for instance—against the partisans, it did not use cruelty towards them. The least we can say is that this was not the case with Russian villagers and Jews in Galician labor camps. Whippings, collective rapes, and strychnine injections followed by observation of the victims' death agonies— which were atrocious, death being preceded by convulsions of bone-breaking intensity[84]—comprise a whole range of practices strictly limited to populations previously subjected to processes of domestication.[85]

Two kinds of administration of violence, used by the same group in the same area, are juxtaposed here. The first, occasional and sporadic, is empirical and tactical. Essentially military, it was sometimes of an extraordinary intensity, though sources are astonishingly silent on this point, even though it always remained exceptional. The second is marked by instrumental rationality and by recourse to an avowed cruelty, in particular with the burning of villages. This latter practice combined the trap-like rationality of the slaughterhouse, incarnated in the gathering of victims, their slaughter in large numbers according to predefined procedures, and the most manifest cruelty on the part of the men who contemplated their victims in the fire and refused to grant them a quicker and less painful death. To find, in the herder's universe, an equivalent of this practice aiming at the complete elimination of a group capable of labor—although considered insufficiently so—we must examine the qualities of these villages doomed to be burned. In dispatches, they were called "bandit villages" or "contaminated by bandits," an expression that calls up the imagery of infection.[86] The only contagious disease legitimizing the massacre of entire flocks in the occidental world until the twentieth century—a perfect parallel to the expression used by the black hunters—was rabies, *Tollwut*. Rabies—foaming rage—holds a central place in the image of the Wild. It is interpreted socially as the breaking into the domestic sphere of the Wild, from which flocks can be protected only by eradication and purification by fire, without shedding blood, of the contaminated beasts, domestic animals returned to savagery by the black invasion of the toxin. It is not by chance that Saint Hubert, the patron saint of hunters venerated in the Tyrol and Bavaria (the region of origin of most of the Dirlewanger poachers), was the principal thaumaturge for infection by rabies.[87] To burn villagers and forest dwellers, to burn them without shooting them first, was thus, in the eyes of the black hunters, to hold back the return of the Wild into the domestic world. Hunters themselves, the men of the unit were impregnated with this imagery. They were cruel beyond a doubt, for they made this incendiary and prophylactic purification their distinguishing sign, laughing sometimes before the bonfires: "Where there's fire, there's Dirlewanger."[88]

It is now time to trace this violence to its origins. As in the imagery that presided over the unit's creation, the latter operated in Belarus in a forest environment, deployed in small groups as tracking or reconnaissance commandos, against an enemy represented as extremely dangerous, of a savagery illustrated perfectly by his "fanaticism" in combat and in particular by his refusal to give himself up alive to the Germans. The second indication of this figurative savagery is thus: the fact that partisan troops mutilated German prisoners or corpses. Transformed, starting in 1942, into a wild animal moving in packs through the depths of the Belarusian forest, the partisan enemy, tracked by small expeditions or major sweep operations, was now perceived as game, and the black hunters applied, to a great extent, cynegetic knowledge and technique to find them. To identify, to track, to kill: such were the missions accepted by reconnaissance commandos and tracking parties in the Belarusian woods.

But the unit took on other missions. Roman agronomists opposed the *Saltus*—the forest—realm of the savage, and the *Ager*, designating space exploited and domesticated by man.[89] The *Ager* of the Germans in Russia was the labor camp for Jews, the forest clearing, and the occupied city. In these three spaces, German control was absolute; in these three spaces, populations were concentrated and put to labor. Only the work camps and the ghettos combined the three elements of the domestication process to which the Germans destined occupied populations. Penning, marking, and labor created the image the occupiers formed of those they lived among, now reduced to human livestock, their value determined by the ratio between production and consumption. The large-scale sweep operations in the Belarusian countryside had a double nature. On the one hand, in the forest, the units, as we have said, hunted partisans. On the other, in the villages of the forest clearings, the herders gathered the fruits of the labor of those whom they considered their livestock. If the latter were suspected of being accomplices of the wild forest enemy, they were then perceived through the lens of a rabies epidemic, and burned, together with their houses, in a massacre meant to be total and purifying—no longer a hunt but a slaughter. Like animals to be butchered, the victims, young or old, were caught in a trap preventing all escape,[90] until the slaughter whose intended totality, although rarely achieved, was characteristic of herders in a time of epidemic.

Behavior and practices of violence were inscribed in a semiotics of Nature, classifying beings and spaces according to their degree of contiguity with the Wild or the Domestic. After this analysis, one question remains. Roman agronomists identified a final space, also populated by animals, with which man had constructed still other relationships: the *Domus*, the home, the seat of familial and familiar relations. French, like German, has retained this threefold ordering of space and nature, connecting the Wild, the Domestic, and the Familiar. Was there also a "human" equivalent of familiar animals in the eyes of the black hunters? What about native populations living beneath the same roof as they and providing services based on an ideology of devotion and a contractual relationship? Why not see in the *Schutzmannschaft* battalions—and in the unit's Russian companies—the human equivalent of these familiar animals? Their missions, which consisted in taking care, in a cynegetic context, of scout and tracker patrols, and in the herding context, missions of encirclement and leading of deported populations, made them strangely resemble a hunting dog in the first case, and a shepherd dog in the second. The nature of relationships between Germans and Russian recruits, mixing daily proximity with punishments and blows, as well as the higher death rate of non-natives during sweep operations, suggest that this analogy is plausible.

The foundation, evolution, and practices of the *Sondereinheit* Dirlewanger may thus be read through the prism of the European cynegetic imagination applied to this "great racial war" waged in the East by the Nazis. Nothing predisposed this war to become a gigantic laboratory of the cynegetic imagination. It was the Germans' perception of the evolution of the situation that led them to look to that analogy for their anti-partisan procedures. Until autumn 1941, security policy was limited to chasing Soviet runaways and monitoring communication lines. Starting in early 1942, the emergence of better-organized partisan groups far from these lines, deep in forests and marshes, led the German authorities to conceive of an operation similar to a battue to finish off these "bands." From the cynegetic imagination were thus born the sweep operations that ravaged Belarus. From another perspective, the policies of occupation and economic predation, consisting of confiscating, of displacing and confining, and of forced labor, led the German authorities and their troops to see their victims in terms of their productivity alone. Perceived initially by the Germans as animals capable of any savagery, three categories of the population were subsequently penned up, sometimes marked, and set to labor: Galician Jews, confined to the labor camps of the economic empire built by Odilo Globocnik, were the first contingent; Soviet prisoners of war, starved to death en masse before their labor began to be exploited in 1943,[91] constituted the second, with which Dirlewanger's men were never really involved; and Belarusian peasants formed the last contingent.

The emergence of this process of domestication and its concomitance with the cynegetic culture of anti-partisan operations models a Nazi representation of the Other—friend or foe—based on the relationship of European societies with nature and animality, a representation that redefines and transcends still-operative racial and social categories; a representation that conforms to the system of practices of violence. Thus we have a dynamic system, representations and practices interacting cumulatively with each other. All, finally, insert themselves in the evolution of a regulatory and hierarchical framework that reflects and conforms to them in turn. The members of the *Sondereinheit* thus operated as hunters of men against partisans transformed into game. Confronted by human masses "domesticated" by the policy of occupation and security, the unit acted as ranchers. When these masses were "contaminated," in their eyes and in the eyes of their hierarchy, by the Wildness of the partisans, the herders of men applied a prophylactic and exterminatory treatment. In this way, the black hunters were transformed into slaughterhouse workers, extreme figures in the world of animal husbandry.

Chapter 6

A New War?

On June 22, 1944, three years to the day from the German army's surprise invasion of Soviet territory, the Red Army threw itself against Nazi positions in Belarus, after forty-eight hours of unprecedented bombardment. From the first days of the ground offensive, defeat turned to collapse for the Central Army Group, which changed the situation radically on the Eastern front. The *Sonderbrigade* had no sooner finished a sweep, Operation Cormorant, than it had to make an urgent detour to Lida, then to northeastern Poland.

On the front, the initiative had long since been out of German hands, but the war of position led by the Central Army Group had until then been able to sustain the illusion of a victorious renewal of operations as soon as reserves and reinforcements were restored. With the encirclement of at least 300,000 men around Minsk, fighting forces along more than a third of the front were out of action. Waging a defensive war for the previous eighteen months and more, the Army Group had progressively experienced the superiority of the Soviets in both troop strength and in armaments.[1] Behind the front lines, better-armed partisans, with air and artillery support for operations near the front, now confronted German units forced to mobilize larger and larger formations in order to fight them.

Lost in the confusion of an army that, in June 1944, began the odyssey that would lead it from Poland to Slovakia, then from Hungary to Saxony, did the *Sondereinheit* continue the hunters' war to which it had dedicated itself for four years? We must first inquire as to the continued use of cynegetic images and practices during the repression of the Warsaw uprising. Did the Polish capital, in this reading, replace the Belarusian forests? Did it become a new territory for the black hunters?

Warsaw: An "Urban Jungle" for the Black Hunters?

Until now, the men of the *Sondereinheit* had moved in a space dominated by forests and occasional clearings. It was a closed space, with many marshes, where the difficulty of movement through the terrain had a central importance. Starting on August 4, 1944, the men of the unit fought in the city, starting from the suburbs of Okhota and Wola, to move towards the Old Town and Pilsudski Square, along LitzmannstädterStrasse.[2] While sweep operations were characterized by the length of the daily marches to reach previously determined objectives—distances that, according to Hannes Heer, played an important part in the fact that villages were systematically burned during the advance[3]—the *Sondereinheit* advanced meter by meter during the first days of the Warsaw operation and had to adjust to a topographically different environment.

It also had to familiarize itself with new armaments, small robot tanks and rocket-launchers, and large-caliber artillery, which annihilated nearly a third of the city center in the first days of the operation.[4] It was a war in an urban environment, more technological than the war against the partisans: this seems to validate the hypothesis of a break in the *Sondereinheit*'s experience. In Warsaw, combat groups advanced under tank protection, as rifle formations deployed in assault waves or as mixed formations advancing under cover of automatic weapons and light artillery. This urban war, deploying practices developed by the *Stosstruppen* during the Great War[5] and in which equipment played an important role, was infinitely more costly in lives than the sweep operations.

At first glance, the Warsaw experience would seem to have had little in common with that of the Belarusian forests. Deceptive impression: the last operations of the unit in Belarus had been marked by the massive use of artillery and armored vehicles, and the partisans were themselves supported by Soviet aviation. As to the use in street combats of robot tanks filled with explosives, the effect was above all psychological, and no known documentation indicates that they were used in the *Sondereinheit*'s sector of operation. These factors put into proportion the novelty of the techniques used in repressing the uprising. More prosaically, the balance of power between the Germans' heavily-armed formations and the insurgents, obviously lacking in heavy weaponry and munitions, was not unlike that existing in 1942–1943 between Belarusian security forces and the partisans. The latter had, like the Polish insurgents, the advantage of knowing the territory. The Germans, for their part, depended on their superior troop strength and weaponry.

The men fought, as well, in the same way. Let us first remark that, as in Belarus, the theater of operations was characterized by the presence of civilians side-by-side with the armed formations. This presence was, of course, far greater in Warsaw, a city of millions, than in the sparsely populated forestland around Minsk. In the two cases, exactions against civilians were routine, though of a different scale. Witnesses' testimony speaks of assaults carried out block by block, house by house. It is not without interest to return to Matthias Schenk's story to detail how these assaults played out. "I would now like to describe the assault on the hospital. As usual, rush to the objective, grenades, and, after they exploded, we went in." Then there was close combat, with automatic weapons and blades, and massive assault by the riflemen. "Then the reinforcements arrived—the SS. It was the Dirlewanger penal battalion. Its soldiers wore no marks of rank. They had drunk a lot and weren't sober. They immediately attacked the Polish positions. They charged the houses, yelling: 'Hurrah!' Just in front of the houses, they fell under Polish fire."[6] This tactic was no different from that used during anti-partisan action. The refusal to change tactic, combined with the inexperience of troops newly arrived in the unit, the insurgents' skilful use of their weaponry in salvos, and the precision of their shooting, explains the unit's numerous losses.

The transfer of the techniques of the *Partisanenbekämpfung* to an urban environment produced extraordinary violence, underlined by Matthias Schenck when he describes the men of the unit taking the hospital by assault and immediately slaughtering all the Polish wounded. The sort of destructive euphoria that takes hold of soldiers after a confrontation and leads them to attack the wounded and kill prisoners was certainly not restricted to the men of the brigade,[7] but such behavior was routine for the unit in the Belarusian woods. The rage of the officers and the fury of the troopers—this empire of black blood—show how their cynegetic imagination transformed insurgent Warsaw into an urban forest, a hunting ground for the *Sonderbrigade*. Had any of the men learned the rudiments of Russian during their stay in the Minsk region and were they intrigued by the cynegetic dimension of their exploits in Warsaw? The name of the neighborhood in which they made their first assaults was Okhota, which means "hunt" in Old Church Slavonic. Toponomic chance or intention, Warsaw had become a territory for predation in the eyes of the black hunters.

The "spoils" were of another magnitude entirely: Warsaw was—as we have said—a city of millions, and the civilian population had not been able to flee. It was the theater for executions in heretofore unknown numbers: post-war Polish investigations, verified by German prosecutors, revealed forty-one mass graves along the 500 meters of the Wolkastrasse, of which sixteen were attributable to the unit alone.[8] We are far from the assault techniques deployed in combat or the killings of combatants. A veteran of the unit, Willy B., tells how, at the end of one of these assaults, those captured were gathered against the wall and executed with a small-caliber bullet to the back of the head, one after the other, in successive rows. He then describes a second execution, also in the Wolkastrasse sector, in which the victims were put in an arrangement like a fish-trap and killed by the crossfire of several automatic weapons shooting blindly into the mass.[9] There is no comparison to be made with the disordered killing of the assault on the hospital. Here, the killers act in coordination, in one case to slaughter their victims at leisure, in a standardized manner, with no concern for speed but thoroughly and surely; in the other, to neutralize them very quickly without really being sure of having killed them all. Two methods, then, using a trap and a rationalization of violence, the first being close to the scientific management usual in slaughterhouses.[10] Numerous testimonies show that this procedure, scarcely different from that put in place starting in autumn 1941 by the *Einsatzgruppen* to exterminate the Jewish communities of Russia,[11] was chosen by the majority of the troops assigned to repress the uprising.[12] Nevertheless, this anthropological constant is not enough to account for the totality of practices of violence.

We must not forget the specificity, for the Nazis, of the Polish capital's insurrection. If the collective violence of the unit finds a coherent interpretation in the anthropology of the Wild and the Domestic, individual practices, those that appear rarely in the testimony of witnesses and experts, are more difficult to grasp. Everything indicates, for example, that rape was frequent and, among others, Matthias Schenck described the nurses stripped and given over to the violence of the drunken soldiers.[13] No doubt rape was widespread in Belarus, predation of women

157

a common occurrence, and trade in them, as we said, a matter of course. We know, furthermore, through inspection reports that the men of the unit employed "housekeepers" who both maintained the buildings and provided sexual entertainment for the men.[14] But these references are more scarce and, more importantly, the intentions of this behavior were different, as we can see if we analyze sexual violence in terms of domination and domestication rather than in terms of sexual entertainment. The rapes committed by the unit in Belarus almost never took place during operations; women were captured, taken back to camp, and then raped. This was not the case in Poland: rape concretized the taking of control, immediately after the assault, and it didn't matter that the women violated were nurses or nuns. On the contrary, the more emblematic their status, the more meaningful the possession taken of the enemy through the bodies of the enemy's women.

Thus *Hauptsturmführer* B. combined rape and brutality centered on the female genital organs by inserting hand grenades in prisoners' vaginas and detonating them.[15] We would be missing the essential if we confined this practice to the sphere of psychopathology. Historical anthropology's analysis sees rather the desire to attack the enemy's womb, in its function of transmission of lineage, of identity.[16] The idea was literally to extirpate the enemy before birth. This violence owed little to chance and much to the way the Nazi authorities thought of the insurrection, the last act of an age-old struggle opposing them to the Poles; a last act that was to settle once and for all the Polish question. "When I learned of the Warsaw uprising," Himmler told a group of local Wehrmacht and training school leaders, "I went immediately to see the *Führer* and I told him: 'My *Führer*, the moment is unfortunate. But historically speaking, what the Poles are doing is a windfall. We can put an end to it in five or six weeks. After that, Warsaw, the capital, the head, the spirit incarnate of this people of sixteen or seventeen millions, of this people who has for 700 years barred our road to the East, who has constantly been in our way since the first battle of Tannenberg, will be annihilated. Then the Polish problem, a historic problem if ever there was, will have been resolved for our children and all who come after us, and will no longer be even the smallest problem for us.'"[17]

In Himmler's mind, the historic reference was central; that's why he gave, according to the declarations of von dem Bach-Zelewsky, the order to raze Warsaw and to execute all its inhabitants.[18] Nevertheless, this historic reference must be situated in the SS imagination. The Poles were the "eternal enemies to the east"; this view was widespread, and the men who, like Dirlewanger, had fought in the *Freikorps* in Upper Silesia, no doubt subscribed more than any others to this representation. But there was added to it a second image, associated with women. The fact that Poles had been tenacious adversaries in the *Volksturmskampf*, the millenary combat of ethnic identity that the two peoples had been waging, in Nazi eyes, was partly due to the supposed excellence of the feminine part of the population. A memorandum of the VoMI, dated the preceding year, confirmed the Polish capacity for this struggle of ethnic identity, and showed that women had been at the forefront of this combat, like those Polish noblewomen who had resisted Prussian domination during the eighteenth and nineteenth centuries.[19] There are other traces of this representation in the writings of historians close to the SS, such as Hans-Joachim Beyer, who popularized the image of a woman of light morals and dubious intelligence, ferociously nationalist.[20] At once harlot and patriotic heroine, the Polish woman thus represented a particular target. This, no doubt, explains the violence directed against the most emblematic among them, nursing the insurgents or manifesting compassion as a Catholic, Catholicism being one of the principal Polish ethnic characteristics in the eyes of the SS.

For it was also a question of destroying what was sacred in the eyes of the enemy, for example the killing of the priest during the assault on the cloister, or the scatological treatment of the crucifix found in the same cloister by the men of the unit. The attack was less on the religious symbol than on the Other's religion. Profanation is not an act of rebellion by a man against a god, but an act of violence by one man against another, a believer. By crushing all resistance, an end would be made to what the Nazis imagined to be the principal character-istics of ethnic identity of "Polishness" (*Polentum*). If the quasi-systematic massacre of the population corresponded to orders given by SS authorities, the leaders and men of the troop shared this representation, which led the Germans to extirpate all trace of enemy identity.

Warsaw thus constituted a break in the black hunters' war. Changing their hunting ground, incapable of adapting to an adversary familiar with the terrain, constrained by a hierarchy no longer concerned with saving its troops, the men suffered heavy losses that accentuated the effects of the same imagina-tive animalization of the enemy as in Russia. The black hunters thus pursued the insurgents like wild animals—smoking them out of the buildings that had become their lairs, making massive use of flame-throwers—prey to a fury of massacre. Confronted by immense groups of civilians fleeing the combat, they treated them, as in Belarus, like livestock, putting them to death by methods aligned with those of the slaughterhouse. Warsaw had become their urban jungle, their hunting ground, but it was also, in Nazi eyes, the end of an age-old struggle between two ethnicities, one of which would now put an end to the other for all time. The fusion of this representation, deeply rooted in historical memory and of the advent of total war, helps us understand why the "hunting ground" that Warsaw had become for the black hunters was transformed into one of the greatest mass graves of the Second World War.

Slovakia: Between Anti-Partisan Action and Frontline Combat

The brigade was in Warsaw for six weeks. It then spent six further weeks in Slovakia, until the beginning of December 1944. Instead of the badly armed cohorts of the AK, it confronted an aggregation of units from the Slovakian army, surrounded by communist partisans from neighboring Galicia.[21] The difference was clear, and the men of the unit soon became aware of it: arriving at the Diviaky railroad station, they were bombarded by Slovakian fighter pilots.[22] In theory, this was an uprising led by irregular elements: the government in place, that of Josef Tiso, had called on Germany for assistance and, in legal terms, it was an action against partisans, but partisans of an unusual kind, equipped with tanks and airplanes. The main actor of the uprising was the Slovakian Army, which had liberated entire sectors of the territory and was trying to keep them out of the hands of both the Germans and the communist partisans who had come from Galicia.[23] The Germans, at any rate, were perfectly aware of this difference. The SD's situation reports carefully distinguished between Slovakian resistance and the inherent instability of the situation, bringing with it desertions, the rebellion of auxiliary troops, and the formation of small bands living off the land.[24] From every direction, routed German or German-allied troops were converging, and the Germans, like those Slovakians remaining loyal to the Tiso regime, had great difficulty controlling the territory.

The Germans were facing a situation rendered yet more complex by the fact that the insurgents had followed the development of the Warsaw uprising, estimated that the German repression had produced more than 30,000 victims, and had identified the units that had participated therein.[25] There was ambiguity, then, of the forces of rebellion among regular army, communist partisan formations and bands of deserters; ambiguity, also, of the behavior of the insurgents, who believed their choice was between stubborn resistance and the same fate as the martyred Polish city, while at the same time maintaining an ambivalent relationship with the Germans, whom they had mixed with during the first four years of the war. This all is reflected in the statistics of the uprising. From September 22 to 28, 1,200 men were put out of action in the Tucs sector.[26] However, the final figures show the involvement of the Slovakian Army, which lost sixty planes, 182 cannons, eighty-one tanks, 200 assorted vehicles, sixty-eight infantry cannons, and 3,000 rifles for 2,000 men killed. But the number of prisoners—820—and of deserters—1,200—shows that executions were incomparably fewer than in Belarus.[27] The Germans, thus, were not waging a war of annihilation.[28]

The *Sonderbrigade* alternated true war operations against the Slovakian army in revolt and its more habitual sweep and patrol operations on the sectors to the south and the east of Slovakian territory. The unit was responsible for no massacre comparable to those of the Okhota and Wola neighborhoods. Sent to the northern part of the sector concerned by the uprising, it arrived when the insurgents had lost, at the moment the city of Banska Bystrica fell. In the first days of their intervention, the men of the Dirlewanger unit waged classic battles, in liaison—theoretically, at least—with other units. There again, it was a matter of assaults by rifle sections supported by integrated elements of artillery and by tank units from the Tatra division. The unit had a few disappointments. These were due, perhaps, as French MacLean claims, to the fact that Dirlewanger wanted to remain independent at all costs;[29] due more certainly to the fact that at least a considerable number of the men thrown into battle lacked experience. Without even speaking of those who had been taken out of concentration camps, lacking any combat practice, the disgraced Wehrmacht and SS soldiers sent to the *Sturmbrigade* as a disciplinary measure lacked any spirit of cohesion. For a battle waged on a plain, in a semi-open environment, the insurgent troops, armed and fortified, had the territorial advantage of the men of the assaulting unit: the latter were held off for several days before breaking through defensive lines over several kilometers and taking control of the cities of Biely Potok and Necpaly.[30] Battles were nevertheless limited in duration and in intensity.

After two weeks the brigade was sent further east, in the mountains, where it rested, added new members—more concentration camp prisoners and disgraced soldiers—and devoted itself to clean-up missions behind the troops on the Hungarian front, closer to its duties in Belarus, such as keeping the population in line. One of the only abuses committed by the unit during its time in Slovakia that was investigated by German and Slovakian magistrates was an execution of civilians occurring in December 1944. The men moved into the village of Marzibrod, arrested three people suspected of passing information to partisans, as well as a Russian partisan caught in the village, and hanged them in the public square. This was not the Dirlewanger unit's usual procedure, although public execution by hanging had been used frequently during the first months of the invasion of the USSR. In Jitomir, for example, *Sonderkommando* 4a had killed Wolf Kieper in this manner, a presumed communist official and agent of an NKVD troika during the Great Purge. The execution, accompanied by loudspeaker propaganda and signboards (including one around the neck of the hanged man) had served as a ritual prelude to the killing of 400 Jews.[31] In Minsk, during the years 1941–1942, German forces made these executions and the display of the bodies a widespread practice. Researchers who contributed to the exhibition on the crimes of the Wehrmacht uncovered thousands of photos showing this strange fruit hanging from tree branches, the balconies of houses, and telegraph poles. Aside from the obvious function of intimidating the populace and staging the power of the occupier—one thinks of the writing hung from the neck of the hanged man, explaining his opposition as a partisan to German authority—these bodies were also hunting trophies. Most of the photos taken by German soldiers follow the same format: a soldier posing in front of the hanging corpse, touching it with his hand, exactly as hunters put their hands on the animal they have killed, the latter being sometimes suspended, sometimes laid on the ground so its antlers are visible.[32] Stéphane Audoin-Rouzeau also sees in the suspension of the corpse a ritual in which the killer reduces his victim to an animal,[33] but he analyzes it as mimetic of slaughter, the animals killed by butchers invariably being suspended.[34]

In the case of the Marzibrod hanging, the desire to animalize the enemy is continued in the treatment of the bodies of the four victims: after having been suspended (like butchered animals) and exposed (like hunting trophies), the four victims were buried in a pet cemetery . . . [35] The various modes of animalization of the other were thus employed, but it is impossible to distinguish the dominant representation, whether hunted wild animal or slaughtered domestic animal. Through this extremely meaningful ritual, the unit returned to a mental universe close to that of its time in Poland and in Belarus. It was not unchanged: the struggle in Slovakia had been a classic military operation during the first weeks, and this hanging, so close to the practices current in the USSR—an interlude—was followed immediately by the Budapest intervention. Before that, however, for a few weeks the unit found itself in a zone farther from combat and alternated brigandage, sweeps, and skirmishes against an elusive enemy whose behavior was almost identical to the unit's.

Rape, pillage, and murder took on a previously unknown amplitude, and, above all, were "privatized." The Dirlewanger unit pillaged as never before, except perhaps in Warsaw during the uprising, even if it was far from alone in that—there was, for example, the Eighteenth SS Division of Galicia, also mentioned in SD reports for its strong propensity to pillage—and without counting deserters who operated in the same way. This was one of the numerous paradoxical changes at the end of the Third Reich. Created to ensure security against the "terror of bands," the *Sonderbrigade* Dirlewanger now lived off the country, just like the "bands" it had fought. The result was not long to wait: an SD report on the mood of the Slovakian population in the path of the invasion stated that the latter preferred the abuses of the partisans to those of the men of the *Sondereinheit*.[36] From now on, they saw little difference between communist or Slovakian partisans, fleeting German army deserters, and the hungry units. All stole, all pillaged. As time worked against the Germans, the behavior of the brigade—and of other units, regular or not—became more and more like that of its prey.

Certainly, poachers were now only a tiny minority within the brigade, but this pillage constituted a sort of gathering strangely reminiscent of the unit's experience in Belarus and in the Lublin district. The leitmotiv in Slovakia—as later, for that matter—was "*Organisierung*," by hook or by crook. Had it ever been otherwise? When Dirlewanger pushed to have the work on the Łahojsk castle finished as soon as possible, did he not enjoin his subordinates to find the necessary materials without looking too closely at their provenance?[37] Wasn't small-scale trafficking one of the constants of the unit's time in Lublin?[38] The same imagery was involved in Slovakia as elsewhere: the exploitation of a population viewed only in terms of its labor potential and of the products of that labor, which were appropriated—gathered—as opportunity provided. The four weeks in southeastern Slovakia, without important skirmishes, much of their activity taking place in barracks in order to integrate reinforcements, must have recalled the time spent in Lublin to the unit's poachers, now all NCOs. These exercises, combined with unrestrained pillage of the peasantry, could certainly appear to be a return to the happy times of the unit's first days. But barely a month later, events were to remind them of the scale of changes in progress.

From Budapest to Cottbus: When Hunters Became Prey

If the *Sondereinheit* Dirlewanger was among the most prominent formations during its time in Belarus, at the head of operations during anti-partisan actions, it had been only one unit among many during the repression of the Warsaw uprising. In Slovakia, it was integrated in a large combat group and drowned in the anonymity of those armies, their existence primarily cartographic, which the Third Reich mobilized in the last months of its existence. In Hungary, the *Sturmbrigade* was dissolved in the Army Group South, where armored units, artillery, and infantry were thrown together. A single report, from a general staff officer, mentions the unit and speaks of Dirlewanger and his adjutant Weisse. While the latter, violent and dangerous, unanimously hated by the men of the troop and unfavorably judged by his superiors, made a rather good impression on the officer, Dirlewanger, on the contrary, is described as a "not particularly likeable *Landsknecht*."[39] His unit never appears in combat reports, except for the Ypolysag episode, where only its defection appears in the Ninth Army's operations journal. Once Soviet troops have moved into Ypolysag, the unit's counterattacks are mentioned, as well as their failure. The unit then disappears from the reports, which concentrate on the encirclement of the Hungarian capital. The case of Lusatia is clearer. Dirlewanger is not mentioned, nor are his operations spoken of, except for a counterattack around Guben, cited in the OKW's operations journal.[40] In Lusatia, the unit was again broken down, part of its infantry formations attached to the *Heeresgruppe* Vistula, while others were integrated in the *Heeresgruppe* Mitte.[41] The unit was not merely cut up and lost in the anonymity of a large formation fleeing in disorder. The size of the battlefield and the scale of the opposing forces also explain the silence surrounding the unit in the archives at our disposition. The Russian attacks engaged battalions, at least, against companies, and clashing armies mobilized hundreds of thousands of men: how to keep track, in these human floods, of the relatively small group that was the Thirty-Sixth SS Division, especially when it never went into combat at full force?

The upheaval caused by the campaigns in Hungary and Lusatia among the men of the unit is now clear. Combined with the radical change of atmosphere within the unit, and its disproportionate increase in troop numbers, such a fragmentation contributed to the definitive break of December 1944. Until that time used to carrying out their assaults, if not to victory then at any rate to the neutralization of their adversaries, the soldiers of the Dirlewanger unit had waged war against partisans in relatively small formations—up to 15,000 men in Warsaw. Now they were lost among human tides among which they had no weight, while up until Slovakia they had been preceded by a certain reputation. Their arrival, as we have seen, never left the other units or their superiors indifferent—but such was now the case. Encroaching defeat overwhelmed all other considerations, authorized all transgressions, rendered superfluous all the warnings issued previously by "classic" army men against the use of poachers, criminals, even prisoners, political or otherwise, in the hopeless campaign of winter 1945. The men of the unit, used to the forests of Belarus, having passed through the urban forest of Warsaw and the mountains of Slovakia, now moved into the plain, against a regular army of invasion. At the moment of the decisive confrontation,[42] in Hungary as well as in Lusatia, battles were desperate and bloody. If some units retired in great disorder, retreat taking the form of panicked flight, the fact is rare enough to be mentioned in operations journals,[43] and the statistics on losses in the German army suggest that troops let themselves be killed on the spot rather than give up an inch of ground.[44] But they were short of everything: artillery, munitions, automatic weapons, fuel, and tanks, not to mention aerial support.

The division was now part of an exhausted, badly trained, poorly equipped army, a mixed army too, cruelly lacking in leadership. Leaving aside the logistical inferiority that granted the Russian adversary a decisive superiority in materiel, the greatest lack was that of NCOs and line officers with experience under fire. The explanation lay in a few figures. Less than five days before the great offensive that would bring the Soviets to the gates of Berlin, the *Heeresgruppe* Vistula had made an accounting of its units' losses: since June 22, 1941, more than half a million men had been put out of action, killed, wounded, or missing, nearly 45,000 for the month of March 1945 alone.[45] The *Heeresgruppe* was incapable of compensating for such hemorrhages: the non-reconstitution of troop numbers automatically affected subaltern officers and NCOs, the fundamental actors of the transmission of that culture of combat, which alone could ensure a minimal chance of survival to newcomers, who therefore fell by thousands in their first engagements. The Ninth Army, to which numerous formations of the division were detached, had thus lost 34,904 men between February 1 and March 1, 1945. During the same period, it had received only 9,990 reinforcements.[46] For the first half of the month of April, the Ninth Army had nonetheless eliminated nearly 800 Russian soldiers—counting only the men killed by the elite riflemen of the army—and had destroyed 120 tanks and eleven planes.[47] Produced by an exhausted army, threatened with destruction where it stood, such numbers showed that the units had not given up the fight, and that they disputed every inch of ground.

None of this, however, was enough to contain the enemy advance. On the morning of April 14, the Soviets attacked with five infantry divisions and 200 tanks, the first attack followed, in the afternoon, by a second, this time with sixty-five tanks. If we follow the detail of the two offensives, the first was directed to a specific sector of the front: the Twenti-eth Grenadier Tank Division bore the brunt of the German defensive effort, repelling the attack of four of the Russian divisions. It gave way that afternoon beneath the pressure of the second attack, concentrated on its sector alone.[48] For an operation of minor importance, the Russians had established a troop ratio of five to one. This augured badly for the great final offensive that everyone, Russians and Germans alike, considered to be imminent.

The lack of weapons and of tanks forced troops on the ground to use new tactics, and the Thirty-Sixth SS Grenadier Division had to adapt. A series of articles detailing its last weeks and obviously written by a veteran mentions the fact that the troops were assigned to anti-tank commandos armed with *Panzerfausts*. A weapon of desperation, the *Panzerfaust* was a one-man rocket launcher equipped with warheads capable, under certain conditions, of penetrating the armor of fighting vehicles. The risks associated with the use of this crude weapon were numerous; launches caused flames to shoot out behind and had a back blast that could decapitate a man. Thus, it was necessary to approach the target alone. The soldiers of the unit practiced what was then called the *Panzerjagd*, the tank-hunt, but between the rifleman and the armored tank who was the prey, who was the hunter? Even if the *Panzerfaust* shooters used techniques of camouflage and stalking similar to those of the *Pirsch*, the danger was incomparably greater for the men than for the tanks that were their targets. After having spent four years fighting an adversary that used the terrain as an ambush for lack of the firepower to sustain a ranked battle, now the *Sondereinheit* Dirlewanger found itself in a similar position, constrained to guerrilla attacks against tanks, unable to sustain a classic battle, and swamped by the enemy's numbers and firepower. The men used, in their turn, the tactics of the partisans; once hunters, now they were prey.

Few sources provide information on the last battles, except for the file, established by the research service of the Red Cross, on soldiers returning from captivity in the USSR. Ordered by unit, the latter were given a questionnaire asking for their unit of origin and their personal status—SS member, Wehrmacht soldier, concentration camp prisoner, poacher—as well as the date and place of their capture. The 634 questionnaires that have been kept tell the story of twofold survivors: they had not been killed during the great Russian offensive and they had survived several years of captivity in economic conditions close to famine.[49] In April and May 1945, in Lusatia, 418 of them fell into the hands of the Soviets. Wehrmacht soldiers and SS men constitute the immense majority of those returning from captivity, not surprising given their preponderance in the unit by the time of their capture. Concentration camp prisoners are under-represented in terms of their place in the unit itself: according to Bruno Wille, they made up nearly a third of the troops in December 1944,[50] but only 3 percent of the returnees.[51] This figure is difficult to interpret: should the high mortality rate of former concentration camp prisoners be attributed to combat or to their stay in Russian prison camps? This second hypothesis is unlikely: coming from a far more rigorous prison environment, to which they had been able to adapt, these men would have survived their captivity in the USSR more easily than others. However, without that culture of combat interiorized by the soldiers of the Wehrmacht and the Waffen-SS, they were no doubt killed in even greater numbers than the others by the gigantic artillery preparation from April 16–18, 1945, than by the flood of tanks and infantry that submerged the German lines.

Let us examine carefully the dates and places of capture of the returnees from Russian camps. The first captures occurred in July 1944 during the summer offensive in Belarus,[52] but the first significant numbers of prisoners—thirty-six men, or 5 percent of the total—appear during the Hungarian campaign, in December. The 164 men captured in April 1945 fell into the hands of Russian scouts before the offensive, or were captured during its course. The 112 men captured in Lusatia in May 1945 survived combat and moved for several days through a hostile environment before being made prisoners. This makes 276 men over these two months.[53] We must still account for 142 more. Twenty-six of them were captured in Lusatia during the period of the war of position, between January and March 1945; the 116 others were captured in May, after the end of hostilities, some in the same region.[54] These had survived both the offensive and the sweep teams of the Red Army, like that soldier arrested in Lusatia in August 1945, or those two others arrested in August 1946 and July 1947, respectively. More remarkable still was the soldier captured by the Soviets in Holstein in June 1945, or that other who got as far as Styria, crossing all of Czechoslovakia and Austria to end by being captured there, like his comrade made prisoner in Hamburg in May 1945, after fleeing more than 500 kilometers. In the hope of falling into American rather than Soviet hands, the men traveled hundreds of kilometers, dodging Russian patrols, living in the countryside and experiencing the lot of those partisans they had pursued—experiencing it with a certain success, despite their final capture.

The poachers of the unit—some fifty of them, if the questionnaires are to be believed—seem to have been among the last to be captured. Not surprisingly, their stories prove their great aptitude for survival in a hostile environment: there is, for instance, the poacher arrested in July 1945 in northern Italy and handed over to the Soviets, or the other who managed to reach the Tyrol, he too crossing hundreds of kilometers of Russian-controlled territory. The majority were captured between Lusatia and Brandenburg in May 1945[55] as they tried to flee the region in order to return to Berlin or to reach the West. Should this be read as a sign of their desire to continue fighting? Nothing is less sure, given that so many chose flight to the west rather than return to Berlin, at that time wallowing in defeat. Anything, including the greatest risks, rather than imprisonment in the USSR.

Certainly some political prisoners profited by the general panic to kill their officers and go over to the Soviets, but the others fought several days more before giving in.[56] The survivors mingled with cohorts of refugees and dazed soldiers, as confirmed by the story of Georg Geipel, a misfit, never really reintegrated after the war, living on his wits, and often in trouble with the police. Enrolled in the summer of 1943 as a civilian prisoner, his presence in Warsaw was the reason he was later called before the Ludwigsburg magistrates: he had publicly boasted of having participated, according to his accuser, in mass shootings.

Geipel fought to the limit in Lusatia. Questioned as to his attitude, he spoke of comrades who were killed with a bullet in the back of the head or by having their throats cut after having been taken prisoner, and he said that he had witnessed Soviet atrocities committed on civilians, atrocities that moved him to do anything to avoid falling into the hands of the Red Army. When he finally was captured, the Soviets took his personal effects and shut him in a barn with other soldiers and a group of women. When night fell, the Russians opened the barn to take advantage of the women, and Georg Geipel profited by this collective rape to escape.[57] There is no reason to doubt this story: the killing of prisoners, including by cutting their throats, was a verified practice, and the belief in the automatic execution of SS men was entrenched among combatants. According to some testimonies, it even led young students of the SS officers' school, newly enrolled in the unit, to commit suicide.[58] We sense the atmosphere of extreme violence, anomie, and despair enshrouding the unit's final days. But, in the case of Georg Geipel, the prey escaped the hunter. Not so for nearly 5,300 members of the unit, dead in combat or behind Soviet barbed wire.

Chapter 7

Post-War

The war ended somewhere between Cottbus and Berlin for Dirlewanger's men. Survivors returned between 1947 and 1955 to a world at peace: first occupied Germany and then, after 1949, the Federal Republic of Germany. They had to reintegrate themselves into a society they had not seen born, but which had taken the place of the one they had known. Then came the time of investigations and questionings, the time of avoidance and lies, the time of imagination and memory. Out of all those came these men's post-war experience. But beforehand, we must determine the exact point where reality and myth blend, where the history of the unit ends and where there begins one of those legends that made it a symbol of Nazi atrocity in West German society.

The Death of Oskar Dirlewanger

Oskar Dirlewanger had accompanied the movements of his unit until its arrival in Lusatia, but his presence at the front was more and more sporadic, between his stays in the hospital and his incessant shuttling between Berlin and his Swabian homeland. In February 1945, a new division commander was named, *Brigadeführer* Schmedes, who had already served in the unit as colonel of one of its regiments.[1] Was Dirlewanger, as some authors claim, preparing an exit in light of the desperate situation of the Third Reich? His absence during the height of the battle for the defense of the national sanctuary is surprising, even if we remember that his position among the Nazi hierarchy was fraught. If Dirlewanger enjoyed the support of Himmler and of Gottlob Berger, to whose eyes he had proved his value by fighting alongside the security troops in Belarus and during the Warsaw uprising,[2] the classic military hierarchy was more and more critical of his lack of seriousness in conducting operations. Several reports stressed his offhandedness and the fact that, under the influence of drink, he had not been in a fit state to lead his troops' assault in Slovakia.[3] Furthermore, Dirlewanger was in no way prepared to manage a unit as large as a brigade, let alone a division. Inheritor of the combat practices developed during the Great War, he was an expert in assault groups and machine gun sections, and he perhaps had a certain familiarity with small artillery formations for tactical support. But managing formations made up of different regiments, of engineering and artillery units, required knowledge and skills, notably in terms of logistics and communications, for which he had never been prepared and to which he had no access. He was a good captain but a miserable division general. Already, in Warsaw, he had sacrificed the men under his command by using them systematically in waves of badly supported riflemen.

By this measure, the use that successive higher commanders made of his division, regularly dismantled so its elements could be assigned to various sectors of the front line, could appear as a penalty, were it not that the urgency of the situation overrode any motivations of the hierarchy, constrained as it was to address the emergencies raised by the threat of dislocation of the front. The responsibilities of commanding general of the Thirty-Sixth SS Grenadier Division were in any event reduced to the bare minimum, given that the division existed only on paper, its members scattered over some hundred kilometers in Lusatia. Its last assignments would have been logistic in nature (supplies and provisions), hardly Dirlewanger's strong point. When the unit was annihilated by the Soviets, he was no longer its *de facto* leader. He had met with Gottlob Berger in Berlin between March 15 and 20, then had left again for Swabia where, according to his sister, "he moved a certain number of items out of [their] residence."[4] Whether these were pillage from his campaigns or compromising documents, Dirlewanger was obviously preparing his flight or disappearance into clandestinity. On April 22, 1945, still in SS uniform, he arrived at one of Berger's hunting lodges in the Allgäu, in the far south of Germany, and asked the caretaker's help in storing various items. He then changed his uniform for civilian clothes.[5] The war, for him, was over.

We don't know what became of Dirlewanger during the next six weeks. There's nothing surprising in this: a new period was beginning for him, marked by clandestinity. He reappears in occupied Swabia in June 1945, where he is imprisoned by the French at Altshausen. The latter delegated the guarding of their prisoners to former concentration camp inmates, in conditions that bespeak the irregularity of the early occupation of defeated Germany. A former Luftwaffe officer was with Dirlewanger during the last days of his detention:

On June 1, 1945, two armed, uniformed Poles, accompanied by a French soldier, came to my parents' house and checked my liberation papers. I showed them the attestations the American authorities had given me at Kempten; one of the Poles tore them up. They grabbed me, but I managed to recover the pieces of my American liberation papers. They told me that I would be back in an hour, and took me in a truck to Altshausen, despite my protests and the fact that that Aulendorf, not Altshausen, had jurisdiction over my case. I was imprisoned there in the local detention center without being interrogated. I was shut in the back cell, where there were already some other prisoners. They were mostly former soldiers, who were taken the next day to Ostrach and freed.

After they left, I was transferred to the front cell, in which Minch and Dirlewanger were already imprisoned. Very soon we began talking and told how we had been captured. Naturally, we were cautious at first, because we didn't really know each other. [. . .]

Dirlewanger said he had been a colonel in the SS, that he had for a short time directed the company of guards at a concentration camp, and that he had been recognized by a Jew, a former inmate of the camp, and that he had been arrested for that reason.[6]

Dirlewanger had been denounced, if this version is correct, by an escapee from the camp at Dzikow or Lutsk. An unlikely meeting but recounted with enough detail to be believed, especially since it seems devoid of any attempt at exoneration. By telling his fellow prisoners that he had had even temporary contacts with the world of the concentration camp, Dirlewanger accorded them a surprising trust, no doubt linked to his analysis of the situation, which the former Luftwaffe pilot described in these terms:

From the first night I joined Minch and Dirlewanger, each of them was taken out and beaten with wooden truncheons. During their ordeal, they were accused only of having been in the Gestapo or the SS. We talked again after they were returned to the cell. We then exchanged our postal addresses, with the vow never to divulge them during an interrogation. We did this at Dirlewanger's suggestion, because he said that he believed that we might not leave the prison alive.[7]

Convinced that he would not emerge from captivity, Dirlewanger remained a rational actor, constructing to the last scenarios based on the survival of one of the three prisoners, and allowing his family to be informed of his death while shielding them from any reprisals. For three nights, the two men were beaten by their guards. Was this a brutal interrogation technique aimed at establishing the truth of the denunciation? The testimony of Anton F., also taken from his cell for "interrogation," contradicts this hypothesis:

During my period of arrest, I never saw a Frenchman, only armed, uniformed Poles. I don't know if they belonged to a company of guards. In the next days, none of us were beaten, with one exception. The second day, after I had been transferred to Minch's cell, there came a young Jew, about sixteen years of age, from Ebersbach in the Saulgau district, who was authorized to hit us in the face, under the Poles' surveillance, until he was satisfied and could do no more. He did so, and we were all badly bruised in the face. I myself was beaten only once by the Poles, with wooden boards, the same day, because I had refused to shout that I was a German pig.

Violence without interrogatory function; violence as vengeance, affirming the superiority of yesterday's victims and seeking, furthermore, to make the former occupying enemy recognize the inferiority of his own situation. It targeted, in this instance, a man compromised simply by his nationality. Dirlewanger and his companion, members of institutions emblematic of Nazi tyranny, were treated in a manner incomparably more brutal: "On the contrary, Dirlewanger and Minch were taken out of the cell every night and struck in the manner described."[8] The results of such a treatment were not slow to be seen. A volunteer Red Cross nurse got access to the prison from

French authorities after having learned, from a Dutch officer, that conditions there were "unbearable." She then asked to feed and care for the prisoners, and thus she could testify to Dirlewanger's condition after two nights of unbroken violence: "Most of the prisoners had black and blue marks on their faces, and Dirlewanger also showed me his back, mottled with hematomas," she declared before describing the mayor's refusal to intervene.[9] The treatment Dirlewanger and his companion received seems to have been still more brutal than that accorded the other prisoners. The Luftwaffe lieutenant describes the third day of detention:

In the night of June 4 to 5, 1945, Minch and Dirlewanger were thrice taken out of their cell and beaten in the manner described. After being brought back to the cell for the third time, they were incapable of speaking or getting up, due to their injuries. A little while later, the guards came back in the cell and ordered them again to get up and go with them. Neither Minch nor Dirlewanger was able to do so. So the guards hit them in the face with their rifle butts until their faces were open wounds. They then stuck them both with their bayonets in the lower part of their bodies, during which Minch, it seemed to me, had several bones broken [unreadable—testimony translator's note]. After this episode, they left them unconscious. I stayed sitting in my corner all this time and didn't dare touch them, for fear of being beaten the same way. In view of my state of mind, it can be understood that I didn't worry much more about the two men. I think they died of the injuries they received during their beatings. But I didn't try to find out if they were really dead.[10]

We know nothing more of Dirlewanger's death and burial. The flagrant irregularity of the incarceration procedure, the great brutality used by those whom the Red Cross volunteer identified as "Polish and Jewish" civilians, whose constant drunkenness she stressed,[11] prevented identification and burial from being carried out normally. It was just this that contributed to the development of the post-war Dirlewanger myth, leading to the judicial investigation of his death.

The latter became all the more easily the object of conjecture and legend as the judicial destiny of the unit took on importance, becoming particularly significant during what was known as the Wilhelmstrasse Trial, held by the U.S. authorities in Nuremberg against various officials of the Ministry of Foreign Affairs, among whom was Gottlob Berger. During the preparatory phase of this trial, the protagonists of the recruitment of the unit were successively interrogated as to the circumstances and the modalities of its formation. Berger's former colleagues, such as Joachim Ruoff and Erwin Walser, or the former SS judge Bruno Wille, were heard together with other protagonists of the affair, such as Hermann Höfle, the former HSSPF of Slovakia.[12] None of them could provide information on Dirlewanger and his fate. Ignorance of what had become of the leader and judicial attention to his violent practices contributed to the growing rumors of his escape. They were encouraged by another escape, that of Dirlewanger's former adjutant, Kurt Weisse, who disappeared from a British camp and of whom even today nothing more is known.[13]

The magazine *Revue* published a sensational article claiming that Dirlewanger had found refuge in Egypt,[14] a hypothesis supported by unit veterans: Berger himself told historians of the *Institut für Zeitgeschichte* that he imagined his former regimental comrade taking refuge in Syria, in contact with members of ODESSA, whose existence invited wild speculations, before declaring in 1965 that he believed him rather to be in the French Foreign Legion, where the experience he had acquired in the *Partisanenbekämpfung* would have been welcome.[15]

Articles repeating the story of Dirlewanger's presence in the Middle East, in Egypt or in Syria, triggered a reaction in the judicial world, the prosecutors of the ZStL launching an investigation of Dirlewanger and his unit. Some veterans did the same: we remember the efforts made by Paul Dorn.[16] As for Wilhelm Rass, his profile did not encourage confidence in his statements, despite their sensational nature: he claimed to have seen Dirlewanger again in 1948, accompanied by two Polish officers in British uniform. Investigators apparently listened to him politely without even pointing out his factual incoherencies.[17] Rass, furthermore, made his declarations at the moment the news of Dirlewanger's death was beginning to circulate, official identification of his body having been made two years before,[18] and it can't be ruled out that he built his narrative from such elements as had reached him.

Belief in Dirlewanger's survival, solidly rooted, thus continued to circulate even after the exhumation and official identification of his body. The legend was more tenacious than even the unit leader himself. It allowed veterans to maintain the fascination he had exercised over them, this man-tamer with his brutal ways. The legend of his survival was further spread by the writer Willi Berthold, author of a novel entitled *Brigade Dirlewanger: A Historical Novel*,[19] who had performed a patient work of investigation and interviews with veterans, a work painstaking enough for its author to be mentioned as the source of important information on Dirlewanger himself in an examination by Fritz Langour, the independent journalist who had interviewed Heinz Feiertag and had published the article giving credence to the escape theory. But reading Berthold's novel suggests that the survival myth itself had a long life. Certainly, the novel theorized that he was living happily ever after in Egypt, but it also mentioned Altshausen, the town in which Dirlewanger had succumbed, as the last place in which he had been sighted. This fiction constructed on the basis of a detailed knowledge of reality marked the last stage of Dirlewanger's career. Passed from life to death, he had entered into the legend of the Nazi refuge, and he ended his existence as the dark figure in a paperback novel.

The Black Hunters in the German Courts: Gone to Ground

Starting in 1945, as we have seen, the *Sondereinheit* had become one of the key pieces of the Wilhelmstrasse Trial. Gottlob Berger was found guilty due to his role in the recruitment of the Waffen-SS, and the Dirlewanger case was quickly seen as one of the best ways of proving Berger's involvement in war crimes committed by SS units. A significant number of the unit's leadership was questioned on this occasion, the American objective being to show the organic relationship between Berger's general staff and the unit, on the one hand, and, on the other, to prove the unit's criminality. This affair marked the beginning of a long judicial pursuit, waged with considerable energy and an impressive attention to detail.

Between 1948 and 1985, the West German judiciary worked on close to forty preliminary investigations, aided in this task by the creation in 1958 of a federal organization, the *Zentralstelle der Landesjustizverwaltungen zur Aufklärung nationalsozialistischer Gewaltverbrecher*, responsible for coordinating these investigations and assigning them to the various prosecutors' offices.[20] This work allowed German police and magistrates to accumulate an impressive amount of documentation and information on the unit. Rare, however, were investigations leading to a full trial, with testimony from witnesses, bill of indictment, and court hearing. This failure is no doubt to be analyzed in light of the practical difficulties of indictment under German law, but also of the strategies used by the black hunters.

The first significant investigation was on the role of the unit in the repression of the Warsaw insurrection. On that occasion, in September 1963, the Flensburg prosecutor delivered a panoramic overview of "facts established" on the unit.[21] This document of some sixty pages was based on the same documentation as Hellmuth Auerbach's article in the *Vierteljahresheft für Zeitgeschichte*,[22] except that Auerbach touched on the recruitment of political prisoners and made more regular use of military and WVHA archives.

Better informed than Hellmuth Auerbach thanks to their use of witnesses, the Flensburg investigators retraced Dirlewanger's steps, supported by the personal dossier of the unit's former leader, copies of the judgments of the court that had condemned him on his morals charge, and his demobilization papers from the First World War. Secondly, they examined the evolution of the unit and the extreme complexity of the institutional and military situation in the summer of 1944, which made it difficult, in their opinion, to qualify the facts then central to the Warsaw investigation. The fact that the unit had not yet, at that time, been transformed into a brigade with a clearly identified general staff, regiments, and battalions, with well-defined chains of command, was one obvious difficulty.[23] To overcome it, the investigators had performed a careful identification of the general staff personnel and the commanders of the two combat groups, led an investigation as to their morality, and questioned unit veterans on their impressions of their leaders.[24] The investigators then attempted to reconstitute the events between the arrival of the unit in the Polish capital and that of Oskar Dirlewanger, in order to understand how far the crimes committed could be attributed to him.

Concluding that it was impossible to establish his responsibility clearly,[25] they next turned to the orders given by the higher echelons, and especially by Himmler. The latter being dead, the investigators tried to establish how far Heinz Reinefarth, the former SS general who had been delegated to quell the uprising (and at the time of the investigation was deputy to the Schleswig *Landtag*), had acted on his own initiative. Reine-farth denied having received an order to destroy the city before August 5, 1944, the date at which he supposedly learned the contents of the order through the intermediary of von dem Bach-Zelewsky.[26] He then declared that he had asked, with von dem Bach's support, that the order be annulled. To the investi-gators, the existence of this order from Himmler was not in doubt: had not the latter given a speech to the local Wehrmacht leaders, on September 21, 1944, in which he claimed responsi-bility for the massacre and affirmed that he had given an order for the total destruction of Warsaw?[27] The content and the form of this order, however, could not be precisely determined: one of the witnesses spoke of a simple sheet of paper on which it was written in pencil that Dirlewanger could kill whomever he saw fit.[28] The question was whether the order implied the destruction of the city as a unit, buildings and all, or the exter-mination of the entire population. The investigators, reviewing the testimonies, concluded that it was impossible to prove without a doubt that the unit had been informed of an order for the systematic destruction of the population issued by Himmler.[29] The question of the responsibility for abuses committed remained unresolved, and the investigation ended with an admission of helplessness.

Nevertheless, the investigators had accumulated valuable knowledge that historians would make use of during the 1990s.[30] In 1971, a second case, this time directed against the *Kampfgruppe* von Gottberg, touched on the unit's activity in the USSR. Even if the prosecutors weren't interested specifi-cally in the unit, we find in the procedural dossiers docu-ments from the Belarusian archives, notably the Minsk Central Archives.[31] Similarly, the massive presence of testimonies gathered by Soviet commissions of investigation in Belarus, particularly in the context of an investigation against the *Sondereinheit* Dirlewanger by the Mogilev judicial authorities, indicates that at least some collaboration took place between justice organizations behind the Iron Curtain, and that documents were circulated among them.[32] This is confirmed by the hearings of one of the principal suspects, Artur Wilke: the man was methodically questioned, operation by operation, and confronted with entries from von dem Bach-Zelewsky's war journal, as well as the troops' combat reports.[33] Knowledge of the chain of command, but also of anti-partisan practices, made great progress. On the judicial level, however, this knowledge was still incomplete. Although the results of operations were clear and the participating units were well known, the names of those responsible for crimes and the role of the chain of command were still obscure. Artur Wilke, for instance, was not called upon by the Hamburg investigators: he had been condemned to ten years in prison during the trial,[34] held in Coblenz, of the Minsk KdS, whose principal defendant was the former Gestapo leader Georg Heuser, for the liquidation of the Belarusian ghettos. Wilke had been condemned for his role in the Slutsk affair at the end of Operation Hornung, but it was not possible to establish his responsibility in the other Belarusian sweep operations, even though he was one of the leaders of reconnaissance and information-gathering units.

Names, dates, places, and numbers of victims were needed to qualify the facts judicially. But these were precisely what was lacking. Soviet testimony gave place names, and often imprecise dates, with just the month during which reprisals had taken place. But these testimonies didn't identify the killers, always described as Germans in combat uniform, without specifying their unit. Collected by Soviet commissions of investigation, they were devoid neither of a certain ideological formalization nor of a haste overriding any systematic exploitation. Even in the infrequent event of a testimony specifying that the massacre had been executed by a penal unit,[35] how could the investigators more clearly identify the black hunters? Incomplete as were the victims' testimonies, those of the killers or the suspects were even more so.

Out of 180 testimonies selected from various investigations of crimes linked to the *Partisanenbekämpfung* in Belarus or pointing directly at the unit, 176 depositions formally deny any involvement in these crimes. Out of the four acknowledging their author's involvement, none admits to more than a single abuse. Certainly, they don't deny an indirect knowledge of the massacres and burnings of villages; none, however, designates direct actors. None has anything to say on the question of the chain of command. None, finally, mentions both the date and the place of an abuse. It is difficult to determine what is due to a deliberate defense strategy and what to German soldiers' experience of the East as a uniform immensity (a perception described in the work of Vejas Gabriel Liulevicius). During the two wars, soldiers' stories and correspondence illustrate a clear tendency over time to no longer differentiate names, dates, and places.[36] How could the black hunters have recalled for the Hamburg investigators, twenty years after the fact, the names of little villages lost in the Belarusian forests, when Dirlewanger himself had found it necessary to ask them, in 1942, to make an effort to learn the names of places so that they could go there immediately in case of an alert?[37] Whether they were really incapable of naming places and dates, or whether they had forgotten them deliberately to avoid future judicial complications, the former members of anti-partisan units gave incomplete testimony, explaining their faulty memory by the time gone by since the events in question. This was the case not only for veterans of the *Sondereinheit*, but for all the units that had operated in Belarus. The specificity of the black hunters was merely their great consistency in the use of these strategies.

Questioned, for example, as to their participation in the assault against the barricades of the Polish capital, they stressed the extreme intensity of combat, as well as the heavy losses sustained. Examined on November 30, 1961, Karl Vieregge, one of the poachers recruited at the unit's inception, carefully builds the argument meant to ward off any possibility of incrimination. He begins by underlining that he was, throughout his time in Belarus, acting as butcher and canteen cook for the unit, and thus could not be implicated in sweep operations. Addressing the investigators' main topic of interest, the repression of the Warsaw uprising, Vieregge describes in detail the different combat missions assigned to the group, while declaring that the latter "wouldn't have had the opportunity" to commit a massacre, given the combat situation and the enormous losses sustained by the group.[38] Peter Erretskamp produces a similar testimony: he commands a company of heavy machine gunners during the assault and is part of the first wave intended to cover the advance of the infantry companies. He partially contradicts Vieregge's testimony, however, speaking of an order that assault companies execute anyone attempting to leave the city, then of a contrary order, issued several days after the first. He denies having been present at any execution, while admitting having seen very many corpses in Warsaw, which he attributes to Stuka attacks on the marketplace.[39]

Rare are the testimonies straying from this line of defense: all the witnesses mention that the extreme combat conditions prevented them from taking part in reprisal actions. Only two of them admit being part of firing squads. The first was careful to recall that they were acting on orders, and on the pretext that the Poles themselves took no prisoners but "hanged [ours] upside down from lamp posts," and he denied that women and children had been massacred by these squads.[40] The second testimony, however, clearly contradicted the unit veterans' line of defense: Willy Brincksmann admitted having participated in the execution by automatic weapon of a hundred Poles against a ruined wall. The document does not identify the men who took the initiative in the execution, nor even date or localize it precisely. If the involvement of the unit's men is again confirmed for the historian, the testimony is useless to the investigators.[41]

Concerning operations in Belarus, the most suggestive case, due to its caricatural nature, is that of Heinrich Kraus. A poacher who had been part of the unit from the very beginning, witness—at the very least—of all the abuses committed by members of the unit, he pushed precaution to the point of claiming to remember neither the responsibilities he had held, nor the code names of sweep operations, nor the places where he was wounded. Confronted with written orders preserved in the Freiburg Military Archives, as well as the testimony gathered by the Mogilev investigatory commission, Kraus stubbornly denied any knowledge of the abuses committed. Examined in 1975, he justified his silence by several head wounds, which had, he claimed, affected his memory.[42] Thirteen years earlier, however, he had already been questioned in the course of the investigation of the suppression of the Warsaw uprising, and he had given details on that occasion, certainly anodyne as to the unit and its leader, but bespeaking his capacity to recall specific events of the period.[43] But in 1975, the very memory of this testimony seemed to escape him. Interestingly enough, the former transporter was assisted by his niece, who reread his deposition for him; the man was pretending to be illiterate. A quick examination of the signature at the bottom of his deposition casts a certain doubt on this assertion. If the writing of his family name is hesitant, that of his first name is childish but well formed, and suggests that the man was deceiving the officials responsible for examining him, on this point at least. They weren't fooled and came back to the matter a year later, in May

1976—without success, however, as Kraus persisted in not remembering a thing.[44]

Some veterans, like Johannes Maas, refused from the first to cooperate and didn't answer the questions put to them;[45] others, like Peter Erretskamp, sent the investigators on false leads. In the investigation of the execution by lethal injection of fifty-seven Jews in Lublin, he was for a long time the only man who would confirm having seen the bodies of the victims, and he testified as to the doctor who was responsible, according to him. He went so far in his declarations as to identify formally one of the doctors on duty in Lublin as the author of the murders,[46] and he supplied sketches of the barracks and of the execution ground. The investigators, however, quickly determined that the doctor in question was not in Lublin at the time the unit was there and thus could not be the author of the murders.[47] Some thirteen years after this first lie, Erretskamp claimed, during the investigation of the *Kampfgruppe* von Gottberg, that he had saved Russian civilians during the burning of their village.[48] The motive for the first lie is a mystery, especially since Erretskamp had not been put on the spot during the investigation. In the second case, the danger was certainly greater for him, but the probability of an NCO being incriminated was small. Erretskamp was not in danger, and he had no apparent reason to want to prolong the investigation—not even personal vengeance, any previous meeting with the doctor he had accused being materially impossible. He had not always been a liar. During the investigation of the suppression of the Warsaw uprising, his testimony on the dissemination of the orders for the destruction of the city was no doubt among those that detailed most precisely the succession of instructions that, between August 5 and 8, 1944, led from an undifferentiated total massacre to a more selective killing of insurgents.[49,50] Between exact testimony and inveterate lying, Erretskamp's motivations defy reason. Was it some sort of game? Nevertheless, the investigators, in the absence of any tangible proof or even of any suspect, abandoned their search.[51]

Rare were the veterans who went beyond a simple recounting of the circumstances of their entering the unit and their career therein. Rarer still were those who broke group solidarity by denouncing their former comrades. To tell the truth, only a single poacher broke this unspoken contract: on September 30, 1969, Franz W., during the investigation of the *Kampfgruppe* von Gottberg, accused Heinz Feiertag of having killed a peasant woman without cause during a routine inspection. In his declaration, W. took his stand on categories of moral judgment: what had shocked him was the arbitrariness of Feiertag, whom he called a "swine."[52] This is the single exception to the law of silence reigning over the poachers' group, but it concerns an NCO who was not a member thereof. Was this practice of *omertà* conscious, even organized? In other affairs, practices of communication between suspects have been remarked. In his biography of Werner Best, Ulrich Herbert describes the great epistolary activity of Heydrich's former adjutant to coordinate the versions of the former heads of local Gestapo bureaus during the "RSHA trial." This, however, was a particular case, in light of the great social and cultural homogeneity of the suspects: all lawyers, all recruited by Best to the Gestapo, and all successfully reintegrated in post-war German society.[53] In an investigation of the Minsk KdS in 1943, targeting former members of *Sonderkommando* 1b and *Einsatzkommando* Five, the investigators noted that at least one of the suspects, a police officer, had been warned by "colleagues" of his upcoming interrogation.[54] In these two cases, however, the preexisting understanding and the solidarity of the group had been generated by the professional identity and cultural proximity between police and suspects.

The men of the *Sondereinheit* did not have access to the social network created in the course of police work. What they did have, as a very special group, was their great experience of police interrogation. Had not most of the unit veterans already been arrested several times? Often sentenced during the 1930s, these men had had to face interrogation methods infinitely more rigorous than those of the criminal police of a democratic Germany. Certainly not all of them had been sentenced twenty-two times in twenty years (between 1939 and 1960), like that Nikolas H. who was questioned during the investigation of the Warsaw uprising, and whose judicial past astonished the investigators themselves,[55] or like Georg Geipel who was in trouble with the police some fifteen times after the war.[56] But none of the members of the *Sondereinheit* Dirlewanger questioned about the unit's activities were faced with an inhabitual and destabilizing experience. This may be one of the factors explaining the investigators' inability to penetrate the unit's criminal practices.

To further analyze this failure would involve taking into account multiple factors: the absence or death of the principal issuers of orders, the destruction of archival materials, the lack of proof and testimony, the resistance of killers to inquisitorial pressure, and the tendency of investigators to be less aggressive regarding this type of crime than those resulting from specifically genocidal orders. Let us limit ourselves to the final result. Some twenty preliminary investigations were undertaken by the ZStL, to which we must add a dozen led by the prosecutors of the West German Länder.[57] Out of thirty-five dossiers, only one case produced a bill of indictment that ended in a trial in criminal court. For their activity as guards in labor camps for Jewish prisoners, Heinz Feiertag and three other unit members received sentences ranging from ten years to life in prison.[58] Feiertag, however, was freed after seven years. The other cases were dismissed, which did not imply that no crimes were committed but acknowledged the difficulty of establishing guilt. Dirlewanger was dead; Kurt Weisse had disappeared without a trace,[59] Gottlob Berger and the other higher officers of the unit could not be condemned for crimes for which they had already been tried at Nuremberg.[60] Pursuing crimes related to anti-partisan actions would mean attempting to place the responsibility for abuses on NCOs.

In 1995, the very long preliminary investigation opened in 1971 by the Hamburg prosecutor's office on the abuses of the *Kampfgruppe* von Gottberg was closed without anyone being brought to trial. Artur Wilke was dead, as were the principals responsible for the crimes, and the magistrates admitted, in their final report, their inability to judge cases that nonetheless were clearly criminal.[61] Dirlewanger's men had successfully resisted the judicial offensive waged by the Germany of 1960–1980. By refusing to collaborate, by clinging to group solidarity, they managed to avoid legal reprisals. The crimes committed by the unit in Poland, in the USSR, in Warsaw, and finally in Slovakia remained largely unpunished.[62]

In the last investigations opened by prosecutors, these old men and retirees gave only the scantiest information as to what had become of them after the war, opposing their interrogators with stubborn silence and flat refusal, without recounting their post-war careers. Let us try, nonetheless, to characterize these careers. A minority, like Nikolas H., never managed to emerge from the marginality that had brought them into the unit, and continued to amass guilty pleas and prison sentences. Others, like Heinz Feiertag, who opened a beer bar in 1960s Berlin, disappeared into certain anonymity without abandoning their pre-war system of representation. A former NCO of the *Leibstandarte* Adolf Hitler, wholehearted subscriber to the values of the *Sondereinheit*, Feiertag remained an anti-Semite, and he maintained a justificatory memory of the war. A brawl with a former prisoner of the Slutsk camp brought about a denunciation and, finally, a condemnation. An ambiguous brawl to begin with, it occurred after several meetings between the former prisoner and his guard, meetings that the former prisoner had described as "friendly"; proof, if such were needed, of the complexity of relationships formed, in post-war Germany, between former oppressors and former victims.[63]

Nevertheless, at a glance the common characteristic of the careers described during the investigations is social marginality. Few of the unit's veterans shared the central experience of post-war Germany: the "miracle" of the rebirth of the two Germanys. The few notable exceptions involve certain political prisoners who joined the unit in late 1944 and who entered politics, some in West Germany, some in East. In the DRG, several members of the central committee of the SED were former members of the unit; Hans Peter Klausch counts nearly nineteen among the founders of the Stasi.[64] In the West, Karl-Otto Watzinger, a former highly placed Social Democratic official, had been part of the concentration camp aristocracy of trustee political prisoners in Dachau. He had joined the unit in November 1944 and rapidly attained the rank of NCO before deserting on the Hungarian front.[65] Elected mayor of Mannheim after the war as a Social Democrat, he was no doubt victim of his excessive visibility and was, in 1970, the object of denunciations by militant anti-fascists who accused him of having participated in several murders of unit members. His participation in these crimes was never established.[66] Militant solidarity played, in this case, the protective role it had already assumed within the world of the concentration camp as within the unit: the investigation was canceled. Aside from these few atypical careers, rare were the veterans of the division who managed to adopt the exterior signs of social respectability. Misfits before the war, the black hunters remained misfits in a post-war Germany that was defining,

notably through these trials, a discourse and memory of its
Nazi past.

In the Margins of Memory

It is not surprising that the black hunters remained marginal
even in the management of the Nazi past: their recruitment
had conformed to a logic based, as we have seen, in an imagination of the hunt and the wild. This continued to play itself
out well beyond the break of 1945 and continued also to
confine them to the margins of society.[67] But their place in the
memory of Nazism was ambiguous for other, more immediate
reasons: they weren't unknown, and in the 1960s many works
for the mass public attested to their special place in European
historical memory. In France, special issues of the popular
magazine *Historia* dedicated to the history of the SS devoted
articles to the unit,[68] and particularly to its recruitment and its
action in the suppression of the Warsaw uprising. The same
may be said for André Brissaud's *L'Histoire de la SS*.[69] Not without reason is the *Sondereinheit* Dirlewanger presented as the
"most famous anti-partisan unit of the Third Reich" by the
historian French MacLean. Its recruitment, its long bloody trail
in Eastern Europe, the personality of its leader, and the interest
shown towards it by Himmler and certain other SS dignitaries
gave it a sinister reputation, certainly not exempt from a certain
fascination. On this basis, Willi Berthold's previously mentioned
novel, *Brigade Dirlewanger*, constitutes a convenient summary
of German representations of the unit.[70] Belonging at once to
a marginalizing image of the unit and to a specific discourse of
interpretation of Nazi violence, it nevertheless presented a
positive hero: Paul Vonwegh, a Republican veteran of the
Spanish Civil War. Vonwegh, hero of the democratic cause in
Spain, returns to Germany for love of a woman, Karen.
Betrayed by the latter's cousin (an up-and-coming prosecutor
in the *Reichssicherheitshauptamt*), he finds himself at Łahojsk,

among the criminals of the *Sondereinheit*. After an initial phase of hostility on their part, Vonwegh gains their respect and loyalty, becomes their leader, and ends by saving them during the final combats in Lusatia, organizing their mass desertion, then dying a hero's death before their eyes as they reach the Russian lines. Describing the unit from Łahojsk to Cottbus, Berthold offered a specific interpretation of the violence in the East, drawing the figures of the "habitual criminal" and "Nazi pervert," while also offering to Federal Germany a positive figure with which Germans could identify, Vonwegh becoming a "man among wolves."

From Willie Berthold's pen emerges the whole SS hierarchy. Some secondary characters are faithfully inspired by real people, such as "Colonel Prinz," a police officer with a military bearing, formerly of the Bavarian political police. It's a barely disguised portrait of what was believed to be known, when Berthold wrote, of Heinrich Mueller or Friedrich Panzinger, respectively numbers one and two of the RSHA Amt IV.[71] As for the young and brilliant prosecutor Wulf-Dieter Brinckmann, black angel of the plot and responsible for the incarceration of Paul Vonwegh, he constitutes a sort of identikit sketch of the lawyers recruited by Werner Best to the Gestapo.[72] The unit leaders, like Weisse and Mueller-Wurzbach, are faithfully described, thanks to the documentation collected by the author. The historical errors—Kube, *Gauleiter*, Reich commissioner in Kiev rather than Minsk—are too flagrant not to be intentional.

Nevertheless, even more than a conscious work of history, the novel was above all an attempt to interpret Nazi violence. Vonwegh's section constitutes a striking collection of hardened criminals as seen by a post-war German: there is Korzetzky, known as "the Gorilla," described as an imposing brute of simian appearance and brutal behavior, condemned to eight years' imprisonment for forcible rape; Petrat, a sadistic murderer, a killer of women, condemned to death; Kirschwein, an epileptic and a coward whose crime is not specified; an embezzler; a former student seized as a scapegoat; and still others who make brief appearances.[73] The members of the unit are *ipso facto* killers: if they are not described in the act of massacring and burning villages (a single action shows them securing the sector whose population will be massacred),[74] it is understood that the unit was the principal actor of the massacres. The men are nonetheless victims of the blind repression rampant in the unit: Is not Petrat at once "a revolting beast and a miserable dog"?[75] They are a band of asocial criminals suffering from neurological or mental disabilities and incapable of internal solidarity before Vonwegh's arrival.

To support this description, a representation of social marginality appears, taken directly from the Weimar period and transmitted throughout the Third Reich, to be inherited finally by Adenauer's Germany.[76] Nowhere does Berthold mention that the greatest sources of recruits for the unit were Wehrmacht and SS prisons, and the majority of recruits were soldiers punished for civil crimes or disgrace in combat. The unit is shown not as a penal battalion but as a swept-together collection of misfits. Thus was developed a first level of discourse on Nazi violence. The latter was the work of criminals from the lower depths of pre-war German society to which a regime, in itself criminal, had given free rein in certain clearly defined spaces. The idea that Nazi violence was the work of social misfits accorded well with a central historical thesis.[77] A kind of *cordon sanitaire* was traced between German society, whose normality was not tainted by twelve years of Nazi rule, and a handful of misfits, in this case criminals, who were to be held responsible for the monstrous crimes of which the regime was guilty. The same mechanism accounted for the presence of young, well-educated men in central positions of SS security organizations.

In the eyes of the author, this feral pack is not irrevocably condemned to do evil. The appearance of Vonwegh, the "man among wolves," puts an end to the denunciations, the racketeering, and the violence prevailing in the section. Even better, he ends by shielding his men, insofar as possible, from the most repugnant duties. So we see him exempt them from the task of executing women and children, and kill an SS man who is raping a woman.[78] But the section commanded by Vonwegh is no longer representative of the unit: other men are responsible for these killings, other criminals, other "fanatics" who kill for pleasure,[79] like the former *Untersturmführer* Exner, a thief by trade, or *Unterscharführer* Belle, a commando veteran already in Poland.[80] Vonwegh has transformed his men. At the end of the Soviet offensive of July 1944, Kordt, the weak, cowardly young student whom the criminals extorted and whose rations they stole, has become an energetic and decisive man; Petrat and Korzetzky, hardened criminals, now follow their leader with blind loyalty, even agreeing to desert in Lusatia to ensure their salvation and escape the curse of the wolf-men. As for Vonwegh, he has even been reunited with his fellow political prisoners from the concentration camp.[81]

Paul Vonwegh is at once a hero, endowed with military capabilities allowing him to save his best men to the end, and an authentic anti-Nazi. But the conservative Germany of those years could not have identified itself comfortably with a communist or a social democrat; therefore it is as a "liberal republican" that Vonwegh went to Spain. He is described as a calm, courageous, virile man who distinguishes himself by speaking formally to his men. A warrior with nerves of steel, he is also capable of sentiment, in those moments when he recalls his fiancée Karen. Positive hero, Paul Vonwegh is also a sort of tragic figure and martyr: after assuring himself that his men have successfully deserted, at the very moment when the assault on Berlin begins, he is killed by the last members of the *Sondereinheit* only 150 meters away from the Russian lines. Despite this ending—this is the discourse of the novel's last pages—the memory of Vonwegh lives on in the memory of the men who reached the Russian lines, those men who would become the pillars of reborn German society.

Brigade Dirlewanger: A Historical Novel was not merely an attempt at a more general interpretation allowing post-war German society to appropriate this traumatic element of the Nazi past while legitimizing its own identity. The author didn't refrain from criticizing the legal apparatus that had ensured the impunity of Reinefarth, the HSSPF who had directed the Warsaw uprising, by closing the case without producing a single Polish testimony.[82] But this criticism itself was subject to caution: a few pages earlier, Berthold cited a Polish testimony he had consulted in the archives of this same case.[83] The novel was, in its very inexactness and misinterpretations, highly representative of the social memory of Nazism. He divided the Dirlewanger men into two groups. The greater part of the recruits were, in the eyes of the author, sadistic brutes, murderers, and alcoholics, encouraged by a perverse hierarchy that practiced murder and rape for pleasure. Wolves among men. Lost in this disturbing environment, other men, often far from honorable themselves, yearned to be rehabilitated if only they could find a leader combining military and human qualities with an iron will and an acceptable political orientation—neither rightwing radical nor communist or socialist. Conveying the values of virility and humanity, as well as a carefully calibrated political discourse, the novel thus provided an interpretation of the unit's history that made it acceptable for the social memory of post-war Germany.

But at the cost of a triple distortion of historical reality: first, Dirlewanger is depicted as human refuse, consumed by drink and sexual orgies, incapable of any military action, and marked by constant sadism. This image denies the indubitable charisma of the unit's leader. Secondly, his men are depicted as the victims of an omnipresent repression, the author continuing the legend of high mortality among the men in Belarus, while the archives show there was nothing of the kind. Finally, this discourse makes sense only by rejecting a particular category of recruits: the black hunters. The latter are mentioned only in the first pages of the book. They have no place in Berthold, implicitly amalgamated with the other criminals, ignoring the dynamics observed in the unit that clearly individualized them, or purely and simply excluded from the author's discourse, their status not fitting in with his system. Their crimes don't stigmatize them like those of Petrat, the woman-killer; their destiny doesn't designate them indubitably as Dirlewanger's victims. Neither born sadists nor pure victims, they can't find a place in the plot. Thus they are rejected to the margins of the construction of memory of which this book is the reflection. And yet, throughout the novel, the cynegetic metaphor is omnipresent.

Considered as the most famous anti-partisan unit,[84] the *Sondereinheit* Dirlewanger was never, like the *Einsatzgruppen* after the Ulm trial or the *Reichssicherheitshauptamt* after the Eichmann trial, the center of one of those public debates that contributed decisively to forming the German memory of Nazi crimes. In this, it remained a marginal element of that memory.

The black hunters thus escaped for the most part both the snares of justice and public debates on Nazi crimes. The survivors had come back to a society that was savoring a recovered normality, an unhoped-for prosperity, and they often had trouble finding their place therein. Whether former poachers or "hardened criminals," they remained on the sidelines of a new Germany that was learning to appropriate its past. The *Sondereinheit* nevertheless remained haloed with a sort of aura mingling violence and repression, an aura of which Berthold's novel gives a detailed version, and which the work of Hellmuth Auerbach and above all of Hans Peter Klausch have contributed to dissipating. Thanks to them the *Sondereinheit* emerged from legend, even if the black hunters remained in the shadow of those heroic victims, the antifascist political prisoners. In the reunified Germany of the 1990s, at the moment when the last case concerning a crime committed by the Dirlewanger unit was closed, it would henceforth be the time for history.

Conclusion

There is a story that is still told today by the hunters of Carinthia, lovers of the *Pirsch*. It is the story of a legendary trophy, a great pale gray chamois, stuffed and shown in the Salzburg *Haus der Natur*. It is said that this beast was, like all white game, marked with the seal of invisibility, protected by the *Salige Frau*, that wild woman, the equivalent of Artemis, who lives on the slopes of the Austrian Alps, whose messenger it was. This exceptional chamois was killed August 27, 1913, by one of the most famous hunters of the Austro-Hungarian Empire: Franz Ferdinand von Österreich-Este. But woe unto him who touched the Salige Frau's white game! Like Rudolf Franz Karl Joseph von Habsburg-Lothringen, found lifeless in Mayerling, or Alexander I of Serbia, assassinated in 1903, Franz Ferdinand died less than a year later, beneath the bullets of Gavrilo Prinzip, at Sarajevo. According to the Austrian hunters, the implacable punishment of this transgressor of the order of the Wild was at the source of the original catastrophe of the century of extremes. The Great War as an ordeal atoning for a transgressed taboo, such is, at heart, the belief of the Tyrolean hunters—a belief that closes the interpretative circle of war as a cynegetic event.[1] For in the beginning was the Great War.

The cortege of desolation and death it left behind gave birth to Oskar Dirlewanger. He had the longest possible and most traumatic war, and this reality was inscribed on his body:

wounded three times, he was one of that smallest minority of soldiers who survived wounds sustained in combat with cold steel. Few men, in short, have seen war at so close a range. "Dog of war"[2] as he was, Dirlewanger never emerged from it, never managed to separate himself from that experience of life under fire, which he transposed after November 1918 into an intense paramilitary activity taking him throughout Germany. An experience he transposed as well into *völkisch*, then into early Nazi political commitment. His doctoral thesis itself constituted a continuation of the war by other means, political, and on other battlefields, academic. Incapable of normalizing his behavior, he then fell into delinquency, financial or sexual.

Extreme illustration of the incapacity of German society to emerge from the lost war, to let go of the representation of a "world of enemies" colluding to bring it to ruin, Dirlewanger also embodied the inextricability of the bonds between cynegetic activity and military practice. All his military activity (in Lublin as in Belarus, and in Southern Germany) was surrounded by the hunt. Beyond the comradeship born in the trenches, Dirlewanger shared with a man like Gottlob Berger a passion for the *Pirsch* and for the wolf hunt,[3] which they practiced together wherever the war took Dirlewanger between autumn 1940 and summer 1944. Landsknecht of another era and passionate hunter, Dirlewanger nevertheless had access to hierarchical connections far beyond those of the mere subaltern officer that he then was, obtaining direct access to Heinrich Himmler, Berger, or von dem Bach-Zelewsky. Pursuing, thanks to these connections, an intense lobbying campaign, Dirlewanger was the principal actor of the unit's development as it grew, in five years, from a commando of a few dozen men to a grenadier division. Between marginality and tenacity, Dirlewanger had thus built a unique career in the Black Order, a career in which militancy, war experience, and social connections mingled, a career inseparable from that of the unit to which he had given his name.

Made up of men perceived through the perspective of that hunting culture that made the Great War the direct consequence of the transgression of a taboo by the Archduke assassinated at Sarajevo, the *Sonderkommando* Oranienburg, soon the *Sondereinheit* Dirlewanger, was constantly viewed in frameworks outside "Nazi normality." Combining, to the eyes of dignitaries as eminent as Hitler or Himmler, cynegetic passion, unbridled violence, and the cruelty of Black Blood, the poachers of the unit were entrusted with the "pacification" and hunting of partisans—partisans assimilated, even before contact with them, to wild animals, prey to be tracked.

In Poland and in Belarus, those extremities of the millennial empire then taking form, the release of the violence that they "had in their blood" was necessary and desirable, while conveniently contained there. Having interiorized a discursive system saturated with representations of the Wild, of the threatening violence of Black Blood, of the hunt as metaphor for war and the image of the fevered warrior, these men established, under Dirlewanger's leadership, very specific gestures of war. To identify and track groups of partisans in the Belarusian forests was a form of war in perfect continuity with the hunting practices observed by ethnologists of the *Pirsch*. A war in which they were expected to express those cynegetic qualities that intimate communion with Black Blood granted them, in the eyes of their superiors as in those of the soldiers they fought beside.

The establishment, starting in January 1942, of sweeps in the form of enormous battues constituted the next step after the *Pirsch*, leading to egalitarian social relationships between the hunters and to practices of mass killing of trapped animals. To the selection-hunt represented by the *Pirsch* and reconnaissance—in which captured weapons, like partisan corpses, were seen as trophies—there was opposed the sweep operation, the collection-hunt, in which the success of the operation was expressed in spoils of farm produce, deported labor, and confiscated cattle. Far from functionally inevitable, this system results from cultural choices based on a specific imagination,[4] adapted, according to Nazi leaders, to a war both new to them and in perfect conformity with the image they had constructed of their adversaries. It was because the enemy was reduced, in their eyes, to the level of wild animals that they envisaged trapping them or tracking them in small groups to the heart of their lairs. It is because the Polish and Russian partisans were *a priori* perceived as wild and cruel that SS leaders conceived the idea of creating a unit of poachers, of black hunters. Black they were because they wore, despite all denials by the SS, the uniform of the order; black they were because within the SS itself, they found themselves stigmatized for their cruelty and their communion with the world of the Wild.

The image of the Wild, however, cannot alone account for all the populations encountered by the unit.[5] The Russian peasants of the villages in the operation zones and the Jewish prisoners of the labor camps shared certain characteristics different from those of the partisan groups. The latter were reputed to be cruel and dangerous; the others were inoffensive domestic "animals." All had been gathered: penned; some, the Jews especially, had been marked; all, finally, had been set to labor.

The scale thus reconstituted, leading from the Domestic to the darkest of the Wild, makes an element on one of its polarities correspond to its equivalent on the other—the dog and the wolf, the stag and the bull. It admits cases of going wild—rabies. Villages suspected of partisan collusion are seen as domestic animals threatened by a return to the savage state due to infection. To eradicate it, the black hunters took great care to spill as little blood as possible from their victims, blood symbolically become black and wild again: the cremation of the living corresponded to an exterminating and purifying imagination of domestic order. Thus, the black hunters behaved according to anthropological codes at once ancient, common to European cultures since prehistoric times, and clear enough to spread their effects throughout the security forces present in Belarus. It is by this standard that we may evaluate the mixture of esteem and reprobation enjoyed by the unit: innovative in its hunting activity (as seen by the "mine-clearing procedure" it developed) and cruel to the extreme in its behavior, even in the eyes of the security troops. The unit was constantly evaluated on the scale of the Wild and the Domestic. This discourse was used at once to stigmatize and to celebrate them. Several decades after the fact, it was still heard in the words of witnesses and accused alike in the investigations of Nazi crimes.

Constructed in constant tension with the daily observation of the real, this system of representations underwent a slow dissolution as German troops withdrew, and it grew unclear when the unit was sent to Slovakia and Hungary. It was not merely the status of the victims that changed with each new displacement of the unit, but the nature of combat as well. This changed inexorably to a war of position in which the Russian assailant had an overwhelming human and material advantage. As time passed, the situation grew worse, and combat less and less like a hunt. Or rather, the black hunters felt less like trackers and more like prey. The unit let itself be annihilated where it stood rather than giving up ground to the Soviet flood that was submerging German territory, illustrating the general behavior of that desperate army that was the *Ostheer* in spring 1945. Of the six thousand recruits of the division, only fifty were still fit for combat on the morning of April 25. The rest, when they were not killed or wounded, were undergoing captivity, including penning up, marking, and enforced labor—a domestication exactly symmetrical with that which the black hunters had imposed on the Belarusian populations. The war practices and collective fates of the Dirlewanger unit are thus analyzable according to the imagination of the hunt and of the Wild, both in "victory" and in defeat.

Are we not in the presence of an extraordinary case forbidding all generalization? Yes, the unit is exceptional. But the question, like the answer, constitutes neither more nor less than a variant of that strategy of separation used by SS dignitaries or officials of the Belarusian civil administration, but also by witnesses and accused during investigations of *Partisanenbekämpfung* crimes. For everyone, yesterday as today, it is crucial to build a protective barrier between the black hunters and "ordinary men," just as it is crucial for European societies to separate the Domestic and the Familiar from the Wild.

If the black hunters and the condemned who populated the *Sondereinheit* Dirlewanger made it a socially unrepresentative unit, its practices of violence resembled in every detail those of other anti-partisan formations. Of the seven hundred villages burned in Belarus, the unit is far from being responsible for the majority of these devastations. Displacement of population, reduction of Russian civilians to the state of herded animals, rapes, markings, and other brutalities, these too were not in any way restricted to the black hunters. At most they played a part in spreading these practices among the units they mingled with. But all the troops engaged in anti-partisan action adopted them, even if western societies of the twentieth century, Nazi or not, would prefer, in accordance with the image of Black Blood, to restrict them to poachers and possessed warriors, to forest spaces and frontier territories.[6]

The second question raised by the present essay in historical anthropology is that of the relationship between decision and practice on the ground. These village burnings may be described with equal legitimacy as the end of a rational process of decision-making, combining security considerations, objectives of economic predation, population selection, and physical constraints of troops on the ground. Christian Gerlach shows this masterfully: one burns a village because its inhabitants have associated with partisans, because one wants to take its cows, pigs, and grain, because one wants to deport civilians who can work and not feed the others. One burns villages, finally, because one has been ordered to do so.[7]

The two interpretative systems do not cancel each other out; each captures a dimension of reality that escapes the other. To combine the tools of social and cultural history with the anthropological analysis of the functional and the symbolic—it seems to me—allows us to distinguish German historians' "history from above" and "history from below."

Seen from above, anti-partisan action had four major periods: during the second half of 1941, the Germans were content to control the main roads of the invaded regions, filtering the floods of refugees and fleeing soldiers, and systematically executing the latter as partisans. In reaction, these fleeing soldiers and units retrenched in hard-to-reach territories, where they formed the nuclei of partisan groups. Starting in January 1942, the partisan movement took form and the Germans began sweep operations, forming vast nets in which the hunt units attempted to catch the partisan groups, while almost systematically executing the populations. In the summer of 1942, these operations were rationalized, combining the preceding objectives with economic considerations—capture of agricultural products and labor. Starting in 1944, finally, the Germans changed strategy and recomposed the entire population of these territories. Deporting it, they replaced it by armed villages populated by collaborators, sometimes from ethnic minorities of the Caucasus, sometimes—this was the case in certain sectors of western Ukraine—by *volkdeutsch* minorities from Baltic countries, the Volga, or Bessarabia. Anti-partisan combat now resembled an enormous game of ethnic dominos.

Historical anthropology thus allows us to distinguish classic historiography of the military practices of the Nazi state and *Täterforschung*, the study of behavior on the ground. It allows us to understand that down below, for the actors on the ground, the sweep operations were at once a hunt for partisans and the penning and slaughter of civilian populations, and that they constituted, seen from above, for the Nazi hierarchy, an instrument of mobilization in the service of the war effort, but also, more deeply, the remodeling of a Europe in need of Germanization. The hunter, omnipresent when seen from below, was doubled above by the engineer—social, statistical, demographic, sociological, and racial.

Notes

Introduction

1. Leonard V. Smith, *Between Mutiny and Obedience: The Case of the French Fifth Infantry Division during World War I* (Princeton, Princeton University Press, 1994). Christopher Browning, *Des hommes ordinaires, le 101e bataillon de police et la Solution finale en Pologne* (Paris: Les Belles Lettres, 1994).

2. For a quick preliminary approach, see Hellmuth Auerbach, "Die Einheit Dirlewanger," in *Vierteljahrshefte für Zeitgeschichte (VfZ)* 10 (1962): 251–263.

3. French L. MacLean, *The Cruel Hunters: SS-Sonderkommando Dirlewanger Hitler's Most Notorious Antipartisan Unit* (Atglen: Schiffer Military History, 1998).

4. Pioneers in this field, Jean-Jacques Becker, Stéphane Audoin-Rouzeau, eds., *Les Sociétés européennes et la Guerre de 1914–1918* (Paris: Université de Paris-X, Armand Colin, 1990); Gerd Krumeich, Gerhard Hirschfeld (eds.), "Keiner fühlt sich hier mehr als Mensch . . . " *Erlebnis und Wirkung des Ersten Weltkrieg* (Frankfurt: Fischer, 1996); Gerd Krumeich, Dieter Langewiesche, Hans Peter Ullmann, Gerhard Hirschfeld (eds.), *Kriegserfahrungen. Studien zur Sozial- und Mentalitätsgeschichte des Ersten Weltkriegs* (Essen: Klartext, 1997).

5. We cite as preliminary suggestions Stéphane Audoin-Rouzeau, *Cinq deuils de guerre 1914–1918* (Paris: Noêsis, 2001) for mourning; for civilians during the Great War, Annette Becker, *Oubliés de la Grande Guerre. Humanitaire et culture de guerre*

1914–1918. Populations occupées, déportés civils, prisonniers de guerre (Paris: Noêsis, 1998); Christian Ingrao, Nicolas Beaupré (eds.) "Marginaux, marginalités, marginalisation en Grande Guerre," special dossier in *14–18. Aujourd'hui. Today. Heute, 4,* 2000. For a full biography, see Stéphane Audoin-Rouzeau, Anne Duménil, Christian Ingrao, Henry Rousso, "Les sociétés, la guerre et la paix, Europe, Russie puis URSS, Etats-Unis, Japon 1911–1946. Bibliographie" in *Historiens et Géographes* 388 (July–September 2003).

6. We will limit ourselves here to mentioning Stéphane Audoin-Rouzeau, Annette Becker, Christian Ingrao, Henry Rousso (dir.), *La Violence de guerre. Approches comparées des deux conflits mondiaux* (Brussels: Complexe, 2002); Bruno Thoss and Hans-Erich Volkmann, ed., *Erster Weltkrieg—Zweiter Weltkrieg: ein Vergleich. Krieg, Kriegserlebnis, Kriegserfahrung in Deutschland* (Paderborn: Schöningh, 2002). For other bibliographical information, cf. Audoin-Rouzeau *et al.*, "Les sociétés, la guerre, la paix."

7. For this concept, see Annette Becker and Stéphane Audoin-Rouzeau, "Violence et consentement. La 'Culture de guerre' du premier conflit mondial," in Jean-Pierre Rioux and Jean-François Sirinelli, *Pour une histoire culturelle* (Paris: Seuil, 1996).

8. This can be seen via the example of the Thirty Years War, for example, where, although without using the concept of a culture of war, all the advances in terms of use of archives described here are employed. Benigna von Krusenstjern and Hans Medick (dir.), *Zwischen Alltag und Katastroph. Der Dreissigjährige Krieg aus der Nähe* (Göttingen: Vandenhoeck und Rupprecht, 1999).

9. On this subject see Sophie Delaporte, *Gueules cassées: les blessés de la France pendant la Grande Guerre* (Paris: Noêsis, 2001); Sabine Kienitz, "Quelle place pour les héros mutilés? Les invalides de guerre entre intégration et exclusion," *14–18. Aujourd'hui. Today. Heute*, 4 (2001). Paul Frederick Lerner, *Hysterical Men: War, Psychiatry and the Politics of Trauma in Germany 1890–1930* (Ithaca: Cornell University Press, 2003); for the Italian case, let us mention Bruna Bianchi, *La follia e la*

fuga: nevrosi di guerra, diserzione e disobbedenzia nell'esercito italiano (1915–1918) (Rome: Bulzoni, 2001), which we have not consulted.

10. Victor Davis Hanson, *Le Modèle occidental de la guerre* (Paris: Les Belles Lettres, 1990); Victor Davis Hanson, *Carnage et Culture. Les grandes batailles qui ont fait l'Occident* (Paris: Flammarion, 2002). Stéphane Audoin-Rouzeau, "Au coeur de la violence de guerre: la violence du champ de bataille durant les deux conflits mondiaux," in Stéphane Audoin-Rouzeau *et al.*, *La Violence de guerre*.

11. So an author like Christian Gerlach unconsciously condemns this type of analysis, preemptively invalidating it in these words: "We have refused to describe in detail these massacres and their cruelty. Their sequence is always the same, and to repeat them adds little to our knowledge," while quoting immediately afterwards a source—Walter Mattner's letter to his wife—that is supremely revelatory of the gestural language of violence and of the psychic mechanisms that make it possible. Cf. Christian Gerlach, *Kalkulierte Morde. Die deutsche Wirtschafts- und Vernichtungspolitik in Weissrusland* (Hambourg: Hamburger Edition, 1999), p. 588, p. 589 for Mattner's text, analyzed in Christian Ingrao, "Violence de guerre, violence génocide. Les pratiques d'agression des *Einsatzgruppen* en Russie," in Stéphane Audoin-Rouzeau *et al.*, *La Violence de guerre*. This remark, obviously, does not reflect on the qualities of Christian Gerlach's book, without which the present work would probably never have seen the light of day.

12. We think here of the work of Olivier Christin, *Une révolution symbolique. L'iconoclasme huguenot et la reconstruction catholique* (Paris: Les éditions de Minuit, 1991); Alphonse Dupront, *Le Mythe de la croisade* (Paris: NRF Gallimard, 1997); and Denis Crouzet, *Les Guerriers de Dieu. La violence au temps des troubles de religion* (Paris: Champs Vallon, 1990).

13. See Stéphane Audoin-Rouzeau, "Au coeur du champ de bataille"; and the pioneering study of John Dower, *War without Mercy. Race and Power in the Pacific War* (New York, Pantheon Books, 1987), on the Pacific Front. In particular, Denis Crouset, *Les*

Guerriers de Dieu. Among others Philippe Descola, "Des proies bienveillantes. Le traitement du gibier dans la chasse amazonienne," in Françoise Héritier, ed., *De la violence*, pp. 20–44; Lucien Scubla, "La proie et son ombre. Traitement rituel et figures symboliques de la relation prédateur/proie chronique," in *L'Homme. Revue française d'anthropologie* 155 (July–September 1999): 277–286. Christian Ingrao, "Les Intellectuels du service de renseignements de la SS 1900–1945," (thesis, Amiens, 2001); for a first published approach, see Christian Ingrao, "Une anthropologie du massacre? Le cas des *Einsatzgruppen* en Russie 1941–1944," in David El Kentz (ed.) *Histoire du massacre* (Paris, Gallimard, 2006). Cf. essentially Allan Kramer and John Horne, *German Atrocities 1914. History of a Denial* (London, New Haven: Yale University Press, 2001). On the relationship between memory of the partisans and Nazi violence, C. Ingrao, "Culture de guerre, imaginaire nazi, violence génocide. Le cas des cadres du SD," *Revue d'histoire moderne et contemporaine*, special number under the direction of Jean Solchany: "La violence nazie," 47-2 (April 2000).

14. On the imposition of forced labor on Jews in the Lublin district and the construction of transportation and military infrastructure in the region by the local SSPF, Odilo Globocnik, see Dieter Pohl, *Nationalsozialistische Judenverfolgung in Ostgalizien 1941–1944: Organisation und Durchführung eines staatlichen Massenverbrechens* (Munich: Oldenburg Verlag, 1996); Thomas Sandkühler, "Endlösung" in *Galizien. Der Judenmord in Ostpolen und die Rettungsinitiativen von Berthold Beitz 1941–1944* (Bonn: Dietz, 1996).

15. On these large-scale sweep operations in Belarus, see Gerlach, *Kalkulierte Morde*, pp. 859–1055.

16. Bertrand Hell, *Le Sang noir. Chasse et mythe du sauvage en Europe* (Paris: Flammarion, 1994).

17. On blood in the Nazi imagination, see Cornelia Essner and Edouard Conte, *La Quête de la Race. Une anthropologie du nazisme* (Paris: Hachette, 1995).

18. There are no fewer than four archival centres in Berlin: the Berlin-Lichterfelde Federal Archives (henceforth BABL), holding

state and military documentation and thus the SS collection [NS-19: Himmler's general staff; R-70 (SU): police units and SS in the USSR; R-20: Plenipotentiary for anti-partisan action; R-19: Central bureau of uniformed police; R-58: Main security office]. The second collection is constituted by the centralized Nazi documentation established by the STASI during its investigations on former Nazi war criminals in the Federal Republic of Germany, situated in Dahlwitz- Hoppegarten (henceforth BADH), filed by name. The third collection is the three million personnel files on SS officers preserved in Zehlendorf, a plush Berlin suburb, consultable since 1998 in Lichterfelde (henceforth BAAZ). The fourth and last Berlin collection is that of the STASI, preserved in the center of Berlin, by the *Bundesbeauftragte für die Stasi-Unterlagen*, federal delegation for STASI documentation, henceforth BStU, which preserves sources from the STASI itself and from East German judicial institutions. At Freiburg, there are federal military archives: *Bundesarchiv-Militärarchiv*, henceforth BA-MA.

19. Henceforth USHMM, with American reference, as well as the original collection, reference, and pagination from the Eastern European archives.

20. *Archywum Glownye Badania Kommissja Zbrodni Hitlerowsky* (henceforth AGKBZH): Commission of Investigation of Hitlerian Crimes in Poland, consulted at the Ministry of Justice in Warsaw, and since transferred to the Institute for National Memory (IPN).

21. Testimony of SS Investigating Judge Konrad Morgen, StA Nuremberg, Nur. Dok. (documents of Nuremberg Trials) NO 1928 and NO 5742, copies in ZStL, 8 AR-Z 28/62 (Case of Dirlewanger and others, Lublin), volume 2 for NO 1928 and volume 6 for NO 5742.

22. We will return to this in the last chapter. For the attitude of the members of the *Einsatzgruppen* on trial, see Ingrao, "Les Intellectuels du service de renseignements SS."

23. For Operation Reinhard, see Pohl, *Nationalsozialistische Judenverfolgung in Ostgalizien*; Sandkühler, "Endlösung" in *Galizien*; Yitzhak Arad, *Belzec, Sobibor, Treblinka. The Operation*

Reinhard Death Camps (Bloomington: Indiana University Press, 1987).

24. Filed under number ZStL, 8 AR-Z 28/62 (Case of Dirlewanger and others, Lublin).

25. Filed under reference StA Hanovre 2Js 460/60 (Case of Feiertag, Hunks and the brothers Zulski).

26. Letter from Dirlewanger to Himmler of 7/10/1944 and reply from Gottlob Berger to Dirlewanger of 15/10, with note from Himmler's head of general staff for personnel, all in BABL, NS 3/401.

27. Hans Peter Klausch, *Antifaschisten in SS-Uniform. Schicksal und Widerstand politischen KZ-Häftlinge, zuchthaus- und Wehrmacht strafgefangenen in der SS-Sonderbrigade Dirlewanger* (Bremen: Edition Temmen, 1993). For the preceding, see particularly pp. 140–141.

28. On the Friedensforschung, see Nicolas Beaupré, Anne Duménil, Christian Ingrao, "Introduction," in the same authors' (dir.), *Expériences de guerre. L'Etat, les hommes, la violence en Europe, 1914–1946* (Paris: Agnès Viénot éditions, 2003).

29. On this subject, and representative of this interpretation, Annette Becker and Stéphane Audoin-Rouzeau, *14–18. Retrouver la guerre* (Paris: Gallimard, 2000).

30. Among them see Rémy Cazals and Frédéric Rousseau, *14–18, le cri d'une generation* (Toulouse: Privat, 2001).

31. This is Hans Peter Klausch's thesis in *Antifaschisten*, 32. The black uniform was theoretical. They never wore the SS runes, and their field uniforms were grey-green, as were those of the rest of the Waffen-SS. They were always separated from the latter by insignia, even if their ranks and assignments were restricted to the SS.

1. The History of a Brigade

1. Cf. testimony of Gerhard Hellkamp, 19/10/62, ZStL, 8 AR-Z 28/62 (Case of Dirlewanger and others, Lublin), vol. 2, folios 401–410, here 401-402, and Johannes Maas, 12/10/62, ibid., folios 395–400, here 395–396.

2. Correspondence in BABL, R-3001 (alt R-22)/1008.

3. Other testimonies from the first recruits date this as November 1940, cf. examination of Karl Vieregge, 10/10/62, ZStL, 8 AR-Z 28/62 (Case of Dirlewanger and others, Lublin), vol. 2, folios 378–383, here folio 379.

4. Id., folios 379–380.

5. On this subject, most recently, see Christopher Browning, *Die Entfesselung der "Endlösung". Nationalsozialistische Judenpolitik 1939–1942* (Berlin: Propyläen Verlag, 2003), pp. 148–172.

6. On this subject, first see Dieter Pohl, *Von der "Judenpolitik" zum Judenmord. Der Distrikt Lublin des Generalgouvernement. 1939–1944* (Frankfurt: Peter Lang, 1993) and Bogdan Musial, *Deutsche Zivilverwaltung und Judenverfolgung im Generalgouvernement: Eine Fallstudie zum Distrikt Lublin* (Wiesbaden: Harassowitz, 2000). On Germanization, particularly in the Zamosc region, see, in French, Cornelia Essner and Edouard Conte, *La Quête de la Race. Une anthropologie du nazisme* (Paris: Hachette, 1995).

7. Examination of Berger, 21/5/48, Nur. Proz. US Government vs. Berger et alii, fall XI, p. 6,137. See also Klausch, *Antifaschisten*, p. 46.

8. Peter Erretskamp, one of the first members of the commando, recalls only this element of the commando's activity. Cf. Examination of Peter Erretskamp, 11/10/62, ZStL, 8 AR-Z 28/62 (Case of Dirlewanger and others, Lublin), vol. 2, folios 384–394, here folio 387. We must not forget that this represents an easy defense strategy during the hearing in progress.

9. We must be on our guard here, this activity appearing to the former commando members as the most banal, the least incriminating, and the most speakable.

10. We may extend this analysis to numerous other SS and General Government police force documents, particularly in Galicia at this time. See for example the final report of the Lemberg SSPF, Katzmann, on "The Final Solution of the Jewish Question in the Lemberg District," in which spoils taken and photographs of "bunkers" built by Jews attempting to escape massacre filled this type of function. Cf. BABL, R-70 (P)/205.

11. Cf. on this subject, Browning, *Entfesselung*, pp. 173–250, and Aly, *Endlösung*.

12. Report by Dirlewanger to SSPF Globocnik, 10/10/1941, USHMM, RG 15.007 M., reels 51 and 52, photocopies of AGKBZH 362/363, no folio number.

13. See the documentation collected by the Sicherheitspolizei and by the SS instructing magistrate in the course of investigating malversations and multiple acts of violence in USHMM, RG-15.007 M. (AGKBZH 362/363), rolls 51 and 52 : [Penal Affairs: Case of Dirlewanger] ; see also USHMM, RG-15.034 M (AGKBZH 185/161), roll 5 [KdS Lublin]. Finally see, for another collection of documents relating to investigations of the unit in the district ZStL, 502 AR-Z 27/73 (Sonderband I: Case of Dirlewanger), vol. 489: a collection of photographs, in very small format and of unknown origin, differing from the two collections of documentation mentioned above. We will return to these judicial episodes in detail in the following chapters.

14. Cf. Order SSFHA Kommandoamt, 1c, of 29/1/1942, which places the Dirlewanger commando under Himmler's general staff for operations, IfZ, MA 329.

15. Globocnik, daily general orders, 22/3/42 in USHMM, RG-15.034 M. (AGKBZH 185/165), roll 6: KdS Lublin. The rest of the collection shows that aside from this cut and dried praise, Globocnik did all in his power to send the commando away.

16. It would seem that the general staff then tried to dissolve the unit and to integrate it into the cavalry brigades that were its spearhead. Cf. Bernd Böll, "Chatyn," in Gerd R. Ueberschär, *Orte des Grauens. Verbrechen im Zweiten Weltkrieg*, (Darmstadt: Primus Verlag, 2003), pp. 19–29, here p. 21.

17. The radio communications concerning men and materiel, as well as their transportation to Belarus, are well documented in BAMA, RS 3-36/11.

18. Cf. on this subject, Gerlach, *Kalkulierte Morde*, pp. 94–111 for the agrarian policy of the occupying forces.

19. Gerlach, *Kalkulierte Morde*, pp. 860–870, here p. 861.

20. Gerlach, *Kalkulierte Morde*, pp. 870–881 for the initial tactics.

21. Cf. on this subject, Gerlach, *Kalkulierte Morde*, p. 885 et seq.

22. Calculations based on summary table in Gerlach, *Kalkulierte Morde*, pp. 899–904, to which we added a few operations not mentioned, such as Regatta, Lenz-Süd, or Föhn, in which the unit's participation has been verified.

23. Proposal for awarding the *Deutsche Kreuz in Gold* to Oskar Dirlewanger, 9/8/43, signed by von Gottberg, IfZ, NO-2923. See also BAAZ, SSO Dirlewanger, particularly folios 4–10.

24. BAAZ, SSO Dirlewanger, folio 5.

25. As it happened, von dem Bach-Zelewsky could not have signed this order personally: he was sick and constantly absent at this period. It must have been his adjutants, Schimana and Gottberg, who supervised the procedure.

26. Letter from HSSPF Central Russia to Kommandostab RFSS, 23/3/42, IfZ, Fa-146 (Special Dossier on Dirlewanger), no folio number.

27. Dirlewanger Commando Activity Report for May 1942, BAMA, SF-02/31684, no folio number. The men perform road work May 7–11 and May 13–24.

28. *Sonderkommando* Activity Report, 27/5/1942, BAMA, SF-02/31684, no folio number. For the unit's use of explosive bullets: Report by the Ukrainian company of the unit on an accident causing the death of one of its members, hit in the abdomen by an explosive bullet fired by a man of the company, BAMA, RS 3-36/20.

29. Cf. Operation Report of SS-Oschaf. Feiertag for the week of 25 to 31/5/1942, 31/5/1942, BAMA, SF-02/31684 [Film sammlung], no folio number.

30. Dirlewanger medal proposal, IfZ, NO-2923, folio 6. See also Gerlach, *Kalkulierte Morde*, p. 899. Christian Gerlach describes the attack on the German policemen as subsequent to the operation, contradicting in this Hans Peter Klausch and the document presented here. Cf. Gerlach, *Kalkulierte Morde*, p. 920. The fact that the unit was transferred overnight from Orscha to the Mogilev-Bobrouïsk railroad supports Klausch's interpretation. War Journal of Erich von dem Bach-Zelewsky (HSSPF Central Russia), entry of 16/6/1942, BABL, R-20/45b, folio 39.

31. Von dem Bach Journal, entry of 17/6/1942. Cf. previous note.

32. Cf. von dem Bach Journal, entry of 11/7/1942, quoted by Hannes Heer, "Die Logik des Vernichtungskriegs. Wehrmacht und *Partisanenbekämpfung*," in his *Tote Zonen. Die deutsche Wehrmacht an der Ostfront* (Hamburg, Hamburger Edition, 1999), pp. 41–79, here p. 70.

33. Dirlewanger medal proposal, IfZ, NO-2923, folios 7 and 14.

34. 286th Security Division, Combat Group Adler, Final Report on Operation Adler, 8/8/1942, BAMA, SF-02/31684, no folio number.

35. Final Report on Operation Adler, annex.

36. The Sipo general staff journal doesn't mention the unit's participation. BABL, R-70 (SU)/16. The reasons adduced for granting a medal to Dirlewanger, IfZ, NO-2923, folio 8, don't mention the operation.

37. Numerous documents, particularly the Minutes of the Meyer-Mahrndorff Examination, 15/9/1942, USHMM, RG-15.007 M (AGKBZH 362/633), roll 52, folios 65–66, as well as combat reports and letter from Dirlewanger sent to Gottlob Berger, dated September 8, 9, and 10, 1942, ibid., folios 58, 59, 62.

38. Letter from Berger to Himmler, 3/10/42, IfZ, Fa-146, no folio number.

39. This is the total reported by Oskar Dirlewanger a year later.

40. As of November 11, 1942 it was designated as Special Battalion Dirlewanger: cf. Message von dem Bach-Zelewsky to Himmler of that day, quoted in von dem Bach-Zelewsky Journal, entry of 11/11/42, BABL, R-20/45b, folio 59.

41. Raul Hilberg, *La Destruction des Juifs d'Europe* (Paris: Folio-Gallimard, 1988); Jürgen Matthäus, "'Reibungslos und planmässig'. Die zweite Welle der Judenvernichtung im Generalkommissariat Weissruthenien (1942–1944)," in *Jahrbuch für Antisemitismusforschung* 4 (1995): 254–274.

42. Execution as described in Hornung: examination of Karl von der Goltz, 5/4/60, StA Hambourg, 147 Js 11/71U (KdS Minsk: examinations in alphabetical order, G-J), Sonderband II, folio 6. See also Gerlach, *Kalkulierte Morde*.

43. "Sumpffieber" order of execution, signed HSSPF North, ZStL, 202 AR-Z 52/59 (HSSPF Russland Mitte: Beweismittel Akten),

vol. 3/2; KTB of the Einsatzstabs Minsk BABL, R-70 (SU)/16; Gerlach, *Kalkulierte Morde*, p. 703.

44. Testimony of Hazkel Kopelowitsch 21/10/1970, ZStL, 202 ARZ 5/1960 (Case of Förster et alii, KdS Aussenstelle Wilejka), vol. 42, folios 8679–8682 and Ilja Wilenskij, 21/10/70, ibid., folios 8683–8685, here folios 8684–8685.

45. The unit in question here is a commando of the KdS Minsk, which provide'd commandos of interrogation officials to the unit. Cf. examination of Artur Wilke of 8, 15, 30/8/1961, StA Hamburg, 147 Js 11/71U (KdS Minsk: examinations in alphabetical order, T-Z), Sonderband 5. SS officer, head of the Minsk anti-partisan center, Artur Wilke was responsible for the executions in Slusk and often worked with Dirlewanger.

46. For all these movements, cf. proposal for awarding the DKG to Oskar Dirlewanger, 9/8/1943, signed von Gottberg, IfZ, NO-2923, folios 8–9.

47. The term used is *Flintenweiber*, "riflewomen."

48. Message from von dem Bach to Himmler, 12/11/1942, quoted in von dem Bach Journal, BABL, R-20/45b, folio 59.

49. Gerlach, *Kalkulierte Morde*, p. 907.

50. Summary table in Gerlach, *Kalkulierte Morde*, pp. 899–904.

51. KTB Einsatzstabs Minsk, 24/9/1942, BABL, R-70 (SU)/16. For conclusions, see Gerlach, *Kalkulierte Morde*, p. 907.

52. One of the operations even was named Fritz as a tribute to Sauckel, Gerlach, *Kalkulierte Morde*, p. 907; Intervention Order for Operation Fritz, in StA Hamburg, 147 Js 11/71U, Sonderband 5, no folio number.

53. Order from von Gottberg, 1/8/1943, IfZ, Fb-85/2, folios 71–77, here folio 71.

54. Gerlach, *Kalkulierte Morde*, p. 1,015–1,017.

55. Cf. proposal for awarding the DKG to Oskar Dirlewanger, 9/8/43, signed von Gottberg, IfZ, NO-2923, folio 10.

56. Morning Report of 30/5/1943, BAMA, RS 3-36/6.

57. Final Report for Operation Cottbus, signed von Gottberg, 28/6/1943, BAMA, RH 26-286/9. See also Gerlach, *Kalkulierte Morde*, p. 969; Klausch, *Antifaschisten*, p. 66.

58. Radio message announcing the death of Kube and the state of emergency in Minsk, 22/9/1943, BAMA, RS 3-36/7, no folio number.

59. Situation Report of 15/10/1943 to Rosenberg, signed Gentz, IfZ, MA249, no folio number, here pp. 4-5 of the report.

60. Letter, Rosenberg to von Gottberg, 24/6/1943, BABL, R-6/492, folio 53, quoted by Gerlach, *Kalkulierte Morde*, p. 162.

61. Order by Himmler, 28/3/1943, BABL, NS-19/2443.

62. On the Unruh Commission, cf. Bernhard R. Kroener, "'General Heldenklau'. Die 'Unruh-Kommission' im Strudel polykratischer Desorganisation (1942–1944)," in: Ernst Willi Hansen, Gerhard Schreiber, Bernd Wegner (dir.), *Politischer Wandel, organisierte Gewalt und nationale Sicherheit. Beiträge zur neueren Geschichte Deutschlands und Frankreichs. Festschrift für Klaus-Jürgen Müller* (Munich: Oldenburg, 1995), pp. 269–285.

63. Letter, von Unruh to the Wehrmacht Commander in Chief for the General Government, 13/5/1943, IfZ, MA300, folio 4044.

64. Letter, Dirlewanger to Berger, 8/6/43, BAMA, RS 3-36/10.

65. Lists of prisoners specifying origin and police record in BABL, NS-31/257.

66. Radio message of 30/10/1943, signed Glücks, BAMA, RS 3-36/1 [Dirlewanger, administrative and other papers], no folio number.

67. On executions in the unit upon arrival of the contingent: Examination of Franz P., 22/9/1946, Nur. Dok. NO-887; see also Examination of Peter Erretkamp, 24/7/1962: he speaks of two executions, including that of a man guilty of sexual abuse of a Russian child, in ZStL, 502 AR-Z 27/73 (Sonderband IV), volume 492, folios 470–479; cf. also Vern. Karl R. Engel, op. cit., folios 34–44. For an example of punishment following the arrival of the new contingent: Battalion Order 12, signed Dirlewanger, 13/8/1942, BAMA, RS 3-36/7, no folio number.

68. SSFHA Order, 10/8/1943, IfZ, Fa-156, folios 140–141.

69. Letter, Dirlewanger to Berger, 8/6/1943, BAMA, RS 3-36/10, no folio number.

70. Correspondence, RFSS to SSFHA, September 3, 1943, with attached copies of agreements and their circulation within relevant institutions, BAMA, RS 3-36/10, no folio number.

71. *Erfahrungsberichte* Operation Günther, 14/7/1943, BAMA, RS 3-36/6, no folio number.

72. Ibid., p. 1.

73. Handwritten, undated totals of the operation in BAMA, RS 3-36/6, no folio number. Christian Gerlach, from the same source, microfilmed and consulted in Potsdam, indicates 3,993 dead, in *Kalkulierte Morde*, p. 902.

74. Figures and calculation derived from a series of situation and personnel reports of the 1st company of the battalion, seventeen reports over the course of April 20–July 12, in BAMA, RS 3-36/15.

75. One of the operations was even named Fritz as a tribute to Sauckel, Gerlach, *Kalkulierte Morde*, p. 907; Intervention Order for Operation Fritz, in StA Hamburg, 147 Js 11/71U, Sonderband 5, no folio number.

76. Daily radio reports of the battalion, 4 and 5/8/1943, BAMA, RS 3-36/18.

77. Combat Report for Operation Hermann, 18/8/1943, BAMA, RS 3-36/7, no folio number. The total must be qualified: the group Dirlewanger directed was made up of the full battalion, 656 men, plus the 595 men of the Kreikenbom Special Commando, made up of *Schutzmannschaft-Männer* and policemen. Even if the Kreikenbom group doesn't mention losses in its own combat report, it is possible that the losses reported by Dirlewanger occurred over the two units he commanded.

78. Ibid., folio 3.

79. Radio message, Dirlewanger to Berger, 5/8/1943, 8 h 20–23, BAMA, RS 3-36/18, no folio number.

80. Daily radio reports in BAMA, RS 3-36/1, no folio numbers.

81. Order, SSPF Minsk, signed von Gottberg, 3/12/1943, IfZ, Fa-156, folio 142.

82. Fourteen thousand men, divided in 17 brigades, according to the information available to anti-partisan units. Report on the Enemy, 11/4/1943, BAMA, RS 3-36/19.

83. Order of engagement, signed von Gottberg, 11/4/1944, pp. 1 and 3, BAMA, RS 3-36/19.

84. *Kampfgruppe* von Gottberg, "Results of Frühlingsfest up to and including 12/5/1944," BAMA RH 19-II/244, folios 48 et seq., quoted by Gerlach, *Kalkulierte Morde*, p. 906.

85. Handwritten list of killed and wounded sent 11/5/1944, BAMA, RS 3-36/19, no folio number.

86. Cf. Essner and Conte, *La Quête de la Race*.

87. For all this, see the very enlightening presentation of Gerlach, *Kalkulierte Morde*, pp. 1,036–1,054.

88. Radio message, Dirlewanger to head of Berger's general staff, 20/5/1944, and radio message of the same day to HSSPF Central Russia, BAMA, RS 3-36/19.

89. Cf., for instance, radio message of the SS official for economic and construction affairs, sent to "Flora," the code name of a detachment of the Sonderregiment assigned to this work, 26/5/1944, BAMA, RS 3-36/19.

90. Letter, Dirlewanger to SSFHA, 19/3/1944, BABL, NS-19/1.

91. Klausch, *Antifaschisten*, p. 94.

92. For poachers, figures quoted derived from daily reports of July 1943, a few days before the enrollment of the first concentration camp prisoners, BAMA, RS 3-36/15; for prisoners, addition of the figure for the first enrollment of July 1943 (Lists of prisoners specifying origin and police record in BABL, NS-31/257) and of the 800 prisoners of the first semester of 1944 (Order of Himmler, 19/2/1944, BABL, NS-19/1); for SS transferred for disciplinary reasons, see preceding note. See Klausch, *Antifaschisten*, p. 98, for the estimation of combat troops.

93. Gerlach, *Kalkulierte Morde*, p. 868.

94. For an outline of this offensive, Richard Overy, *Russia's War* (London: Penguin, 1997), pp. 241–244.

95. It's difficult to produce an exact figure for the unit's victims. It left its own figure—15,000 killed—for its first year of activity, which was not its most murderous, given that its largest operations—Cottbus, Hornung, Erntefest, Draufgänger—came in its second year. It seems reasonable to give, as a minimum figure, the original figure multiplied by two and perhaps a hundred villages burned; nevertheless, we must insist that this figure is a guess.

96. Cf. Notice of summary of information gathered on Special Unit Dirlewanger by the Flensburg prosecutor's office during the investigation of the Warsaw uprising, ZStL, 502 AR-Z 27/73 (Sonderband II: Dirlewanger), vol. 490, folios 127–196, here folio 150.

97. On all this, Beevor, op. cit., pp. 244–246.

98. KTB 9th Army, entry of 6/8/1944, BAMA, RH-20-9/205.

99. Examination of Karl Vieregge, 30/11/61, ZStL, 502 AR-Z 27/73 (Sonderband IV: examinations of former brigade members [Warsaw uprising]), vol. 492, folios 74–86, here 81.

100. Notice Flensburg Prosecutor's Office, ZStL, 502 AR-Z 27/73 (Sonderband II: Dirlewanger), vol. 490, folios 127–195, here folios 174 et seq. For the date of the end of their stay, Examination of Joanna K. 14/3/1947, ZStL, 502 AR-Z 27/73 (Sonderband II: Dirlewanger), vol. 492. Joanna K. was one of the hospital nurses. She had to act as Dirlewanger's interpreter, cf. for this Klausch, *Antifaschisten*, p. 116.

101. Jerzy Kirschmayer, *Powstanie Warszawaskie*, Warsaw, 1959, p. 245, quoted by Klausch, *Antifaschisten*, pp. 120 and 453.

102. This calculation represents a minimum, since when the prosecutors identified transports of reinforcements arrived in Warsaw without being able to estimate the number of men included, I didn't count them in the estimation. Notice Flensburg Prosecutor's Office, Notice Flensburg Prosecutor, ZStL, 502 AR-Z 27/73 (Sonderband II: Dirlewanger), vol. 490, folios 127–195, here folios 150–154 et seq.

103. Figure given by Klausch, *Antifaschisten*, p. 111.

104. Press notice in BAAZ, SSO Dirlewanger, no folio number.

105. On the relationship between Nazi Germany and Slovakia, the latest reference to consult is Tatjana Tönsmeyer's thesis, *Das Dritte Reich und die Slowakei. Politischer Alltag zwischen Kooperation und Eigensinn* (Paderborn: Schöning Verlag, 2004). The book only touches briefly on the uprising.

106. Klausch, *Antifaschisten*, p. 130, quoting Wolfgang Venohr, *Aufstand für die Tschekoslowakei. Der Slowakische Freiheitskampf* (Hamburg: Christian Wegner, 1969), pp. 259–272.

107. Klausch, *Antifaschisten*, p. 131.

108. Radio message AOK 9, 9/10/1944, BAMA, RH 20-9/217. See also Klausch, *Antifaschisten*, p. 123.

109. Letter, Dirlewanger to Himmler, 7/10/1944, BABL, NS-3/401.

110. Ibid.

111. Letter, Wolff to Berger, 15/10/1944, BABL, NS-3/401.

112. On all this, see Klausch, *Antifaschisten*, pp. 178–183 and 184–188.

113. Affidavit, Bruno Wille, 28/6/1946.

114. KTB *Heeresgruppe* Süd, entry of 5/12/1944, BAMA, RH 19 V/43, folio 111.

115. KTB *Heeresgruppe* Süd, BAMA, RH 19 V/43, folio 156, also quoted by Klausch, *Antifaschisten*, p. 227.

116. Cf. for all this, KTB *Heeresgruppe* Süd, folios 111, 122, 216 to 228. On the desertion of political prisoners, to which we will return, see Klausch, *Antifaschisten*, pp. 225–271, which gives the most detailed information, though tinged with a propensity to exaggerate the importance of this desertion.

117. Krisztian Ungvary, *Die Schlacht um Budapest. 1944–1945. Stalingrad an der Donau* (Munich: Herbig, 1999).

118. Overy, *Russia's War*, pp. 257–260.

119. Ibid., pp. 263–267.

120. "Bewährungseinheiten der ehemaligen deutschen Wehrmacht," in *Mitteilungen der VVN Niedersachsen* 21 and 22, 1950. Quoted by Klausch, *Antifaschisten*, p. 312.

121. Cf. Affidavit, Bruno Wille, 28/6/1946, for the period of December 1944.

122. Calculation based on information from the archives of the German Red Cross research department (henceforth DRK-SD), file on persons carried and declarations of soldiers returned from Soviet captivity, DRK-SD, File: File on declarations of prisoners returned to Germany. DRK-SD, VML, Band WE577 et seq. (list and photographs of soldiers reported missing).

2. THE DIRLEWANGER CASE

1. On this debate, essentially structured by Daniel Goldhagen, *Les Bourreaux volontaires de Hitler. Les Allemands ordinaires et l'holocauste* (Paris: Seuil, 1997), and by the book against which Goldhagen was reacting, Christopher Browning, *Des hommes*

ordinaries, we may turn to (in French) Edouard Husson, *Une culpabilité ordinaire? Hitler, les Allemands et la Shoah* (Paris: François-Xavier de Guibert, 1997), and in German to Christopher Browning, "Die Debatte über die Täter des Holocausts," in Ulrich Herbert, ed., *Nationalsozialistische Vernichtungspolitik, 1939–1945. Neue Forschungen und Kontroversen* (Frankfurt: Fischer, 1998), pp. 148–169. See also Klaus-Michael Mallmann, "Were the Perpetrators of Genocide 'Ordinary Men' or 'Real Nazis'?: Results from Fifteen Hundred Biographies," in *Holocaust and Genocide Studies* 14, no 3 (2000), pp. 331–366, more critical towards Browning, but not espousing Goldhagen's excessively simplistic conclusions. For a recent overview of research on the actors of practices of genocidal violence, see Gerhard Paul, "Von Psychopathen, Technokraten des Terrors und 'ganz gewönhlich' Deutschen. Die Täter der Shoah im Spiegel der Forschung," in Gerhard Paul, ed., *Die Täter der Shoah. Fanatische Soldaten oder ganz normale Deutsche?* (Göttingen: Wallstein, 2002), pp. 13–92.

2. Exhumation and autopsy report, 24/10/1960, ZStL, 502 AR-Z 27/73 (Sonderband I: Case of Dirlewanger), vol. 489.

3. All his biographical data come from his SS personnel dossier, consulted at the BAAZ, as well as in copy in ZStL, 502 ARZ 27/73 (Sonderband I: Case of Dirlewanger), vol. 489.

4. Notice of the Prosecutor, "Results of investigations on the Dirlewanger Commando," undated, ZStL, 502 AR-Z 27/73, vol. 489.

5. For all this, see the questionnaire completed by Dirlewanger upon entering prison, as well as his identification record, also produced by the penitentiary administration, 28/1/1935, in ZStL, 502 AR-Z 27/73, vol. 489.

6. On the structure of the losses, see Stéphane Audoin-Rouzeau, "La violence du champ de bataille," in Stéphane Audoin-Rouzeau, Annette Becker, Christian Ingrao, Henry Rousso (dir.), *La Violence de guerre. Approches comparées des deux conflits mondiaux* (Bruxelles: Complexe, 2002).

7. Information collected in SA-*Führer* Fragebogen, March 20, 1934, certificate of the demobilization cell of the 7th Württemberg Security Division, article in the *Sangerhausener Zeitung* of

14/7/1932, and for the wounds, autopsy report of 24/11/1960, all in ZStL, 502 AR-Z 27/73 (Sonderband I: Case of Dirlewanger), vol. 489. See also Klausch, *Antifaschisten*, p. 35.

8. On this critical question and the wide circulation of this experience of psychosis on the subject of snipers, Allan Kramer and John Horne, *German Atrocities 1914. History of a Denial* (London, New Haven: Yale University Press, 2001).

9. *Allgemeine Vorschrift fuer den Stellungskrieg*, 1917, § 155, quoted by Anne Duménil, *Le Soldat allemand dans la Grande Guerre*, unpublished thesis, 2001, unpaginated copy, pp. 167–179.

10. Duménil, *Le Soldat allemand*, pp. 31–32.

11. SA officer's questionnaire, March 20, 1934, copy in ZStL, 502 AR-Z 27/73 (Sonderband I: Case of Dirlewanger), vol. 489. The type of wound received by Dirlewanger is specified only in the Proposal for Awarding the *Deutsche Kreuz in Gold* to Oskar Dirlewanger, 9/8/43, signed von Gottberg, IfZ, NO-2923.

12. On the question of edged weapons, see Stéphane Audoin-Rouzeau, "Pratiques et objets de la cruauté," in Anne Duménil, Nicolas Beaupré, Christian Ingrao (dir.), *1914–1945 : l'ère de la guerre* (Paris: Agnès Viénot Editions, 2004), *Vol. I : Violence, mobilisations, deuil 1914–1918*, et Duménil, *Le Soldat allemande*, pp. 217–220. Anne Duménil shows that in the German army, soldiers were trained to inflict infallibly mortal blows, concentrating on the head and more particularly on the eyes and the neck.

13. On all this, Duménil, *Le Soldat allemand*, 4th part, pp. 85–185 and 481–528 for the year 1918.

14. Ibid., pp. 334–335.

15. We are reminded of the Proposal for awarding the *Deutsche Kreuz in Gold* to Oskar Dirlewanger, 9/8/1943, signed von Gottberg, IfZ, NO- 2923 and of the article in the *Sangerhausener Zeitung* of 14/7/1932, in ZStL, 502 AR-Z 27/73, vol. 489, folio 40, in which he himself mentions his stiffened hand in passing.

16. Report of the University Medico-Legal Institute of Freiburg to the Ravensburg Prosecutor's Office, 24/11/1960, ZStL, 502 AR-Z 27/73, vol. 489, folios 104–110.

17. Certificate of the demobilization cell of the 7th Württemberg Security Division, 20/6/1919 and article in the *Sangerhausener Zeitung* of 14/7/1932, in ZStL, 502 AR-Z 27/73, vol. 489, folio 37.

18. See especially Vejas Gabriel Liulevicius, *War Land on the Eastern Front. Culture, National Identity and German Occupation in World War I* (Cambridge: CUP, 2000).

19. Klaus Latzel, *Deutsche Soldaten—nationalsozialistischer Krieg? Kriegserlebnis—Kriegserfahrung 1939–1945* (Paderborn: Schöning Verlag, 1998). Latzel concludes that after all racist prejudice was far less widespread during the Great War than during the Second World War.

20. Article in the *Sangerhausener Zeitung*, 14/7/1932, in ZStL, 502 AR-Z 27/73, vol. 489, folio 37.

21. Political evaluation report on Dirlewanger by the SD Oberabschnitt SW, 14/5/1938, in BABL, NS-19/1207. Copies in ZStL, 502 AR-Z 27/73 (Sonderband I: Case of Dirlewanger), vol. 489, as well as in IfZ, Fa-146.

22. For this episode, see Dirk Schumann, *Politische Gewalt in der Weimarer Republik 1918–1933. Kampf um die Strasse und Furcht vor dem Bürgerkrieg* (Essen: Klartext, 2001).

23. Ibid., pp. 127–131.

24. For all this, see Schumann, *Politische Gewalt*, as well as Gerd Krumeich, "Versailles. Der Krieg in den Köpfen," in Gerd Krumeich, ed., *Versailles 1919. Ziele—Wirkung—Wahrnehmung* (Essen: Klartext, 2001).

25. SA officer's questionnaire, March 20, 1934, and report of the SDOA SW dated 14/5/1938, copies in ZStL, 502 AR-Z 27/73 (Sonderband I: Case of Dirlewanger), vol. 489.

26. Report of the University Medico-Legal Institute of Freiburg to the Ravensburg Prosecutor's Office, 24/11/1960, ZStL, 502 AR-Z 27/73, vol. 489, folios 104–110, here folio 106.

27. *Sangerhausener Zeitung*, 14/7/1932, ZStL, 502 AR-Z 27/73, vol. 489.

28. The parallel between combat during the interwar period and anti-partisan action was drawn *a posteriori* by the leaders of anti-partisan operations in the East, cf. undated report by the BdS Riga on "Partisans and their Methods of Operation," in

which the author writes that "combat against the Spartacist uprising was nothing more nor less than anti-partisan action," in USHMM, RG-11.001 M.05, roll 74, [Osobyi Arkhiv, 504/1/2], folios 1–10 for the report, folio 4 for the quotation.

29. Richard Bessel, *Germany after the First World War* (Oxford: Clarendon, 1993); George L. Mosse, *De la Grande Guerre au totalitarisme. La brutalisation des sociétés européennes* (Paris: Hachette, 1999).

30. For this movement, see Ulrich Herbert, *Best, eine Biographische Studien über Radikalismus, Weltanschauung und Vernunft* (Bonn: Dietz, 1996) and Christian Ingrao, "Les étudiants allemands, la mémoire de la Grande Guerre et le militantisme nazi," in John Horne, ed., "Démobiliser les esprits," special number of *14–18. Aujourd'hui. Today. Heute*, no 6 (2002).

31. Friedrich Meinecke, "Der Geist der akademischen Jugend in Deutschland. Zur Erklärung der politischen Ursachen des Rathenau- Mordes (1922)," in Georg Potoski, ed., *Friedrich Meineckes politische Reden und Schriften* (Darmstadt: 1968), pp. 338–343, here p. 340. Quoted by Herbert, *Best*, p. 65.

32. For this see Jürgen Schwartz, *Studenten in der Weimarer Republik. Die deutsche Studentenschaft in der Zeit von 1918–1923 und ihre Stellung zur Politik* (Berlin: 1971), pp. 232–244.

33. See Norbert Kampe, *Studenten und "Judenfrage"* (Vandenhoeck & Ruprecht: 1988).

34. Herbert, *Best*, p. 68.

35. Vote results and participation rates given by J. H Mitgau, "Studentische Demokratie," in *Süddeutsche Akademische Stimmen, 1/3/1921, Nachrichtenblatt des DHR*, February–March 1921. Quoted by Herbert, in *Best*, p. 551, note 69.

36. For Heydrich, see Shomo Aronson, *Heydrich und die Frühgeschichte der Gestapo und des SD, 1931–1945* (Berlin: Ernst Reuter Gesellschaft, 1967). For Höhn, *Lebenslauf*, Reinhard Höhn, undated, BAAZ, SSO Höhn.

37. Oskar Dirlewanger, *Zur Kritik des Gedankens einer planmässigen Leitung der Wirtschaft*, thesis (Frankfurt: Wirtschaft- und Sozialwissenchaftliche Dissertationen, 1925).

38. For all this, see the SA officer's questionnaire and the SDOA SW report of 28/5/1940, in ZStL, 502 AR-Z 27/73, vol. 489.

39. Sangerhausener Zeitung, 14/7/1932, ZStL, 502 AR-Z 27/73, vol. 489.

40. We speak here of contemporary opinion; we will not speak of the critical judgment that an early twenty-first century Western observer might bring to bear on a work of evident shoddiness.

41. Oskar Dirlewanger, *Zur Kritik des Gedankens einer planmässigen Leitung der Wirtschaft*, thesis (Frankfurt: Wirtschaft- und Sozialwissenchaftliche Dissertationen, 1925), here pp. 6–7. This thesis appears in the files of the Staatsbibliothek de Berlin, the copy consulted bears the stamp of the Frankfurt University Library and is in ZStL, 502 AR-Z 27/73 (Sonderband I), vol. 489, annex 5.

42. For Gerhard Ritter, see the thesis of Christoph Cornelissen, *Gerhard Ritter, Geschichtswissenschaft und Politik im 20. Jahrhundert*, (Dusseldorf: Droste, 2001). For Best, cf. Ulrich Herbert, *Best*, pp. 74–75 in particular.

43. Dirlewanger, *Kritik*, p. 8.

44. For these men and their doctoral theses, see Michael Wildt, *Generation des Unbedingtes. Das Fürungskorps des Reichssicherheitshauptamtes* (Hamburg: Hamburger Edition, 2002), and Christian Ingrao, *Les Intellectuels dans le service de renseignements de la SS*, thesis, Université de Picardie, 2001.

45. Dirlewanger, *Kritik*, p. 100.

46. Ibid.

47. Memorandum "Initial Conclusions of Investigations on the Dirlewanger Special Commando," in ZStL, 502 AR-Z 27/73, vol. 489, here folio 2.

48. Report of SDOA SW, 14/5/1938, ZStL, 502 AR-Z 27/73, vol. 489.

49. Judgment of the Heilbronn Landgericht, 12/10/1936, in ibid.

50. Judgment of the Heilbronn District Court, 21/9/1934, in ibid.

51. Judgment of the Heilbronn District Court, 12/10/1936, in ibid.

52. For Murr, see his biography in Herrmann Weiss, *Biographisches Lexikon zum Dritten Reich* (Frankfurt: Fischer, 2002).

53. Letter of complaint to Himmler, signed Brandenburg, BABL, NS-19/1207.

54. Letter, Himmler to Dirlewanger, 4/8/1944, IfZ, Fa-146.

55. See the extremely voluminous investigation of Dirlewanger in AGKBZH 185/61 and 65, USHMM, RG-15.034 M., rolls 5 and 6, and AGKBZH 362/633, USHMM, RG-15.007 M., rolls 51 and 52.

56. Letter, Dirlewanger to the RFSS, 4/7/1939, and letter of the Party Chancellery to Berger, signed Victor Brack, in ZStL, 502 AR-Z 27/73, vol. 489.

57. Judgment of the Heilbronn District Court, 13/5/1937.

58. Letter, Dirlewanger to Himmler, ZStL, 502 AR-Z 27/73, vol. 489.

59. Correspondance on the investigation of Sarah Bergmann in AGKBZH 185/61, USHMM, RG-15.034 M., roll 5; letter, Berger to Dirlewanger, in AGKBZH 185/65, USHMM, RG-15. 034 M., roll 6.

60. For these efforts, see Dirlewanger's correspondence with the HSSPF for Ruthenia, Gottlob Berger, and Himmler in IfZ, Fa-146. For Dirlewanger's promotion, see the note on the results of the investigations of the Dirlewanger unit in ZStL, 502 AR-Z 27/73 (Sonderband II: Dirlewanger), vol. 490.

3. CONSENT AND CONSTRAINT

1. Examination of Oskar Henning, 5/3/1962, ZStL, 502 AR-Z 27/73 (Sonderband IV), vol. 492, folio 18.

2. Exhumation report of 24/11/1960, in ZStL, 502 AR-Z 27/73, vol. 489.

3. Examination of Paul Dorn, 4/7/1962, ZStL, 502 AR-Z 27/73 (Sonderband IV), vol. 492, folios 431–448.

4. Testimonies in ZStL, 502 AR-Z 27/73, vols. 492 and 493.

5. Helmut Heiber, *Universität unter dem Hakenkreuz* (Munich: Saur, 1991-1992).

6. Testimony of Berger before Helmut Heiber in IfZ, ZS-427/2. Cf. also examination of Berger, 29/7/1965, ZStL, 8 AR-Z 28/62, vol. 7, folios 1197–1200, in which he says that Dirlewanger had been given refuge by the grand mufti of Jerusalem.

7. Quoted by Klausch, *Antifaschisten*, p. 42. The observation, as it happens, was that of political prisoners with the same profile as the future recruits of the unit's final period.

8. Minutes of examination of Meyer-Mahrndorff, 15/9/1942, USHMM, RG-15.007 M. (AGKBZH 362/633), roll 52, folios 65–66.

9. Examination of Vieregge, November 3, 1961, ZStL, 502 ARZ 27/73 (Sonderband IV), vol. 492, folios 2–13, here folio 4.

10. Examination of Gustav Strumpf, 17/1/1962, ZStL, 502 ARZ 27/73 (Sonderband IV), vol. 492, folios 87–102.

11. Examination of Adalbert Deschner, 5/4/1962, ZStL, 502 ARZ 27/73 (Sonderband V), vol. 493, folios 61–62.

12. Numerous testimonies in ZStL, 502 AR-Z 27/73, vols. 492 and 493; cf. also testimony of Berger before Helmut Heiber in IfZ, ZS–427/2.

13. Examination of Franz Beuser, 5/2/1962, ZStL, 502 AR-Z 27/73, vol. 492, folios 184–185.

14. On the Thirty Years' War, see, for latest scholarship, Benigna von Krusenstjern and Hans Medick (dirs.), *Zwischen Alltag und Katastroph. Der Dreissigjährige Krieg aus der Nähe* (Göttingen: Vandenhoeck und Rupprecht, 1999), which reviews the problematics and particularly the practices of violence. Although only one of these soldiers dared to mention it in his presence, it is obvious that many observers, historians included, still had this model in mind when they described Dirlewanger's personality. Hans Peter Klausch himself uses the expression as a chapter title. Besides Klausch, *Antifascisten*, p. 35, which makes Dirlewanger a "Landsknecht of the counterrevolution," we may note that Artur Wilke, the head of the Minsk SD, also used the term "prototypical Landsknecht" to qualify Dirlewanger; cf. Examination of Wilke, 5/6/1974, StA Hamburg, 147 Js 11/71U, vol. 5, folios 723–749, here p. 735.

15. Cf., on this subject, testimonies on Dirlewanger's attacks in Slovakia in Klausch, *Antifaschisten*, pp. 130–131. It must be borne in mind, however, that Klausch attempts throughout his work to demonstrate Dirlewanger's tactical inefficiency and military incompetence. Even admitting a lack of sources on this point, the testimonies and the archives available to us seem nevertheless to suggest that this evolution is genuine.

16. Examination of Bruno Wille, 31/7/1947, IfZ, ZS-1638, folios 1–7, here folio 3.

17. Ibid., folio 6.

18. Affidavit, Bruno Wille, 28/6/1946.

19. 3.69 percent per year, assuming the number of executions to be even distributed over the year and the troop numbers of the unit to be stable, both assumptions obviously false.

20. Based on Jean-Noël Biraben, *Les Hommes et la Peste en France et dans les pays européens et méditerrannéens* (Paris-La Haye: Mouton, 1975–1976) and Elisabeth Carpentier, *Une ville devant la Peste. Orvieto devant la peste noire de 1348* (Brussels: De Boeck Université, 1993). Pierre Chaunu, *Eglise, culture et société. Essais sur Réforme et Contre-réforme, 1517–1720* (Paris: SEDES, 1981), p. 69, shows that a social group's adaptive limits are reached starting at a mortality of 1 percent per day—it is that point that Marseille, in 1720, stopped enshrouding its dead—and that mortality climbed to over 5 percent per day in July and August 1348 in Orvieto, at the height of the Black Plague. This rate was never reached in any battle of the total wars of the twentieth century. Cf., on this subject, Stéphane Audoin-Rouzeau, "La violence du champ de bataille," in Stéphane Audoin-Rouzeau, Annette Becker, Christian Ingrao and Henry Rousso (dirs.), *La Violence de guerre. Approches comparées des deux conflits mondiaux* (Brussels: Complexe, 2002).

21. Detailed account in Deposition of Karl Richard Engel, 24/8/1961, ZStL, 502 AR-Z 27/73, vol. 492, folios 34–44.

22. One example in Franz Pavela, examination of 22/9/1946, in IfZ, NO-887 also copied in ZStL, 502 AR-Z 27/73 (Sonderband V), vol. 493, folios 269–277.

23. Order, Dirlewanger, 24/10/1941, USHMM, RG- 15.007 M. (AGKBZH 362/633), roll 51, folios 177 et seq., also quoted in Klausch, *Antifaschisten*, p. 50.

24. Correspondence, Dirlewanger to Berger, in USHMM, RG- 15.034 M. (AGKBZH 185/61), roll 5.

25. Affidavit Konrad Morgen, 28/1/1947, IfZ, NO-1908. Hans Peter Klausch is wrong, it seems to me, to refuse to see in Morgen's testimony a proof of the sexual dimension of the unit's practices of violence in Lublin. Other testimonies, however, though their focus is Belarus, confirm that this type of criminality was part of the unit's practice. Cf. Déclaration W.B., 22/1/1946, IfZ, NO-867,

and Examination, Albin Vogel, IfZ, NO-1716, both quoted by Klausch, *Antifaschisten*, p. 87.

26. Examination of Adalbert Deschner, 5/4/1962, ZStL, 502 ARZ 27/73, vol. 493, folios 27–33.

27. Correspondence of the RFSS of 17 and 28/10/1940, BABL, R-3001 (alt R- 22) 1008, folios 237 et seq.

28. SS investigators were unable to confirm any accusation contained in the anonymous letter due to the silence of Dirlewanger's men. Final reports of the investigators in USHMM, RG- 15.007 M. roll 51, AGKBZH 362/363.

29. See, for a quick and synthetic approach, Ian Kershaw, *Hitler. Essai sur le charisme en politique* (Paris: Gallimard, "NRF essays," 1995).

30. Letter, Dirlewanger to Berger, 10/9/1942, USHMM, RG- 15.007 M. roll 51, AGKBZH 362/363, folios 62–63, here folio 63.

31. SSHA Notice of 14/8/1942, USHMM, RG-15.007 M., roll 51, AGKBZH 362/363, folios 21–34, here folio 32.

32. The four cases of killing or return to the KL for probable execution are mentioned in the list, maintained by the Ministry of Justice, of men transferred to the special unit, in BABL, R-3001 (alt R-22) 1008.

33. Daily general orders 13/8/1943, BAMA, RS 3-36/7. Cf. also Klausch, *Antifaschisten*, p. 82.

34. Testimony of Johann W., in ZStL, 502 AR-Z 27/73, vol. 492, quoted by Klausch, *Antifaschisten*, p. 109.

35. Testimony of Paul Dorn, 4/7/1962, ZStL, 502 AR-Z 27/73, vol. 492, folios 431–448.

36. Examination of Bruno Wille, 31/7/1947, IfZ, ZS-1638, folios 1–7, here folio 3.

37. Examination of Oskar Blömer, 6/1/1967, ZStL, V 117 AR 395/65, vol. 1, folios 126–131.

38. For indications of the discovery of the Ninth Army's leadership of Dirlewanger's inability to control his troops, see KTB *Heeresgruppe* Süd, BAMA, RH 19 V/43, folios 111, 122, 216 to 228.

39. For the Wehrmacht's military justice and its overwhelmingly repressive character, see Omer Bartov, *The Eastern Front, 1941–1945: German Troops and the Barbarisation of Warfare* (Oxford:

Saint Antony's-Mac Millan Series, 1985), and by the same author, *L'Armée de Hitler. Les soldats, les nazis et la guerre* (Paris: Hachette, 1999).

40. Testimony of Harald Momm, 28/5/1962, ZStL, 502 AR-Z 27/73, vol. 492. Cf. also Klausch, *Antifaschisten*, p. 134. The description of the camp beating is exactly the same as that described by Momm in Wolfgang Sofsky, *L'Organisation de la terreur* (Paris: Calmann-Lévy, 1995), pp. 274–275.

41. We can follow the premonitory symptoms, in the wake of the Bayern Projekt of the Institut fuer Zeitgeschichte, in Ian Kershaw, *L'Opinion allemande sous le nazisme* (Paris: CNRS éditions, 1995), pp. 13–20, and Ian Kershaw, *Qu'est-ce que le nazisme? Problèmes et perspectives d'interprétation* (Paris: Folio-Gallimard, 1992, 2nd edition revised in 1997), here pp. 317–321.

42. Correspondence, HSSPF Russland-Mitte of 5/7/1943, IfZ, NO-761.

43. Klausch, *Antifaschisten*, p. 100.

44. Ibid., p. 103, although he mentions that partisans often killed their German prisoners for security reasons.

45. Ibid., p. 104.

46. Let us recall that the unit lost, in all, nineteen out of 195 poachers, and perhaps a hundred (the minimum figure was forty-one in December 1943, it may have doubled between time) soldiers from other categories (SS transferred for disciplinary reasons, asocials or criminals). CF. the notes on the list of poachers sent to the unit in BABL, R-3001 (alt R-22) 1009, and the correspondence mentioning the unit's losses on 4/12/1943, in BAMA, RS 3-36/10. See also Klausch, *Antifaschisten*, pp. 68 and 88.

47. The troop numbers of the unit, particularly the wounded, the sick and those under arrest may be followed for several months, from January through March 1944, in the weekly reports in BAMA, RS 3-36/11. Over the course of these three months, there are never more than three men under arrest at a time, the equivalent of fewer than 1 percent of combat troops and fewer than 0.4 percent of total troops.

48. Menus of 11 through 20/12/1943 in BAMA, RS 3-36/1.

49. See on this subject, described as power-drunkenness, the articles of Hannes Heer, *Tote Zonen. Die Wehrmacht an der Ostfront* (Hamburg: Hamburger Edition, 1999).

50. In this sense, and as to this contractual relationship, the hierarchical organization of the *Sondereinheit* may usefully be compared to that studied in Leonard V. Smith, *Between Mutiny and Obedience*, of the Fifth French Infantry Division during the Great War.

51. Out of the unit's approximately 1,650 German recruits present in Belarus, or fewer than 0.5 percent of the total.

52. Radio messages June 1 and 5, 16 and 18, 1944, BAMA, RS 3-36/19, no folio number.

53. Result based on the number of men present after the incorporation of the first 321 prisoners in July 1943 (237 poachers and SS + 321 criminals = 558 recruits) from which we subtract the men mentioned in the report of 29/9/1943, in BABL, RS 3-36/11.

54. Reports on troop numbers of 1/4/1944 in BAMA, RS 3-36/15.

55. According to the German-Polish historian Hans von Krannhals, *Der Warschauer Aufstand 1944, Francfort, Bernhard und Graefe Verlag fuer Wehrwesen* (Frankfurt: Bernard & Graefe Verlag,1962) p. 240, and Klausch, *Antifaschisten*, p. 98, 881 men as of 1/8/1944, to which are added 1,650 soldiers from Wehrmacht detention centers and 200 criminals from the KZs. After Warsaw, troop strength is only 648 men, according to Kirschmayer, *Powstanie Warszawskie*, p. 245, quoted by Klausch, *Antifaschisten*, pp. 120 and 453.

56. Klausch, *Antifaschisten*, p. 136.

57. Klausch, *Antifaschisten*, p. 262.

58. Klausch, *Antifaschisten*, p. 309.

59. Klausch, *Antifaschisten*, p. 261.

60. Report by Bruno Meyer, undated and incomplete, quoted by Klausch, *Antifaschisten*, p. 246.

61. KTB *Heeresgruppe* Süd, entry of 10/12/1944, BAMA, RH 19 V/43, folio 156.

62. We cannot consider the "covert strike" of the German combatants in 1918 described by Wilhelm Deist, "Verdeckter Militärstreik im Kriegsjahr 1918?," in Wolfram Wette (ed.), *Der Krieg des*

kleinen Mannes. Eine Militärgeschichte von unten (Munich: Piper, 1992), pp. 146–168, as a refusal to fight, but rather as a consequence of defeat, as justly pointed out by Christoph Jahr, *Gewöhnliche Soldaten. Desertion und Deserteure im deutschen und britischen Heer 1914–1918* (Göttingen: Vandenhoeck und Rupprecht, 1998) and Duménil, *Soldat allemand.*

63. Cf. on this case, the admirable article by Nicolas Werth "Un état contre son people," in Stéphane Courtois et alii, *Le Livre noir du communisme* (Paris: Robert Laffont, 1995), as well as Nicolas Werth, in Audoin-Rouzeau et alii (dirs.), *La Violence de guerre*, and Nicolas Werth, "Soldats-paysans et déserteurs de l'Armée russe durant la Grande Guerre," in Jean-Jacques Becker, Stéphane Audoin-Rouzeau (dirs.), *Dictionnaire de la Grande Guerre* (Paris: Bayard, 2004).

64. We will return to this in the last chapter. More generally, see Christian Ingrao, "Le suicide comme sortie de guerre. Allemagne, Japon 1945," in *Annales. Histoire. Sciences sociales*: 2006.

4. POACHERS IN THE POLIS

1. Notice, Ministry of Justice, 23/3/1940, BABL, R-22/1008, folio 23.

2. Notice, Ministry of Justice, 28/3/1940, BABL, R-22/1008, folio 24 et seq.

3. Notice, Ministry of Justice to Ministerialdirektor Crohne, 5/4/1940, BABL, R-22/1008, folios 28–32, here folio 29.

4. Letter, SS *Reichsführer* to the Minister of Justice, March 29, 1940, BABL, R-22/1008, folio 23.

5. Notice, Ministry of Justice to Ministerialdirektor Crohne, 5/4/1940, BABL, R-22/1008, folios 28-3, here folios 30–31.

6. Correspondence in BABL, R-22/1008, folios 149-160: letters with nominative lists, sent particularly to Wolff.

7. For the RSHA, Correspondence of Amt V of 2/7/1942, BABL, R-22/1009, folio 3. Berger, for his part, personally selected the men for the first contingent heading to Oranienburg.

8. Notice "Specifications given by the Reichsmarschall, "24/9/1942, BABL, R-22/5015, folio 60, quoted in Klausch, *Antifaschisten*, p. 31.

9.   For the war of Secession, see the marksmen's units recruited by Hiram Berdan. See also and above all MGFA (dir.), *Handbuch zur deutschen Militärgeschichte*, vol. V, p. 168 et seq. See also the bibliographical clarifications in Klausch, *Antifaschisten*, p. 422, note 9.

10. Claus Meyer, "Geschichte der Feldjägertruppe. Teil 1," in *Deutsches Soldatenjahrbuch 1984* 32:163–168, and Klausch, *Antifaschisten*, pp. 28–29.

11. Erwin Eberl, "Graue Falken im schwarz-gelben Feld. Errinerungskizze au Bosnien und Herzegowina, als diese noch österreischich waren" in ibid., p. 334. Quoted by Klausch, *Antifaschisten*, p. 422.

12. Werner Jochmann (dir.), *Adolph Hitler, Monologe im Führerhauptaquartier* (Hamburg, 1980), entry of 28/10/1941. For all this, see Klausch, *Antifaschisten*, p. 30.

13. Jochmann, *Monologe*, entry of 20/8/1942.

14. Michel Tournier, *Le Roi des aulnes* (Paris: folio Gallimard, 1976).

15. For Goering and the hunt, see Heinrich Rubner, *Deutsche Forstgeschichte 1933–1945: Forstwirtschaft, Jagd und Umwelt im NS-Staat* (St. Katharinen: Scripta-Mercaturae-Verlag, 1997).

16. Full dossier in BABL, NS-19/3371: Himmler's correspondence, hunt invitations. I warmly thank Fabrice d'Almeida for drawing my attention to this dossier.

17. Invitation addressed to Karl Wolff, Himmler's chief of personal staff, signed Globocnik, in ibid., folio 160.

18. Spiritual Canticle of Saint Hubert, quoted by Bertrand Hell, cf. following note.

19. Bertrand Hell, *Le Sang noir*, p. 314.

20. For *Einsatzgruppen*, see Helmut Krausnick and Hans Heinrich Wilhelm, *Die Truppen des Weltanschauungskrieges: Die Einsatzgruppen der SIPO und des SD, 1938–1942* (Stuttgart: DVA, 1981); Peter Klein (ed.), *Die Einsatzgruppen in der besetzten Sowjetunion 1941–1942. Die Tätigkeits- und Lageberichte des Chefs der Sicherheitspolizei und des SD* (Berlin: Edition Hentrich, 1997); and finally Andrej Angrick, *Besatzungspolitik und Massenmord. Die Einsatzgruppe D in der südlichen Sowjetunion 1941–1943* (Hamburg: Hamburger Edition, 2003).

21. Cf. Christian Ingrao, "Pour une anthropologie historique du massacre. Le cas des *Einsatzgruppen* en Russie," in David El Kentz (ed.), *Histoire du massacre* (Paris: Gallimard, 2005); and Christian Ingrao, "Violence de guerre violence génocidaire. Le cas des *Einsatzgruppen* en Russie," in Audoin-Rouzeau et alii (dirs.), *La Violence de guerre*.

22. See, for example, the reaction of the Minsk KdS to the accusations of Commissioner General Kube in Minsk KdS Report to HSSPF Russland- Mitte, Nur. Dok NO-4317.

23. Examination of Ludwig Sparrwasser, ZStL, 202 AR-Z 96/60 (Case Sk 7a, Rapp and others), vol. 8, 5/12/1962, folios 3029–3037, here folio 3031.

24. See Ingrao, *Les Intellectuels*, third part, for the use of cruelty and its discourse in the *Einsatzgruppen*.

25. Jochmann, *Monologe*, entry of 20/8/1942.

26. Ministerialrat Joel, notice "Specifications given by the Reichsmarschall," 24/9/1942, BABL, R-22/5015, folio 60.

27. Ibid.

28. Bertrand Hell, *Le Sang noir*.

29. Bertrand Hell, *Le Sang noir,* p. 55.

30. Bertrand Hell, *Le Sang noir*, p. 101 et seq.

31. Ministerialrat Joel, "Specifications given by the Reichsmarschall," 24/9/1942, BABL, R-22/5015, folio 60.

32. Cf. Hannes Heer, "Die Logik des Vernichtungskriegs. Wehrmacht und Partisanenkampf," in Heer, *Tote Zonen*.

33. This representation was extremely common and was rooted in the experience of German soldiers in the First World War. For its circulation in the representation of soldiers, see Latzel, *Deutsche Soldaten,* and for the genesis of this representation during the Great War: Vejas Gabriel Liulevicius, *War Land on the Eastern Front: Culture, National Identity and German Occupation in World War I* (Cambridge: CUP, 2000).

34. Order, Globocnik to the KdS, 6/9/1941, USHMM, RG-15.034 M., roll 5, AGKBZH 185/61, anonymous letters of 24/7 and 3/8/1941, ibid., folios 1, 3 to 6, and requisition reports, ibid., folios 8 et seq.

35. For an overview of the behavior of security institutions in Galicia, see Klaus Michael Mallmann, " 'Mensch Ich feiere heut den tausendste Genickschuß': Die Sicherheitspolizei und die Shoah in Westukraine," in Paul (ed.), *Die Täter der Shoah*, pp. 109–136.

36. Letter, Dirlewanger to Friedrich, 20/3/1942, USHMM, RG- 15.034 M., roll 6, AGKBZH 185/65, folio 132.

37. Hell, *Le Sang noir*, pp. 55–57.

38. Dieter Pohl, *Nationalsozialistische Judenverfolgung in Ostgalizien 1941–1944. Organisation und Durchführung eines staatlichen Massenverbrechens* (Munich: Oldenburg Verlag, 1996).

39. For Globocnik and Germanization in the very region the unit was stationed, see Czeslaw Madajczyk, *Die Okkupationspolitik Nazideutschland in Polen 1939–1945* (Berlin (E): Akademie Verlag, 1987) and the document collection Czeslaw Madajczyk (ed.), *Vom Generalplan Ost zum Generalsiedlungsplan* (Munich: Saur Verlag, 1994); but also, in French, Essner and Conte, *La Quête de la race*.

40. Cf. Gerlach, *Kalkulierte Morde*, pp. 950–951 and especially 907-909.

41. RKO report to the Ostministerium, 4/10/1943, in IfZ, MA-249: RmfdBO.

42. Sworn declaration by Höfle, quoted from Klausch, *Antifaschisten*, pp. 129 and 457. Cf. also Ek Report 13, 9/12/1944, in BABL, R-70 (Sl)/195, for the description of problems caused by the Dirlewanger in Slovakia.

43. Anonymous letters of 24/7 and 3/8/1941, USHMM, RG- 15.034 M., roll 5, AGKBZH 185/61, folios 1, 3 to 6, and letter handing over dossier to the SS judge of Himmler's personal staff, 3/3/1942, announcing the opening of a case against the author of the anonymous letters, in USHMM, RG- 15.034 M., roll 6, AGKBZH 185/65, folio 128.

44. HSSPF Russland Mitte, Proposal for awarding the cross of the Reich in gold, 9/8/1943, IfZ, NO 2923, folio 4.

45. HSSPF Russland Mitte, 23/3/1942, BABL, R-70 (SU)/38.

46. Journal of von dem Bach-Zelewsky, 5/8/1942, BABL, R-20/45b.

47. Report of Combat Group Adler of the 286th Division, 8/8/1942, BAMA, RS 3-36/5.

48. Ibid.

49. Final Report on Operation Cottbus, 28/6/1943, signed von Gottberg, in BAMA, RH-26-286/9.

50. Deposition of von Gottberg's adjutant, Weber-Bergfeldt, 25 and 26/10/1973, StA Hambourg, 147 Js 11/71U, vol. 4, folios 619–636. Note that not only are civilian populations suspected of being accomplices in placing mines, but among them, children are suspected in particular. Here folio 630.

51. Cf. Gerlach, *Kalkulierte Morde*, p. 969 and Heer, *Vernichtungskrieg*, pp. 130–131.

52. Notice, Minsk Prosecutor, undated, StA Hambourg, 147 Js 11/71U (main dossier, case of von Gottberg. Investigation: examinations), vol. 5, folios 811–812.

53. Testimony of Alexander Mironov, 16/1/1961, StA Hambourg, 147 Js 11/71U (*Kampfgruppe* Gottberg, Dirlewanger unit), Sonderband I, folio 100.

54. Examination of Iwan Boranow, 20/7/1968, Mogilev Investigation Commission, in StA Hambourg, 147 Js 11/71U, Beiheft 5, folios 6–7.

55. Examination of Franz Wegschneider, 16/9/1969, StA Hambourg, 147 Js 11/71U (*Sondereinheit* Dirlewanger, alphabetical entries), SB 1 bis (2), folio 47.

56. Told by Matthias Schenck, quoted in Klausch, *Antifaschisten*, pp. 113–114.

57. The verb is *toben*, implying madness, possession, fulmination.

58. Schenck, in Klausch, *Antifaschisten*, p. 108.

59. This passage is not the only one in which Schenck brings together cruelty, rage, and alcohol: he describes the attitude of Dirlewanger himself in related terms when he has a wounded Pole executed. Schenck, in Klausch, *Antifaschisten*, p. 118.

60. The reference here is to French MacLean's book, to which we will return, which includes a chronological history of the unit: MacLean, *The Cruel Hunters*.

61. Hell, *Le Sang noir*, pp. 131–145 in particular.

62. Hell, *Le Sang noir*, p. 114.

63. "Ganz allgemein hiess es, dass Dirl. in den Dörfern fuerchterlich 'gehaust' habe," Examination of Paul Rumschewitsch, 10/6/1974,

StA Hambourg, 147 Js 11/71U, vol. 5, folios 750–760, here folio 756.

64. Ibid.

5. A HUNTERS' WAR?

1. André Leroi-Gourhan, *Le Geste et la Parole* (Paris: Albin Michel, 1964), vol. II, p. 237. Leroi-Gourhan's starting point is an equivalence between the social group responsible for cynegetic activities and a developing warrior caste. Pierre Clastres, in a critique of Leroi-Gourhan's thesis, which he considered excessively naturalistic, reformulated it crudely as "War is a man-hunt." Cf. Pierre Clastres, "Archéologie de la violence: la guerre dans les sociétés primitives," in Clastres, *Libres 1*, Payot, 1977, pp. 137–173.

2. Report, *Spähtruppe*, on the operation of 2 and 3/6/1944, BAMA, RS 3-36/17, no folio number.

3. Intervention order signed by von Gottberg, 15/5/1943, USHMM, RG-11.001 M.01, roll 10: ASM 500/1/769, folios 125–132, here folio 128.

4. Intervention order for Operation Cottbus, signed by von Gottberg, 15/5/1943, IfZ, Fb 101/13. Incident reports of the Dirlewanger unit in BAMA, RS 3-36/6; also see Gerlach, *Kalkulierte Morde*, pp. 948–951, for a detailed retelling of the operation.

5. A certain number of testimonies give an idea of the tornado of violence that the *Sondereinheit* unleashed during Operation Cottbus, StA Hambourg, 147 Js 11/71U (Sonderbat. Dirlewanger, translated Russian testimonies), Beiheft 5. The 15,000 dead must be considered as a minimum figure. One *Sondereinheit* incident report alone claims 14,000 killed and thirteen prisoners, in Incident report for the period 20/5 to 2/6/1943, BAMA, SF-02/31686, folio 710 (microfilm version, RS 3-36/7). Also quoted by Gerlach, *Kalkulierte Morde*, p. 950. Slightly different figures: Total Figures for Operation Cottbus, signed Hstuf Artur Wilke, 18/6/1943, USHMM, RG-11.001 M.01, ASM 500/1/769, folios 164–165. Wilke reports a total of 9,818 dead for the operation.

6. Hell, *Le Sang noir*, Introduction.

7. BABL, NS-19/3371: Correspondence, Himmler, hunt invitations.

8. Hell, *Le Sang noir*, Introduction.

9. Invented at the end of the Mousterian by *Homo Sapiens* and differentiating him as certainly as his cranial morphology from his cousin *Neanderthalis*, the hunt *en battue* constitutes the first example of the practice of mass killing; it is for this also that it constitutes an analogical reference for large-scale sweep operations. André Leroi-Gourhan, *Les Chasseurs de la préhistoire* (Paris: Métaillié, 1992).

10. Letter, von Gottberg, 27/11/1942, StA Hambourg, 147 Js 11/71U (Documents from the archives of the StAs [StA Munich, 118 Js 6/71, StA Coburg, Js 296/65]), Beiaktenordner 2, no folio number.

11. For the image of the boar in the Germanic hunt, see Hell, *Le Sang noir*, pp. 67–69.

12. Ernst Jünger, *La Chasse au sanglier* (Paris: Christian Bourgois Editeur, 1968). I thank Ronald Wood for drawing my attention to this text.

13. A theme that has been well explored outside the cynegetic context by Liulevicius, *War Land on the Eastern Front*.

14. One example among many: on May 23, 1943, a section of the Wehrmacht, no doubt misled on purpose by the local population, is encircled and attacked by a group of partisans. Panicked, the Wehrmacht men leave behind eleven dead, three missing, and all their weapons. A *Spähtruppe* of the *Sondereinheit* finds the bodies "horribly mutilated." Radio message 11 of 24/5/1943, 10:00, in BAMA, RS 3-36/6. Closer still to the unit: a truck of men returning from leave was attacked near Minsk by a partisan unit, killing three men, on May 25, 1942. A letter from Dirlewanger to the HSSPF Russland Mitte dated the next day reports that the bodies of the men, killed by explosive bullets, had been mutilated post mortem. Letter in BAMA, RS 3- 36/4, no folio number.

15. The 57th Schuma Battalion fought regularly beside the unit, particularly during Operations Cottbus, Günther, and Hermann, cf. Bill of Indictment in StA Hambourg, 147 Js 11/71U, Beiaktenordner 1; numerous documents in ibid., vol. "Einheiten" 1 ; cf. Gerlach, *Kalkulierte Morde*, p. 902, and Martin Dean, *Collaboration in the Holocaust: Crimes of the Local Police in Bielorussia and Ukraine, 1941–44* (New York: Saint Martin's Press, 2000).

16. Examination of Hans Siegling, [date missing], StA Hambourg, 147 Js 11/71U, vol. 8, folio 1240 ; cf. also Examination of Hermann G., 10/8/1976, in ibid., vol. 7, folios 1093–1098, here 1095. In the second case, a member of the unit tells of a case of partisan atrocity without using it as part of a strategy of exoneration.

17. Bertrand Hell notes, in an article in *Dernières nouvelles d'Alsace*, the resurgence of this belief in an animal punishing a hunter who has transgressed a taboo in a hunting accident during the 1990s. Hell, *Le Sang noir*, p. 326.

18. With this exception: these hunting tales had a moral function, in that the hunters who were victims of the fury of the game were guilty of transgressions due to a lack of control of black blood and of the passion of the hunt. All, thus, described the black-blooded game as punishing that passion. Cf. Hell, *Le Sang noir*, p. 327. It is difficult, however, to find such a function in the stories of partisan atrocities: the victims are often presented as innocent—female—and the lack of security is rarely brought out in the narration, even when it is probably flawed, as in the case of the unit's men on leave during the summer of 1942.

19. Ibid., folio 1241.

20. Correspondence, HSSPF Russland Mitte to the SSFHA, 19/6/1942, IfZ, Fa-146.

21. Correspondence, Dr. Dirlewanger to the SSFHA, 14/3/1944, ibid.

22. Klausch, *Antifaschisten*, p. 68.

23. A belief highlighted and brilliantly deconstructed, Christian Gerlach, *Kalkulierte Morde*, pp. 128–222.

24. Creation order for the medal sent to the unit 26/3/1944, in BABL, R-70 (SU)/38.

25. ZStL, 202 AR-Z 5/60 (Case of Förster et alii, KdS Aussenstelle Wilejka), vol. 42. Eighty Russian testimonies of which more than half use the term "to hunt."

26. Cf. Gerlach, *Kalkulierte Morde*, pp. 859–974, awaiting the publication of Masha Cerovic, whose graduate work includes a promising study of the partisans based on Russian and German archives.

27. Ingrao, *Intellectuels*, chapter 12.

28. Hell, Le Sang noir, pp. 30–31.

29. Letter from the *Sonderkommando* to the HSSPF, 9/9/1942, BAMA, RS 3-36/4, no folio number.

30. A contrary example, but in another sector than that of the *Sondereinheit*: a Russian agent employed as a radio operator and returned by the Germans in Crimea is interrogated BABL, R-70 (SU)/18, no folio number.

31. Cf. Gerlach, *Kalkulierte Morde*, p. 890.

32. Affidavit Waldemar B., 22/9/1946, IfZ, NO-867; Examination of Albin V., 29/5/1945, IfZ, NO-1716.

33. Examination of Werner W.B, 25 and 26/10/1973, StA Hambourg, 147 Js 11/71U (Main dossiere, case of von Gottberg. Investigation: examinations), vol. 4, folios 619–636, here folio 633.

34. Cf. Affidavit Waldemar B., 22/9/1946, IfZ, NO-867.

35. An argument which is nevertheless systematically used by torturers to justify the practice of violence against civilians. In an entirely different context, the practice of torture and sexual violence has been analyzed in detail in Raphaëlle Branche, *La Torture et l'armée pendant la guerre d'Algérie. 1954–1962* (Paris: Gallimard, 2001).

36. In his thesis, Jacques Pernaud has shown that, on the Pleistocene site of Tautavel, predation on deer was essentially anthropic and concerned almost exclusively adult deer. The population of hominids was primarily Neanderthal, but the arrival of *Homo Sapiens* at the end of the period does not seem to have changed this predation centered uniquely on adults. Jacques Pernaud, *Les Cervidés du site pleistocène moyen de la Caune de l'Arago à Tautavel (Pyrénées-Orientales). Paléontologie, étude des populations, approche paléoethnologique*, thesis (MNHN, 1993).

37. Hell, *Le Sang noir*.

38. Hannes Heer has shown that notes or orders of this type corresponded to phases of radicalization of anti-partisan methods. Cf. Hannes Heer, "Die Logik des Vernichtungskriegs. Wehrmacht und Partisanenkampf," in Heer, *Tote Zonen*, pp. 41–79, here pp. 60–64. See also Gerlach, *Kalkulierte Morde*, pp. 971–974.

39. Correspondence, HSSPF Russland Mitte, 7/09/1942, BABL, R-20/6, folios 167–168.

40. Gerlach, *Kalkulierte Morde*, p. 972.

41. Gerlach, *Kalkulierte Morde*, pp. 1,088–1,092.

42. Correspondence between Brandenburg and Himmler, 9/06-13/07/1944, in IfZ, Fa-146, no folio number.

43. Rain shower.

44. Spring fest.

45. Instruction notice, 11/4/1944, BAMA, RS 3-36/16.

46. Testimony of Alexander Mironowitsch, 16/1/1961, StA Hamburg, 147 Js 11/71U, Sonderband 1, folio 100.

47. Testimony of Maria Sosnjowska, 3/7/1961, ZStL, II-202 AR-1957/58 (*Kampfgruppe* von Gottberg), vol. 1, no folio number: a little girl is seized by a member of the unit and her head smashed against a tree, her body then being thrown in the face of the villagers.

48. Testimony of Sunaida Soljar, 17/1/1961, StA Hamburg, 147 Js 11/71U (*Kampfgruppe* Gottberg, Dirlewanger unit), Sonderband I, folio 107: she escaped the execution in which her son was executed. She describes women trying to shield their children from the bullets with their own bodies.

49. Examination of Zinaida Piluj, 15/4/1961, ZStL, II-202 AR-1957/58, vol. 1.

50. Combat report, Draufgänger 2, 1 to 9/5/1943, BAMA, RS 3-36/4, no folio number.

51. This was already the case for Operation Cottbus: in his incident report, the *Sondereinheit* claimed the capture of an anti-tank gun and a mobile howitzer, in Report on Operation Cottbus, 20/5-2/6/1943, BAMA, RS 3-36/4.

52. Gerlach, *Kalkulierte Morde*, pp. 975–1,010.

53. Battalion orders 37 and 40, BAMA, RS 3-36/7.

54. Operation Bamberg, a test of the sweep system, the only operation performed before the unit arrived in Belarus (26/3- 6/4 1942) brought the Germans 5,061 cattle, 115 tonnes of grain, and 120 tonnes of potatoes. Cf. Gerlach, *Kalkulierte Morde*, p. 899.

55. Ibid.

56. Experience report, Operation Günther, 14/7/1943, BAMA, RS 3-36/6, no folio number.

57. Intervention order for Operation Senkewitsch, 22/5/1944, BAMA, RS 3-36/2, no folio number.

58. Bertrand Hell analyzes the hunt in terms of gathering and harvesting, in apparent contradiction with the model developed here, because he makes the southern European battue hunt, which owes a great deal to chance, a gathering hunt. The *Pirsch* is considered by Hell to be a harvest hunt. But it seems to us that the battues which the "*Pirsch*ers" must perform to respect their hunting plans are part of the same harvest. Hell, *Le Sang noir*, chapter 1.

59. Order of von Gottberg, 1/8/1943, IfZ, Fb-85/2, folios 71–77, here folio 71.

60. Pierre Clastres criticized André Leroi-Gourhan's theses in these terms: "If war is a hunt, then it is a man-hunt." [. . .] Unless we suppose that the purpose of war is always alimentary and that the object of this type of aggression is man as game to be eaten, this reduction of war to hunt has no basis." Clastres, in fact, only criticizes the assimilation of war with predation, not with the hunt. Although his analysis of the goals of these two phenomena is correct, he is not interested in the analogy existing between these two cultural practices of killing, and particularly not in their symbolic backgrounds, in the social discourse surrounding the hunt, preoccupied as he is by demonstrating the specificity of war as a cultural practice—as opposed to a natural one. He forgets that the hunt itself is not a "natural" practice, but a cultural one, at the very least since the appearance of *Homo Sapiens*. Cf. Clastres, "Archéologie de la violence."

61. Ibid.

62. Report of July 1943 in BAMA, RS 3-36/5, no folio number.

63. Telegram from Dirlewanger to Stubaf. Blessau, Berger's adjutant, 11/3/1943, BAMA, RS 3-36/19, quoted in Klausch, *Antifaschisten*, p. 86.

64. On the policy of anti-Semitic repression, and particularly on acts of pillage, marking with the yellow star, enclosing Jews in ghettos and submitting them to forced labor, see Bogdan Musial,

Deutsche Zivilverwaltung und Judenverfolgung im Generalgouvernement: Eine Fallstudie zum Distrikt Lublin (Wiesbaden: Harassowitz, 2000), particularly pp. 124–144 for marking and enclosure, pp. 164–169 for forced labor.

65. For this camp, and the mention of a unit commando responsible for guarding the camp, see Thomas Sandkühler, *"Endlösung" in Galizien. Der Judenmord in Ostpolen und die Rettungsintiativen von Berthold Beitz 1941–1944* (Bonn: Dietz, 1996) pp. 125, 185. See also p. 491, note 45, for the Lutsk camp.

66. We will return to these practices of violence. For beatings in Galicia, for participation in the selection of Jews in the Lutsk ghetto, see the bill of indictment against Feiertag et alii, in IfZ, Gh 05.10. For the whip-marking by the Dirlewanger unit, in Galicia as well as in Belarus, see the deposition of Konrad Morgen, IfZ, NO 1908, folio 1, and the examination of Albin V., IfZ, ZS-1560, folio 1.

67. Examination of Albin V., 19/3/1948 IfZ, ZS-1560.

68. Daily general orders signed by Dirlewanger, 25/5/1943, ZStL, 502 ARZ 27/73 (Sonderband II: Dirlewanger), vol. 490.

69. Journal, von dem Bach-Zelewsky, entry of 23/6/1943, BABL, R-20/45b, folio 79.

70. BAMA RH 26-403/7. Quoted by Heer, *Vernichtungskrieg*, pp. 130-131 and note 49.

71. Vern. J. B. SS Pol. Reg. 2 14/10/63, BStU ZUV 9, 17, Bd. 1, folio 172, quoted by Gerlach, *Kalkulierte Morde*, p. 969.

72. As expressed, in an entirely different historiographical context, by Crouzet, *Les Guerriers de Dieu*.

73. See particularly the incident reports in BAMA, RS 3- 36/21.

74. See the final report on Operation Cottbus by Artur Wilke, 18/6/1943, USHMM, RG-53.002 M., roll 6, ZstA Minsk 845/1/206, folios 165–166. See also the testimonies of Russian survivors, especially Vern. Iwan Baranow, 20/7/68, StA Hambourg, 147 Js 11/71U, Beiheft 5, folios 5–6.

75. Ibid. Also StA Hamburg, 147 Js 11/71U (Sonderbat. Dirlewanger, translated Russian testimonies), vol. Beiheft 1-5.

76. Examination of S., 21/2/1977, StA Hamburg, 147 Js 11/71U (Main dossier, case of von Gottberg. Investigation: examina-

tions), vol. 7, folios 1177–1182, here 1181. The execution involves only some thirty people.

77. Cf. final report of the commission of investigation in ZStL, II-202 AR-Z 177/67, vol. 24, for the regions of Tschervenj and Beresino, and Russian testimonies in StA Hamburg, 147 Js 11/71U, vol. SB 1 bis (2); see also and above all the summary notice of the Minsk prosecutor, undated, in ibid., vol. 5, folios 811–812.

78. For these latter practices, see bill of indictment against Feiertag in IfZ, Gh 05.10.

79. This, at any event, is how Dirlewanger justified the use of poison. Letter from Dirlewanger to Friedrich, 20/3/1942, USHMM, RG- 15.034 M. roll 6, AGKBZH 185/65, folio 132.

80. The victims, in any event, were stripped, according to some testimonies: Examination of Peter Erretskamp, 11/10/1962, ZStL, 8 AR-Z 28/62 (Case of Dirlewanger and others, Lublin), vol. 2, folios 384–394, here folio 390. Erretskamp doesn't specify whether the victims were stripped before the execution, but this is undoubtedly the case: otherwise, he would have been assigned to the stripping and handling of the bodies, not just the latter. His testimony is nevertheless subject to caution: the prosecutors themselves were surprised by his propensity for fabulation. Report on closing of the case in ibid., vol. 8. For stripping preliminary to execution in genocide: cf. Raul Hilberg, *Destruction des Juifs d'Europe*, vol. I, chapter. "Les opérations mobiles de tuerie."

81. Cf. IfZ, Gh 05.10, particularly.

82. Examination of Werner Weber-Bergfeldt, 25 and 26/10/73, StA Hamburg, 147 Js 11/71U, vol. 4, folios 619–636, for a blatant case including use of the whip, cigarette burns, and execution by lethal injection, all in the presence of Gottberg and of Artur Wilke. For other cases in the presence of Dirlewanger, cf. Déclaration W.-B., 22/1/1946, IfZ, NO-867, and Examination of Albin V, IfZ, NO-1716, both quoted in Klausch, *Antifaschisten*, p. 87.

83. Hell, *Le Sang noir*, pp. 25–34.

84. This is what emerges from the testimonies of W.-B. and of Albin Vogel quoted above. Hans Peter Klausch believes to be unfounded this dimension of cruelty—"sadistic," he writes—in

the unit's practice of violence, but without proposing a convincing argument: cf. Klausch, *Antifaschisten*, p. 49.

85. In the European cultural arena, one of the cruelest sacrificial rites is for example that of a bear, captured, tamed, domesticated, adopted as one of their own by Spanish villagers, then tortured and beaten to death by the very people who had tamed it. Described by Bertrand Hell, in *Le Sang noir*. The example, described by the writer Nicolaï Bounine, of Russian peasants trying to dismember bulls alive, constitutes a second illustration bringing us closer to the arena in question. Nicolaï Bounine, *Zakhar Varobiev* (Moscow, 1912). Zakhar Varobiev is the eponymous peasant hero of Bounine's novel; he and his fellow villagers flay a bull alive for amusement. The case was noted by V. Doineo, "The Russian Peasant: Who Is He?" in *The New Russia*, no. 22 (July 1, 1920), pp. 264–269. Bounine's *Le Village* (Paris, 1922) is available for further reading. I am most grateful to Nicolas Werth, who drew my attention to this case and gave the details here. Farther from us, in Madagascar, young men, as part of their rites of passage, torture with an axe cattle dedicated to this sacrifice. Maurice Bloch, "La consommation des 'jeunes hommes' chez les Zafimaniry de Madagascar," in Françoise Héritier, *De la violence* (Paris: Odile Jacob, 1996), pp. 201–222, here p. 206. The anthropologist Catherine Rémy, finally, shows us, in an as-yet unpublished thesis, that cruelty, despite strict regulation, is standard practice in the slaughter of cattle, and that it serves a function of differentiation within the social group of slaughterhouse workers. Until her thesis is available, see Catherine Rémy, "Une mise à mort industrielle 'humaine'? L'abattoir ou l'impossible objectivation des animaux," in *Politix*, vol. 16, no 64/2003:51-73; p. 71, for a sequence showing the upwelling of cruelty.

86. See, for example, the liquidation orders issued by Dirlewanger 1/3/1944, in BAMA, RS 3-36/2 for "Banditendorf;" for "Bandenverseucht," for instance, see Hitler's order for the evacuation of territories contaminated by partisans in the summer of 1943, in StA Hamburg, 147 Js 11/71U (Documents [provenance: Nuremberg Fürth 12 Js 300/67]), Beiaktenordner 3/1, folios 24–32.

87. For all this, see Hell, *Le Sang noir*, pp. 147–201; for the cult of Saint Hubert, pp. 177–188.

88. Examination of Paul Rumschewitsch, 10/6/1974, StA Hamburg, 147 Js 11/71U, vol. 5, folios 750–760, here folio 756.

89. See Philippe Descola, *Par-delà nature et culture* (Paris: Gallimard, 2005), pp. 58–90, and particularly pp. 80–88. Philippe Descola is studying here the modes of appropriation of space by approaching the European case through Roman agronomy, with emphasis on the specificity due to the Neolithic revolution.

90. Cf. on this subject, Noëlie Vialles, *Le Sang et la chair. Les abattoirs de l'Adour* (Paris: MSH, 1991).

91. Cf. Gerlach, *Kalkulierte Morde*, as well as Christian Streit, *Keine Kameraden. Die Wehrmacht und die sowjetischen Kriegsgefangenen 1941–1945* (Stuttgart: DVA, 1978).

6. A NEW WAR?

1. For all this, Overy, *Russia's War*.

2. Cf. on this subject, Hans von Krannhals, *Der Warschauer Aufstand 1944*, (Frankfurt: Bernard und Graefe Verlag fuer Wehrwesen, 1962), and Wlodimierz Borodziej, *Der Warschauer Aufstand 1944* (Frankfurt: Fischer, 2001).

3. Heer, *Tote Zonen*.

4. Photos published in MacLean, *The Cruel Hunters*, between pages 160 and 161. The photos were consulted at the Bundesbildarchiv, Berlin. Their references are mentioned. For the use of artillery and buildings destroyed, see Borodziej, *Der Warschauer Aufstand*, p. 144.

5. Cf. on this subject, Duménil, *Le Soldat allemand*.

6. Schenck, in Klausch, *Antifaschisten*, p. 113.

7. John Dower observed this among American soldiers in the Pacific. Dower, *War without Mercy*.

8. Borodziej, *Der Warschauer Aufstand*, p. 123; see also, for the number of mass graves attributable to the unit, Klausch, *Antifaschisten*, p. 111.

9. Examination, incomplete and undated, of Willy B. in ZStL, 502 AR-Z 27/73, vol. 492, (Sonderband IV), at the very end of the volume.

10. Vialles, *Le Sang et la chair*.

11. Ingrao, "Une anthropologie du massacre?" in El Kentz (ed.), *Histoire du massacre*.

12. Cf. for instance examination of Walter F., 23/11/1961, ZStL, 502 AR-Z 27/73 (Sonderband V), vol. 493, folios 8–19.

13. Schenck, in Klausch, *Antifaschisten*, pp. 113–114 et infra, preceding chapter.

14. Cf. infra, preceding chapter.

15. Practice attested to in Examination of George S., 6/5/1965, ZStL, V 117 AR 395/65, vol.1, folios 23–36, here folio 28.

16. On the question of attack on women as elements of the transmission of lineage: Véronique Nahoum-Grappe, "L'usage politique de la cruauté: l'épuration ethnique (ex-Yougoslavie, 1991–1995)," in Héritier (dir.), *De la violence*, pp. 273–323.

17. Speech, Himmler, quoted in Borodziej, *Warschauer Aufstand*, p. 121.

18. Hans von Krannhals, *Der Warschauer Aufstand 1944* (Frankfurt: Bernard und Graefe Verlag fuer Wehrwesen, 1962), p. 308 et seq., p. 327 et seq., p. 420 et seq.

19. Memorandum on women in the Volkstumskampf in BABL, R-59/65.

20. Hans Joachim Beyer, *Das Schicksal der Polen. Rasse—Volkscharakter—Stammesart* (Leipzig, Berlin: Teubner Verlag, 1942), p. 158. Quoted by Karl-Heinz Roth, "Heydrichs Professor: Historiographie des 'Volkstums' und der Massenvernichtungen. Der Fall Hans Joachim Beyer," in Peter Schöttler (ed.), *Geschichtsschreibung als Legitimationswissenschaft, 1918–1945* (Frankfurt: Suhrkamp, 1997), pp. 262–342, here pp. 292 and 332.

21. This migration was in effect in 1943, as revealed by the questioning of arrested partisans, in BABL, R-70 (Sl)/84.

22. MacLean, *Cruel Hunters*, p. 200.

23. Radio message from Ek 14, 30/9/1944, BABL, R-70 (Sl)/87, folio 15. The SD men detect an evolution, a "bolshevization" of the situation, concomitant with the German military victory: radio message of 2/10, ibid., folio 89.

24. Situation report, Einsatzgruppe H., in BABL, R-70 (Sl)/83, folio 62; numerous other reports in BABL, R-70 (Sl)/170.

25. Copy of a report found in the archives of Slovakian insurgents on the Warsaw uprising in BABL, R-70 (Sl)/95, folios 65 et seq.

26. Daily report, Ek 14, 28/9/1944, BABL, R-70 (Sl)/196.

27. Final numbers of the operation to put down the Slovakian uprising in Daily report, Ek 14, 27 and 28/10/1944, in BABL, R-70 (Sl)/196, no folio number.

28. We are not denying the scale of the massacres committed by the Germans in occupied Slovakia, particularly during the retreat, massacres abundantly documented in ZStL, I- 505 AR-Z 284/77, particularly vols. 1 and 9. The victims are nevertheless estimated at "only" 2,000.

29. MacLean, *Cruel Hunters*, p. 201.

30. Klausch, *Antifaschisten*, p. 130, quoting Wolfgang Venohr, *Aufstand fur die Tschechoslowakei. Der Slowakische Freiheitskampf* (Hamburg, 1969), pp. 259–272.

31. The execution is described in Bernd Boll and Hans Safrian, "Auf dem Weg nach Stalingrad. Die 6. Armee 1941–42," in Klaus Naumann and Hannes Heer, *Vernichtungskrieg. Verbrechen der Wehrmacht 1941–1944* (Hamburg: Hamburg Edition, 1995), pp. 260–296. French translation in Anne Duménil, Nicolas Beaupré, and Christian Ingrao (dirs.), *L'Ere de la guerre, t. II Nazisme, occupation, pratiques génocides* (Paris: Agnès Viénot éditions, 2004). An analysis in terms of demonstrative violence towards civilian populations and Germans in the Wehrmacht and the SS in Ingrao, "Violence de guerre, violence génocide."

32. For all this, see the catalogues of the two exhibitions, *Vernichtungskrieg. Verbrechen der Wehrmacht*, published in 1994 and 2000, as well as Naumann and Heer, *Vernichtungskrieg*.

33. Stéphane Audoin-Rouzeau, "Corps en guerre," in Alain Corbin (dir.), *Histoire du corps* (Paris: Seuil, 2006). I thank Stéphane Audoin-Rouzeau for showing me this text before its publication.

34. Cf. on this subject, Vialles, *Le Sang et la chair*.

35. Examination of Angela Svoboda, 14/12/1972, ZStL, I-505 ARZ 284/77 ([Einsatzkommando 14 Slovakia]: Case of Dirlewanger), vol. 33, folios 5951–5954.

36. Report, Ek 13, 9/12/1944, BABL, R-70 (Sl)/195, folios 58–67.

37. Order, Dirlewanger to Praefcke, BAMA, RS 3-36/5, no folio number.

38. Cf. on this subject, Klausch, *Antifaschisten*.

39. Quoted by Klausch, *Antifaschisten*, p. 228.

40. Percy Ernst Schramm (ed.), *Kriegstagebuch der OKW*, (Frankfurt; 1961), vol. 4, entry of 16/2/1945, folios 1099–1100. Quoted by Klausch, *Antifaschisten*, p. 296.

41. BAMA, RH 19 XV/4, folio 179.

42. Cf. on this subject, Hanson, *Le Modèle occidental de la guerre*; Hanson, *Carnage et culture*.

43. This was the case of the 31st SS Grenadier Division, whose units, over 50 percent destroyed, fled the Budapest conflict on 28/11/1944, KTB *Heeresgruppe* Süd, entry of 28/11/1944, BAMA, RH 19 V/42, folios 156–164.

44. This, it seems to me, was one of the reasons for the colossal losses in the German armed forces during the last year of the conflict: Rüdiger Overmans, *Deutche Militärverluste im Zweiten Weltkrieg* (Munich: Oldenburg, 2000); pp. 238 and 269. The German army lost, in that last year alone, 2,500,000 hommes, or 50 percent of its total losses. See Ingrao, "Le suicide comme sortie de guerre."

45. Statistical report on losses, HQ of HG Weichsel, 13/4/1945, in Annexes to the KTB, BAMA, RH 19 XV/9a, folios 65–67.

46. Statistical report on troop replacements as of 1/3/1945, in Annexes to the KTB of *Heeresgruppe* Weichsel, BAMA, RH 19 XV/9b, folio 10.

47. Enemy losses from 1 to 14/4/1945, undated, in Annex to the KTB of *Heeresgruppe* Weichsel, BAMA, RH 19 XV/9b, folio 98.

48. Daily report, 9th Army, 14/4/1945, BAMA, RH 19 XV/9b, folio 20.

49. Cf. on this subject, William Moskoff, *The Bread of Affliction: Food Supply in the USSR during World War II* (Cambridge: CUP, 1990)

50. Affidavit of Bruno Wille, 28/6/1946. TMWC, vol. LXII, p. 528 et seq.

51. Calculations based on forms completed by prisoners returned from Russia, Red Cross research files consulted in Munich.

52. Fewer than ten individuals.

53. 165 men were taken prisoner in April, more than 90 percent of them during the two last weeks of the month, as against 111 in May, during the first week of the month.

54. Twenty-two of them were captured in Lusatia after the end of hostilities.

55. Three were captured in Belarus.

56. Klausch, *Antifaschisten*, pp. 311–314.

57. Examination of Georg Geipel, 12/7/1962, ZStL, II-211 AR 1210/62, vol. 1, folios 11 et seq. for the escape, and folios 15 et seq. for the violence inflicted on prisoners by the Russians.

58. Letter Helmut Fs. of 6/3/1965 to the Red Cross research department, quoted by Klausch, *Antifaschisten*, p. 312.

7. POST-WAR

1. Klausch, *Antifaschisten*, p. 300.

2. A letter from Himmler recalling Dirlewanger to order demonstrated his satisfaction with Dirlewanger's combat performance, but also the fact that Himmler expected immediate and total obedience. Letter of August 8, 1944, in ZStL, 502 AR-Z 27/73, vol. 489.

3. Cf. on this subject, Klausch, *Antifaschisten*, p. 131. Klausch quotes the former second in command of the 14th SS Division, made up of Ukrainian collaborators, who wrote a hagiography of this unit in 1973. Cf. Wolf-Dietrich Heike, *Sie wollten die Freiheit. Die Geschichte der ukrainischen Divisionen, 1943–1945* (Dornheim, 1973).

4. Examination of Maria Dirlewanger, StA Nuremberg, War Crime Accusations, Examinations D.45, quoted by Klausch, *Antifaschisten*, p. 302.

5. Klausch, *Antifaschisten*, p. 303.

6. Examination of Anton F., undated, ZStL, 502 AR-Z 27/73, vol. 489, folios 101–106, here folio 102.

7. Ibid.

8. Ibid.

9. Testimony of Betty A. 22/1/1958, ZStL, 502 AR-Z 27/73, vol. 489, folio 99.

10. Examination of Anton F., undated, ZStL, 502 AR-Z 27/73, vol. 489, folios 101–106, here folio 103.

11. Testimony of Betty A., 22/1/1958, ibid., folio 100.

12. IfZ, NO-2 959 for Reinecke, IfZ, NO-2 895 for Hermann Höfle, IfZ, ZS-1 570 for Erwin Walser; IfZ, ZS-427/1 for the collected examinations of Gottlob Berger IfZ, ZS-1 638 for Bruno Wille ; Ruoff is interviewed by IfZ historians, in IfZ, ZS-1 399.

13. ZStL prosecutors recognized in the 1960s that they had no way of finding Weisse again, not knowing if he was even alive. Cf. the search for him in the context of the investigation of the Warsaw uprising, in ZStL, 502 AR-Z 27/73, vol. 491.

14. Article reproduced in ZStL, 502 AR-Z 27/73, vol. 489, no folio number.

15. IfZ, ZS-427/2. For the testimony on the Foreign Legion, Berger said he had visited the grand mufti of Jerusalem and thus had stayed in the Near East, and he couldn't imagine that his "old friend" hadn't contacted him. Cf. Examination of Berger, 29/7/65, in ZStL, 8 AR-Z 28/62, vol. 7, folios 1197–1200.

16. Examination of Paul Dorn, 4/7/1962, ZStL, 502 AR-Z 27/73, vol. 492, folios 431–448.

17. Examination of Wilhelm Rass, 16/3/1962, ZStL, 502 AR-Z 27/73 (Sonderband V), vol. 493, folios 121–129. Examiners' note, folio 130.

18. Exhumation and autopsy report, 24/10/1960, ZStL, 502 AR-Z 27/73, vol. 489.

19. Willi Berthold, *Brigade Dirlewanger. Roman* (Köln: Lingen, [probably 1963]). Subsequent editions have an expanded title: *Brigade Dirlewanger. Roman nach Tatsache*.

20. For the description of these trials, see Frank M. Buscher, *U.S. War Crimes Trial Program in Germany, 1946–1955* (New York, Westport, London: Greenwood Press, 1989); Norbert Frei, *Vergangenheitspolitik. Amnestie, Integration und die Abgrenzung vom Nationalsozialismus in den Anfangsjahren der Bundesrepublik* (Munich: Oldenburg, 1996); and Donald Bloxham, *Genocide on Trial: War Crime Trials and the Formation of Holocaust History and Memory* (Oxford: Oxford University Press, 2001).

21. "Collected Information on the Dirlewanger Special Unit," undated 68 page report, in ZStL, 502 AR-Z 27/73, vol. 490.

22. Hellmuth Auerbach, "Die Einheit Dirlewanger," in VfZ 10, 1962, pp. 251–263. This is an abridged version of a report produced by Auerbach and available in BAMA, RS 3-36/23.

23. Emphasized by investigators in the Flensburg prosecutor's report quoted earlier, p. 29.

24. Ibid., pp. 30–32.

25. Ibid., p. 49.

26. Ibid., p. 50.

27. Ibid., p. 52, quoted here from Borodziej, *Der Warschauer Aufstand*, p. 121.

28. Testimony of von dem Bach and his head of general staff Rohde, quoted in ibid., pp. 52 and 53.

29. Ibid., p. 55.

30. Investigations on Belarus and anti-partisan action were, together with the newly opened Eastern European archives, the main source for the principal works marking the historiographic renewal of the 1990s. Cf. particularly Gerlach, *Kalkulierte Morde*, and Ralf Ogorreck, *Die Einsatzgruppen und die Genesis der "Endlösung"* (Berlin: Metropol Verlag, 1996).

31. These documents are found in three specific dossiers called *Sonderbaende*, in StA Hambourg, 147 Js 11/71U, *Sonderbaende* 3-5 and unnumbered *Sonderbaend*.

32. Testimonies systematically translated by investigators in Hamburg and collected in six special volumes in StA Hambourg, 147 Js 11/71U, Beihefte 1-6.

33. Cf. in particular, Examination of Artur Wilke, 7/6/1974, StA Hambourg, 147 Js 11/71U, vol. 5, folios 770 et seq.

34. Cf. Judgment in ZStL, 202 AR-Z 282/59, vol. 1.

35. Cf. for instance, in another case, for the Lida ghetto, testimony of Hazkel Kopelowitsch 21/10/70, and Ilja Wilenskij, 21/10/70, ZStL, 202 AR-Z 5/60 (Case of Förster et alii, KdS Außenstelle Wilejka), vol. 42, respectively folios 8679–8682 and folios 8683–8685, here folios 8684–8685.

36. Cf. Liulevicius, *War Land on the Eastern Front*, cf. also Latzel, *Deutsche Soldaten*, for the two conflicts.

37. Daily general orders of 23/2/1942, BAMA, RS 3-36/4, no folio number. Let us note that Dirlewanger's order dated from the period the unit was adapting to a new environment, that it had nearly thirty months to do so, and that the order was never repeated.

38. Examination of Karl Vieregge, 30/11/1961, ZStL, 502 ARZ 27/73, vol. 492, folios 50–61.

39. Examination of Peter Erretskamp, 28/2/1963, ibid., folios 74 et seq.

40. Examination of Alfred Weber, April 10, 1962, ZStL, 502 ARZ 27/73, vol. 492, folios 337–341.

41. Examination, undated and unpaginated, of Willi Brincksmann, ZStL, 502 AR-Z 27/73, vol. 492. The first three pages of the testimony, containing the place, the date, and the identity of the witness, were missing. Klausch, *Antifaschisten*, p. 110, examined under the same reference, which he attributes to Willibald A., dated 6/3/1963. The importance of this testimony is relative, given the numerous material indicators of the unit's participation in the massacres, from the exhumation reports on mass graves supplied by the Polish investigation commission on Nazi crimes in Poland to the testimony mentioned by Klausch, *Antifaschisten*, pp. 105–120, also quoted by von Krannhals, *Der Warschauer Aufstand*, and also those, from the Polish side, quoted by Borodziej, *Der Warschauer Aufstand*.

42. Examination of Heinrich Kraus, 17/10/1975, StA Hambourg, 147 Js 11/71U (*Sondereinheit* Dirlewanger, alphabetical entries), SB 1 bis (2), folios 929–934.

43. Examination of Kraus, 3/4/1962, ZStL, 502 AR-Z 27/73, vol. 492, folios 103–109.

44. Examination of Kraus, June 1976, StA Hambourg, 147 Js 11/71U, vol. 6, folios 1006–1011.

45. If this is not the case for the investigation of the poisoning of the fifty-seven Lublin Jews, he refuses to cooperate during an investigation on the liquidation of the Jews of the Tscherwenj ghetto. Cf. Examination of Johannes Maas, 16/2/1977, in ZStL, II-202 AR-Z 177/67, vol. 2, folios 401 et seq.

46. Examination of Peter Erretskamp, ZStL, 8 AR-Z 28/62 (Case of Dirlewanger and others, Lublin), vol. 2, folios 384–394; Examination of the same suspect, 15/12/1964, ibid., vol. 7, folios 1187–1196; for the impossibility of incriminating the doctor, see the documents produced during the Dortmund investigation (reference: 45 Js 30/64), in Prosecutor's Note, undated, StA Hamburg, 147 Js 11/71U, SB 1.

47. Note from the case prosecutor, ZStL, 8 AR-Z 28/62, vol. 2, folios 307–310.

48. Examination of Erretskamp, 11/8/1976, StA Hamburg, 147 Js 11/71U, vol. 7, folios 1109–1116, here folio 1112.

49. Examination of Peter Erretskamp, 28/2/1963, ZStL, 502 AR-Z 27/73, vol. 492, folios 74 et seq.

50. von Krannhals, *Der Warschauer Aufstand*.

51. Concluding Report, StA Dortmund, 45 Js 30/64, consulted in StA Hamburg, 147 Js 11/71U, SB 1.

52. Examination of Franz W., 16/9/1969, StA Hamburg, 147 Js 11/71U, SB 1 bis (2), folios 42–46, here folio 45.

53. Herbert, *Best*.

54. Examination of Ernst R., 6/2/1959, ZStL, 2 AR-Z 21/58 (Ehrlinger, [BdS Kiew, Sk 1b.]), vol. 2, folios 639–676.

55. Examination of Nikolas H. and investigators' note recapitulating Nikolas H.'s condemnations in ZStL, 502 AR-Z 27/73, vol. 492, folios 165–172.

56. ZStL, II-211 AR 1210/62, vol. 1.

57. Estimation based on Flensburg prosecutor's report in ZStL, 502 AR-Z 27/73, vol. 490, and "units" file, ZStL.

58. Judgments and appeal of the trial may be consulted in StA Hamburg, 147 Js 11/71U SB 1 (2).

59. Cf. Archival dossier and biographical note on Weisse in ZStL, 502 AR-Z 27/73, vol. 491.

60. These were the conclusions drawn by the Flensburg magistrates in the early 1960s during the investigation of the Warsaw uprising. Cf. ZStL, Report of the Flensburg StA on information available on the Dirlewanger unit in ZStL, 502 AR-Z 27/73, vol. 490, no folio number.

61. StA Hamburg, 147 Js 11/71U, unnumbered volume on investigation conclusion.

62. The trial concerning Warsaw ended with a dismissal of the charges against Heinz Reinefarth. Indictment may be consulted in IfZ, Gf 01.05.

63. Summing up of charges against Feiertag, Hunke et alii in IfZ, Gh 05.10; judgments of first instance and revision in StA Hamburg, 147 Js 11/71U, SB 1 bis (2).

64. Klausch, *Antifaschisten*, p. 414 and p. 547.

65. On Watzinger, ibid., pp. 245, 333, 358–359.

66. ZStL, I-110 AR 686/70.

67. See above, chapter on "Poachers in the Polis," conclusion.

68. *Historia*, special issue no 21, 1971, pp. 70–73.

69. André Brissaud, *L'Histoire de la SS* (Paris: Stock, 1973).

70. Berthold, *Brigade Dirlewanger*.

71. Berthold, *Dirlewanger*, pp. 103–104 and 229. For Mueller, see the biographical notice in Hermann Weiss, *Biographisches lexikon zum Dritten Reich* (Frankfurt: Fischer, 2002), pp. 326–327.

72. Ibid., pp. 216–217. For a generational portrait of the young lawyers, see Herbert, *Best*.

73. Ibid., pp. 5–9.

74. Ibid., pp. 61–62.

75. Ibid., p. 281.

76. For this subject, and for both Weimar and the Third Reich, Patrick Wagner, *Volksgemeinschaft ohne Verbrecher. Konzeptionen und Praxis der Kriminalpolizei in der Zeit der Weimarer Republik und des Nationalsozialismus* (Hamburg: Christians Verlag, 1996), pp. 137–149 and 180–190.

77. Cf. on this subject, Pierre Ayçoberry, *La Question nazie. Les interprétations du national-socialisme, 1922–1975* (Paris: Seuil, 1979).

78. Berthold, *Dirlewanger*, p. 82.

79. Ibid., p. 253, for the link between "fanaticism" and murder for pleasure.

80. Ibid., p. 244, for the murder of a Russian peasant by Belle, following page for the murder of a man, two women, and two children by Exner.
81. Ibid., p. 269.
82. Ibid., p. 288.
83. Ibid., p. 286.
84. This is highlighted both by MacLean, *Cruel Hunters*, and by the cover of Berthold's novel. Here historians and novelists agree.

CONCLUSION

1. Story mentioned by Hell, *Le Sang noir*.
2. I borrow the expression of Lawrence Keeley, *War before Civilization* (Oxford University Press, 1996), translated into French as *Les Guerres préhistoriques* (Paris: Editions du Rocher, 2002).
3. Telegram from Dirlewanger to Ostuf Blessau regarding a wolf hunt with Berger, 11/3/1944, in BAMA, RS 3-36/19.
4. Hell, *Le Sang noir*, conclusion.
5. Bertrand Hell reaches the same conclusion as to the inseparability of these two elements of Eurasian societies' relationship with nature. In ibid.
6. It is this which justifies in our eyes the project of a global study, using similar conceptual tools, of the policies of anti-partisan action on the Eastern front, which will constitute the subject of a forthcoming book.
7. Gerlach, *Kalkulierte Morde*.

Thanks

Sing, O Muse, the wrath of Achilles, the son of Peleus; hateful wrath, which brought to the Achaeans sufferings without number, and threw as fodder to Hades so many proud heroes' souls, while these same heroes were the prey of dogs and of all the birds of the sky.

Homer, *The Iliad*, 1.1-5

Is it surprising, on the threshold of these thanks, that my words refuse to come to me? That the shade hovering over this book cannot find its way?

Come to me the words to say Laetitia, She Who Is Absent . . .

Come to me the words to speak the immense impulse that carries us—our children ourselves—through this voyage; the impulse expressed by Stéphane Audoin-Rouzeau on September 16, 2005, when he confided to the community there present the mission of bringing forth together what should be.

Come to me the words to say that the community then assembled has fulfilled its mission, that this book is testimony thereto.

This book would never have emerged from the desk drawers where fate shut it in September 2005 without that community, that circle at once pleasant and painful to number. For I

261

must name first of all those—Roland Beller, Xavier Escure, and Marie-Louise Prévot—who are no longer members, except in the memory of those who have known and lost them.

I must next cite those who permitted and followed the development of this book, and among them the archivists or librarians of the centers of Washington (USHMM), Hamburg, Berlin-Lichterfelde, Dahlwitz-Hoppegarten, Berlin-Mitte, Freiburg, Ludwigsburg, Warsaw; the *Hamburger Stiftung zur Foerderung von Wissenschaft und Kultur*, which generously granted the financial means necessary for three years of investigation; the Catholic University of the West, which welcomed me at the IALH from September 2004 to August 2005, and finally the IHTP, the true home of this book . . . I must speak here of the fundamental debt which binds me to Stéphane Audoin-Rouzeau, to Nicolas Werth, to Henry Rousso, and to Gerd Krumeich. Nicolas Beaupré, Benoît Majerus, Raphaëlle Branche, Christian Delage, Elisabeth Claverie all reviewed this work in part or in total. I must also say what this publication owes to Anthony Rowley and to Fabrice d'Almeida. May all those, family or friends, who cannot be named here pardon me, may they know that this anonymity is not forgetfulness on my part, may they know that, thanks to them, trial is not disaster.

Come to me the words to say that I now feel I can bring forth the future.

Come to me, finally and above all, the words to speak what was to Esteban, Nathan, and Gaïa; to speak radiance and JOY, grace, truth, and heritage; to say that there is an answer to the "May it be?" of the song, and that this answer, we will live it together, beyond loss.

Paris, June 28, 2006